Really?

Really?

A traveller's guide to
strange things in the Bible

JOHN MURFITT

ISBNs: Paperback: 978-1-80541-344-8 eBook: 978-1-80541-345-5

British Library Cataloguing-in-Publication Data. A catalogue record for this book is available from the British Library.

Front cover: 'A Jewish writing tablet in Israel. Photo kindly supplied by Mark Murfitt.'

For more information, please email:
johnmurfitt@hotmail.com.

This book is dedicated to Geoff, my friend and example in the Christian faith.

Contents

The New Testament

About the Author

John is enthusiastic about the subject of this book as with his others: *Two Destinies (2022)* and *The Kingdom (2023).*

After extensive research, each is a subject which he is burdened to share.

His past includes experience in the ministry, education and family life, meeting the challenges all these have presented.

He lives near the south coast of Cornwall and in his retirement he attends local churches, undertakes DIY, dog walking, reading, writing, works with various village committees, Parkinson's UK in Cornwall, and keeps Pekin bantams. Occasionally he plays golf, and he likes to travel.

He has been married to Ruth for more than fifty years and is proud of four sons and eight grandchildren.

When and where possible, he points others towards Christ.

Cornwall, 2023

Foreword

Really? is a book investigating the extraordinary and helps to prove the workings of a wider, bigger, more glorious world outside the physical dimensions of which we are familiar, which is governed by One called the King of Kings and Lord of Lords. Those who pay homage to Him may well find things happen to them which makes unbelieving people react when told about them as saying, "Really?" in a tone of voice suggesting they don't really accept it at all.

When I was doing my "O" Levels many years ago, I was as worried as I could be, knowing how important the results were for whatever future I might have, so much so that my parents got the doctor to prescribe tranquilisers for me to slow me down. They did help when I was panicking over some of the questions!

In the two years before I took my "A" Levels, I became a Christian and read a chapter in the Bible each morning. The exams were in June but early May that year I was reading for the very first time the story of Joshua, and how he was told to conquer all the territory the Israelites were to inhabit. God was encouraging Joshua and said to him, 'As I was with Moses, so I will be with you. I will not fail you or forsake you.' (Joshua 1: 5). The words 'I will not fail you' jumped out at me as I was reading and I was certain God was saying that precisely to me that morning.

I still swatted like mad for the exams, but when I was in the exam room I was completely calm knowing I was going to pass them. My mother couldn't believe it when I told her. I did pass (got 100% in Pure Maths!) and got a scholarship which enabled me to go to university (which is another story). *Really?* Can that be true? Yes, it was me – and so I commend this collection of Bible stories for you to read and react the same or differently as you may. There really is another world out there!

Dr Peter Brierley
Statistical Consultant

Acknowledgements

I would like to sincerely thank those who have helped and encouraged me with this book.

I must especially thank Geoff Fox who has been a special Bible teacher and always being willing to help me with theology when I have needed it. He is the leader of an evangelical free church in Cornwall and a successful businessman daily living out his faith in the work place. He has challenged me as a respected critical friend to examine very carefully the Word of God, make adjustments to my written texts where necessary, and present my content in a truthful, clear and concise way. He has always inspired me to go forward. I am so thankful for all the time he has given me.

I would also like to thank Peter Brierley, who very modestly describes himself as a statistical consultant and has written for me the excellent Foreword to this book. Whilst statistical analysis is part of what he is and does, he is also a skilful writer and author. He also advises influential national groups in trends of faith and matters of national importance in secular and Christian circles. He is the founder of a well-established charity working in Kenya touching many lives, both children and adults. Over a number of years I was privileged to work with him.

In addition, I am grateful to Ben and PublishingPush for their invaluable support and direction to enable this to be a book and not just a manuscript, and especially to Phil Hadley for his brilliant proof-reading and editing based on years of experience and knowledge of God and his Word. He has done an amazing job leaving no stone unturned.

I would especially like to thank my studious and ordained wife, Ruth, who carefully checked this work line by line and has always been an inspiration to me and a wonderful sounding board in all aspects of my script, more helpful and more challenging than she realises. She has patiently supported my progress at every stage and made useful suggestions in every chapter for which I am grateful. She has willingly understood the time I have needed for my hours of writing. I wish to say to her: "Thank you!"

If any mistakes, weaknesses or inaccuracies have slipped through, I take full responsibility for them and I do apologise to you, the reader.

Lastly I would like to thank unnamed people in this text whom I have encountered on my Christian journey and who have been a fitting example and encouragement to me. Without them I wouldn't be where I am and this book would not have been written. Some have been especially patient with me over the years, keeping my feet on the ground and showing me by their lives and words the faithfulness of God, how to live as a Christian and how to love the Word of God. I couldn't begin to apply theory to practice without them – and I am still very much a learner! I am blessed indeed, and I thank you, the reader, for taking on this book to consider its content and reach an informed decision about strange things encountered in the Bible. I can only imagine that you are as mystified as I am about some of them but also trust you are as impressed as I am and in awe of our great God.

Textual Note:

1. References are taken from the New International Version of the Bible, Anglicised, referred to as NIVUK, (The New International Version; Biblica; 1973, 1978, revised 1984 and 2011). For conciseness, the Old Testament and the New Testament are referred to as OT and NT.
2. References appear in the familiar format of book, chapter, verse (as in John 3:16). If already referring to John chapter three, then reference to a verse will be indicated as, for example (v16). Occasionally there may be reference to KJV: King James Version; 1611. Other versions, where used, will be explained.
3. Old Testament dating relies on John C. Whitcomb; Old Testament Kings and Prophets; BMH Books; 1977; and: bookshop.org/books/chart-old-testament-kings-and-prophets-paper; 2021. John C. Whitcomb (1924-2020) was professor of theology and *Old Testament* at Grace Theological Seminary, Winona Lake, Indiana, for 38 years.
4. On occasions, the full or concise Bible commentary of Matthew Henry (1662-1714), a theologian and non-conformist minister of a church in Chester, England is referred to. The complete commentary was first published in 1706 in six volumes, entitled: *Exposition of the Old and New Testaments*. The edition I have mostly used in the one volume concise edition published by Marshall, Morgan and Scott; 1980. Matthew Henry was competent in Latin and Greek from the age of nine.

He had a wife and nine children and all his life had poor health and died aged 51.

5. If the reader follows up my source references used in the Notes at the end of the text, please note a reduced reference Web address system is used such as *christianity. org.* The user's computer should then automatically add the prefix www. via the search engine used.

Introduction

A personal testimony

As the year of 2011 progressed, I felt unusually short of energy and I seemed to get breathless on quite a number of occasions. On a Wednesday near the middle of December I attended a communion service at my local parish church and then went with a team of four or five people to the local school, about half a mile away, to conduct collective worship (an assembly) featuring the Christmas story using the Storyteller Bible[1], designed for use with primary aged children. In this there is a re-telling of 70 key Bible stories. The team did an excellent job reading and acting out the main details of the Christmas story. I had no idea what lay ahead.

In the communion service I didn't feel quite right but worked through it and put it down to tiredness, but when I got home from the school I had a pain across my chest and told Ruth, my wife, I needed to sit down and have a cup of tea to revive me as I was feeling unexpectedly tired. I never drink tea during the day. I began to realise something was not quite right.

The ambulance service was called and a local First Responder was soon with me caring for me before the ambulance arrived. I was then taken to the local hospital in Truro twenty miles away and admitted to a cardiac ward. After a couple of days my pain greatly increased and was hardly eased by a strong pain killer which I had to spray under my tongue. It exploded into action so I nicknamed it *nitro-glycerine*. This was my way of coping. By Saturday, my consultant was summoned to my bedside, and he said I needed to have an urgent operation. For that I had to travel with a nurse allocated to care for me on a journey of 60 miles to a specialist unit at Plymouth. To use a common phrase, this was 'a blue light' journey.

Despite being a nearly-new vehicle, on the way the ambulance developed serious engine trouble and instead of being able to complete its journey, was directed to go back to an ambulance station at Bodmin, 30 miles back on my journey from the outskirts of Plymouth to where there was a 'spare' ambulance. This is not what you need to be part of when you are in heart failure! My ambulance crawled along and limped into the car park. I walked with a blanket wrapped around me across the compound on a bitterly wintry morning to change to another ambulance. All the way on the journeys my vital heart condition and other readings were being measured and recorded and I heard my nurse warning Plymouth staff to get ready for my arrival.

I was naturally praying about these events and felt I should contact my wife to warn her not to go west in Cornwall to Truro but to go east to Devon to meet me at Plymouth. On the journey, the only possession I had was my mobile phone and I clutched it in each ambulance. I was asking God to assure me he had my life in his hands when a text came in from a Pastor friend I hadn't had any contact with for quite some time. He simply wrote, 'John, I believe the Lord has everything under control, "My times are in your hands" (Psalm 31:15).'

As I was being prepared for the operation in a small room by the theatre, my wife sent a text telling me she and two of my four sons were on their way to Plymouth. At the same time a heart surgeon was contacted doing his grocery shopping with his wife and children in a large supermarket and he was summoned to quickly get to the hospital for an emergency operation. It is an understatement to say I didn't feel at all well, nor did I feel any better when he said I had about three weeks to live if I didn't have the operation. I was asked by him to sign the permission letter to give him the go-ahead to do the operation and I had to accept the risk involved. He told me, because I asked him, that 5% of patients didn't survive. Again I was praying.

He wanted to go ahead and start (and later said in confidence to my wife, he preferred to be with me rather than shop with his wife in a well-known supermarket!) I persuaded him to delay a little *until* my wife arrived. At worst, I wanted to say good-bye to her and to my sons who had been able to make the long journey down-country to see me. To my surprise and initial dismay, the surgeon said after about ten minutes he must get started and couldn't wait any longer. As I lay there trying to accept I wouldn't see my family again before the operation, the Lord gave me two things. First, a wonderful peace that when my eyes opened after the operation I would either see my wife or Jesus (depending whether I was on earth or in heaven). Second, God caused me to notice the only thing on the walls: a clock. I believe God then said to me, 'Remember the words I have given you, "My times are in your hands."' I thanked God for that clock. I knew I was safe. If I awoke on earth I would see Ruth. If I awoke in heaven, I would see Jesus. Soon I was asleep.

Just before I was awakened from a three day induced coma, I had a wonderful vision of my guardian angel. He was standing at the foot of my bed with a solemn and controlled expression. He held a sword by its handle vertically down from his chest to the floor. I asked him his name and he said 'David.' I asked if my wife was all right and he said 'She is fine. Her angel, called Genesis is with her.' I was then conscious of hearing my name said with some determination and brought round gradually from unconsciousness by a specialist nurse. Shortly after, my wife came in to see me with my sons. I was still on earth. As I looked at Ruth with my tubes, wires and machines attached, my first words to her were, 'If I've missed Christmas, your present (which I had made for her), is in the shed.' She assured me it wasn't yet Christmas Day but would be soon.

I found out from the surgeon he had to lower my body temperature and stop my heart to work on it for seven hours or so, and re-start it. It was also stopped and re-started several weeks later back at the Truro hospital to get the rhythm more even.

What an experience all this was. I had top quality surgery and care from brilliant staff and was surrounded by my loving family and unbeknown to me at the time, underpinned by lots of praying friends and several churches. When I returned to my village, I was made very welcome by neighbours and friends. They all seemed to know what had happened to me.

From the Wednesday Communion to my uncomfortable return journey home in my wife's car, about twelve days later, there were some strange things which happened. The ambulance broke down! The surgeon was 'available' but in a supermarket! The clock linked to the text I received! The peace I had before the operation! The vison of my guardian angel! The sight of my wife and sons, and others, who came to see me, and whom I thought I may never see again!

Really? Yes, really!

I know I have experienced God's goodness to me, but there are some very strange details. The Bible is unusual and has some very strange details of people and incidents, in this factual book conveying attributes of God: his love, his justice and his plan of salvation. It is some of these strange things I want to explore in this book.

As a teenager I once worked in Barnsley Market, Yorkshire, on Saturdays selling flowers cut from a flower farm. I helped to cut them, pack them for transporting and unload. Flower holding bags were readied and loose cash filled my pouch for change. All was prepared. All had to be ready before the customers arrived. The flowers had to be presented well to sell. The stall was set.

Similarly, in looking at the strange things in the Bible, the stall needs to be set, so first we must look into what the Bible actually is, and for this I refer to a church in New Zealand writing that the books of the Bible were:

'Written under the supernatural guidance of the Holy Spirit by laymen and scholars, commoners and nobility, the Bible is as unique as it is profound, containing 66 ancient books that have shaped laws, influenced culture and inspired billions to faith over three millennia.'[2]

I therefore need to examine this unique library of books and look into their authority.

Old Testament Books

The OT is a collection of 39 divinely inspired spiritual books written between 1445 BC (the commonly accepted date of the Exodus from Egypt, as explained by Don Stewart of the Blue Letter Bible group)[3] and 415 BC (when Malachi was prophesying during the temple rebuilding encouraged by Ezra and Nehemiah).[4]

I believe the OT is an accurate historical record of God's people, their laws, writings and prophecies. It details promises of the Messiah to come to earth as human and yet as God and alludes to his Second Coming in glorious triumph and splendour at the end of the age. It acts as a model for faith and conduct. It reveals God and shows many insights into his chosen people and their needs and experiences. It details sin and a holy God.

New Testament Books

The NT is a collection of 27 divinely inspired spiritual books. It covers history in the four Gospels of Matthew, Mark, Luke and John, and the early church in the book of Acts. It tells of the birth, life, death and resurrection of Jesus Christ, God's Son as the only Saviour from sin for all people for all time. It tells how God loved the world and everyone in it, but despite all the healing, help and hope which Jesus brought to so many, most people rejected him and his message and plotted to have him killed. It tells how he was crucified and died on a cross and how God brought him back to life again after three days and was seen by hundreds of people over a period of forty days before going back to heaven. These historical facts are well supported by the historians of the day. The amazing spread of the Christian faith, and some of the persecution and troubles its followers faced, are told in these books.

The 21 letters from Romans to Jude give guidance and teaching for Christian living. They were written to correct weaknesses and mistakes made by early Christians and to point them in the right direction in their faith.

The last NT book is Revelation. It tells of things that are yet to happen in God's plan for the human race. It describes, using a mixture of facts, visons and symbols, the future of God's people in the new heaven and new earth and the final defeat of Satan and evil. It concludes by reinforcing the warnings of the whole Bible regarding the consequences of rejecting God and his love.

The Bible's authority

Though the Bible was written by people, mostly men as far as we know, unlike any other book, it was guided and planned by God the Holy Spirit from beginning to end. Paul describes this to his youthful Pastor and friend whom he is overseeing as, 'Holy Scriptures…' and 'God-breathed' (2 Timothy 3:15-16) (see also 2 Peter 1: 20-21). Christians say that the Bible is 'inspired,' meaning that God spoke his message through the people he chose to act as authors. This makes the Bible very special indeed, and other than the most minor of infrequent copyist errors and translation challenges from the original language into our own language, I believe the Bible is inerrant. It has to be if it is the basis for our salvation and faith. This is why we call it 'The Word of God.' Jesus believed this and so used it constantly in his teaching and preaching.

Each time he made reference to the Bible (often called the Scriptures) it was the OT (the Jewish Torah) and this gives me great confidence to trust it because Jesus believes its infallibility and therefore reliability. In every case, Jesus' words show that he believes in its historic accuracy and divine authority. The Jews often referred to their Scriptures as 'the law and the prophets.' The gospel writers record the words of Jesus giving his authority:

> *Matthew*: 'Do not think that I have come to abolish the Law or the Prophets; I have not come to abolish them but to fulfil them' (Matthew 5:17).
> *Mark*: 'Are you not in error because you do not know the Scriptures or the power of God?' (Mark 12:24).
> *Luke*: 'Beginning with Moses and all the Prophets, he explained to them what was said in all the Scriptures concerning himself' (Luke 24:27).
> *John*: 'You study the Scriptures diligently because you think that in them you have eternal life. These are the very Scriptures that testify about me' (John 5:39-40).

Jesus also gave his seal to the whole of the NT before it was written, telling the disciples: '…obey everything I have commanded you' (Matthew 28:20). He re-assured them the Holy Spirit would: '…teach you all things and will remind you of everything I have said to you' (John 14:26). He re-assured them that the Holy Spirit would guide his own people to understand the truth, 'But when he, the Spirit of Truth comes, he will guide you into all the truth' (John 16:13a). As time passed after his ascension, the Holy Spirit would prompt their memories, but Jesus also knew that the NT would be written during the following 60 years, and so he is giving his authority to both the prompting and to the writing of the NT.

In concluding his Gospel John, one of the three senior Apostles and closest friend of Jesus writes: 'Jesus performed many other signs in the presence of his disciples, which are not recorded in this book. But these are written that you may believe that Jesus is the Messiah, the Son of God, and that by believing you may have life in his name' (John 20:30-31).

I am therefore using the Bible respectful of its relevance and reliability, taking care not to 'distort' it, as Paul said to the Christians in Corinth.[5] I am also mindful that readers will hold or arrive at their own conclusions and I respect their views and the right to form their own conclusions; a good principle is '...to work out your own salvation with fear and trembling' (Philippians 2:12b). However, may I humbly also say to those unsure what to believe, as Paul instructed the Philippian Christians, that if '...you think differently, that too God will make clear to you' (Philippians 3:15b).

Some things are strange

Did a donkey *really* speak? Did the sun *really* stand still at the command of a warrior-leader? Did a Judge *really* destroy a temple by physical strength? Did a prophet *really* make an iron axe head float on water? Did the heat of a furnace which killed those stoking it *really* not touch three men thrown into it? And where did the fourth man come from? Did a fish *really* swallow a man? Did a professional soldier *really* come to know the Son of God when Jesus' own disciples failed to do so? Was a woman *really* the first missionary after meeting Jesus because of her love for Jesus and courage to tell of his resurrection and because she was in the right place at the right time? Did Jesus *really* walk through walls after his resurrection? Did Jesus *really* stand to see the first Christian martyr die? Did John *really* see Jesus ride on a white horse? These and many other strange people, events and teaching will be examined and won't fail to challenge our thinking and our faith.

What we know is that God is almighty, omnipotent ('unlimited power')[6] and omni-present ('present everywhere')[7] and has his own way of doing things at a point in time. This is sometimes within the laws of nature he has created and sometimes outside these laws. His actions and the actions of ordinary men and women which don't fit our normal understanding and experience form the subjects of this book. Things which are strange can sometimes be understood when the context is seen and reflected on with careful consideration and believed by faith, other things will remain as a mystery and will only be understood when we arrive in heaven. Even there, we would need God in his grace to explain his actions and reasons. The psalmist says, 'When I consider your heavens, the work of your fingers, the moon and the stars, which you have set in place, what is mankind that you are mindful of them, human beings that you care for them?' (Psalms 8:3-4)

The scope and aim of this book

The scope of this book is to see if there is a challenge in a strange person, event or teaching in each of the books of the Bible (and the word **strange**, presented in **bold,** as here will make an appearance in every chapter which in length are more like vignettes![8]). Some books will have many examples and others very few. However, as already indicated, the Bible is the main source book for this study and indicates: (i) the truth about God, (ii) the truth about the character of human beings, and (iii) the truth about all we need to know about salvation. As an older and experienced teacher once said to me when I began my first teaching post in London teaching pupils with challenging behaviour, 'Expect the unexpected,' and 'Always face the enemy!' These maxims are certainly influencing my present investigations.

The aim of this study is to see God at work and to know he is sovereign and in control of all things including this world and the people in it. God acts in, with and for others because he loves us and cares for us. He wants us to receive his love and for us to love and worship him not as a duty but as a joy and pleasure. We will then grow in faith, grace and experience, and in love for him and others. As Jesus said to Jairus, the Jewish synagogue leader, '…Don't be afraid; just believe' (Mark 5:36b). That is a challenge from Jesus.

Really? Really!

The Old Testament

1 Genesis - *Two people sinned and the whole of mankind fell.*

*'Now the snake was more crafty than any of the wild animals the Lord God had made. He said to the woman, "Did God really say, You must not eat from any tree in the garden?" The woman said to the snake, "We may eat fruit from the trees in the garden, but God did say, You must not eat fruit from the tree that is in the middle of the garden, and **you must not touch it, or you will die**." "You will not certainly die," the snake said to the woman. "For God knows that when you eat from it your eyes will be opened, and you will be like God, knowing good and evil." When the woman saw that the fruit of the tree was good for food and pleasing to the eye, and also desirable for gaining wisdom, she took some and ate it. She also gave some to her husband, who was with her, and he ate it. Then the eyes of both of them were opened. The Lord God called to the man, "Where are you?"*

To Adam he said, "Because you listened to your wife and ate fruit from the tree about which I commanded you, You must not eat from it, Cursed is the ground because of you; through painful toil you will eat food from it all the days of your life. It will produce thorns and thistles for you, and you will eat the plants of the field. By the sweat of your brow you will eat your food until you return to the ground, since from it you were taken; for dust you are and to dust you will return."'

(Genesis 3:1-7a, v9b, v17-19)

15

Daily news in Britain always seems to say that someone else in the public eye has been found out for trying to deceive others. They are discovered as the Bible predicts they will be: '…you may be sure that your sin will find you out' (Numbers 32:23b). Sin cannot be hidden for ever; God will expose it eventually: 'Nothing in all creation is hidden from God's sight. Everything is uncovered and laid bare before the eyes of him to whom we must give account' (Hebrews 4:13). The Apostle Paul put it strongly to the Christians in Rome that sin has a consequence: 'For the wages of sin is death' (Romans 6:23a) (see also Romans 7:11). This is the position that God holds. He sees sin and deals with it. Sin pays a price. The result is non-negotiable. But why? Where did sin come from?

I find it difficult to understand how anyone can believe in the theory of evolution. It is a deception. To me it is illogical that human beings evolved from other creatures and they somehow developed a moral framework and, unable to maintain moral purity, descended into self-centredness which, if we give it the Bible's name, we simply know as sin. No! The Bible's explanation, as seen in the passage from Genesis three above, is much easier to understand and believe to be the truth as to where sin came from.

This key passage shows that Satan, who was strong-willed and resented God, also resented his Creator creating people and giving them free-will. The only condition placed on the first people was that they must not touch one particular tree in the garden of Eden. If Adam and Eve touched it, they would die.

In heaven, Satan had challenged God and been expelled and so from his kingdom of Earth tempted Adam and Eve to cause them to do what he did: rebel against God. This led the first people into selfishness and sin which would lead to their death. The effect on creation was also dramatic. All the world created by God was affected, and is summarised in the few words that the world developed 'thorns and thistles.' Instead of tending the garden they were placed in as a joy and delight, demanding work, discomfort and painful child births would all precede death and destruction of a once perfect body and a once perfect life in a once perfect environment. As Paul describes the result of sin: '…the whole creation has been groaning as in the pains of childbirth right up to the present time' (Romans 8:22).

One of the saddest details of the descent into sin by Adam and Eve was, as Matthew Henry records in God's searching words, followed by his own comment. God asked:

> '"Adam, where art thou?"[9] Those who by sin go astray from God, should seriously consider where they are; they are afar off from all good, in the midst of their enemies, in bondage to Satan, and in the high road to utter ruin.'[10]

The first created people, subsequent people, and the whole of the physical creation is subject to *The Fall*, as theologians express it. There is shame and embarrassment and a failure to live in harmony with God. This is why Paul tells the Roman Christians, '…all have sinned and fall short of the glory of God' (Romans 3:23). 'Therefore, just as sin entered the world through one man, and death through sin, and in this way death came to all people, because all sinned' (Romans 5:12).

Whether we like it or not, and whether we agree or not, the fact is that sin has been inherited by the whole human race for all time and all of creation has been affected. This is **strange** but true and is why there is distress, disease and death, and weather and geological events on and in the Earth. As the Apostle Paul wrote to the Christians in Rome, 'We know that the whole creation has been groaning... not only so, but we ourselves... groan inwardly...' (Romans 3:22-23).

All have sinned, so all need a Saviour. God knows that and from the beginning of time has had it all under control.[11]

2 Exodus - *The sea stands like a wall to right and left as the people cross on dry ground.*

'Pharaoh king of Egypt… pursued the Israelites… As Pharaoh approached, the Israelites looked up, and there were the Egyptians, marching after them. They were terrified and cried out to the Lord. They said to Moses, "Was it because there were no graves in Egypt that you brought us to the desert to die? What have you done to us by bringing us out of Egypt?"

Moses answered the people, "Do not be afraid. Stand firm and you will see the deliverance the Lord will bring you today. The Egyptians you see today you will never see again. The Lord will fight for you; you need only to be still."

Then the Lord said to Moses, "Why are you crying out to me? Tell the Israelites to move on. Raise your staff and stretch out your hand over the sea to divide the water so that the Israelites can go through the sea on dry ground."

*Then Moses stretched out his hand over the sea, and all that night the Lord drove the sea back with a strong east wind and turned it into dry land. The waters were divided, and **the Israelites went through the sea on dry ground**, with a wall of water on their right and on their left.'*

(Exodus 14:8; v10-11; v13-16; v21-22)

After 430 years the Israelites left slavery in Egypt once Pharaoh, the King of Egypt, had suffered enough from the ten plagues inflicted by God upon him and his people and so he let the people leave. They numbered about 2.5 millions and, leaving, with vast numbers of flocks and herds, they travelled on foot 250 miles in about 25 days, as far as a town near the Red Sea called Pi Hahiroth. Pharaoh, realising he had lost a massive workforce he was using to build new cities, changed his mind and decided he wanted the people to return and continue working for him.

Close to the Red Sea, the Israelites realised they had a challenging situation with the sea in front of them and the Egyptian army behind them. Their lives and futures were in the balance. They were in despair with no obvious way out. They couldn't return to slavery in Goshen and couldn't go forward into the Promised Land. So, as the Egyptians closed in on them, God provided an impenetrable cloud to separate the army from the Israelites as a temporary measure. Matthew Henry[12] in his commentary on Exodus 14, makes an interesting point: 'He, who divided between light and darkness, *(at Creation)* (Genesis 1:4), allotted darkness to the Egyptians, and light to the Israelites. Such a difference there will be between the inheritance of the saints in light, and that utter darkness which will be the portion of hypocrites for ever.' (*Emphasis mine*). Their outlook was desperate; God's intervention was needed!

The people complained to Moses and he relayed their anguished concerns to God. Indicating he would enable them to cross the Red Sea, God said to Moses, "Raise your staff and stretch out your hand over the sea to divide the water so that the Israelites can go through the sea on dry ground" (Exodus 14:16).

Moses did as he was commanded (v21), he raised his hand and God worked all night and drove back the sea and Pharaoh and his army followed with hearts hardened and an arrogant attitude and charged at speed after the Israelites. They started to cross on dry ground. In the middle of the sea God '…threw (*the Egyptians*) into confusion. He jammed the wheels of their chariots so that they had difficulty driving.' (*Emphasis mine*). They knew that something was seriously working against them. 'And the Egyptians exclaimed, "Let's get away from the Israelites! The Lord is fighting for them against Egypt"' (v24b, v25). Moses raised his hand and staff for a second time, and the sea 'went back to its place' (v27), swallowing up and destroying Pharaoh and his entire army.

The crossing of the Red Sea is mentioned a number of times in the OT and NT as a fact and to encourage God's people to trust him and to assure them he would be with them in every situation. They were reminded to look back into their history to see what happened at the Red Sea crossing. Joshua was there at the time as assistant to Moses and so, having taken over the leadership, he addresses the people from experience telling them, '… the Lord dried up the waters of the Red Sea before you when you came out of Egypt' (Joshua 2:10). In the NT Luke repeats this statement (Acts 7:36).

The water deserves a special mention. It stood up each side of the Israelites as a wall. It came into being because '… Moses stretched out his hand over the sea, and all that night the Lord drove the sea back with a strong east wind and turned it into dry land. The waters were divided, and the Israelites went through the sea on dry ground, with a wall of water on their right and on their left' (Exodus 14:22 and v29).

The parting of the sea at just the right time and the water acting as if it were ice defying gravity and standing like a wall to each side of the large nomadic nation on the move is a miracle in which God is active and overrules his own laws of nature. He can do that because he is God. He did it because he was providing for and protecting his own treasured possession; his people.

Charlie Garrett; Ordained Minister of a Grace Baptist Church, Florida,[13] writes: 'Whether God does it (*parting the waters*) through a natural means or through a miracle which transcends nature, there is always the miraculous associated with it. God causes things to occur at specific times to show that he was behind it and it wasn't just arbitrary.' (*Emphasis mine*).

The Hebrew word for 'dry land' (v21) shows that the sea bed was not only dry it was totally free from water as if drained. It was as dry and compacted as if it were a desert path. For this reason, the Egyptians with their heavy iron chariots had no reason to hold back from following the Israelites and could easily drive their chariot wheels on the sea bed (v23). Sadly for them God threw them into confusion and caused their chariots to be immovable (v25). They knew without a doubt that God was fighting for his people against Egypt and in a panic made this clear to each other (v25). Meanwhile, the wall of water defied them. It was there for God's people to provide a safe passage through the sea, and when they were safely across (v29), then the walls of water collapsed and the entire Egyptian army drowned. None survived (v28).

The *walls* of water were **strange** and cannot be logically explained except that they were the result of an intervention by God. Charlie Garrett[14] puts this succinctly:

'Therefore, unless one just dismisses this account as an outright fabrication, the only logical deduction is that the waters were actually a wall, exactly as described. They were supernaturally being held in place, not by a mere natural occurrence, but by that which transcends the natural.'

We therefore conclude that just as the cloud at Pi Hahiroth was light to the Israelites but darkness to the Egyptians (v19-20), so the water brought life to God's people but death to their enemies (v22 and v28). This miracle had the immediate effect of challenging and strengthening the faith and trust of the Israelites in both their Lord and in his servant, Moses (v31). They went through the sea and into the Promised Land. God's people were saved from harsh treatment as slaves in Egypt. They were saved from death or capture by the Egyptian army. They were saved from drowning, and even getting wet, in the Red Sea. This is a picture of spiritual salvation. There is no wonder Paul, aware of God's power to save, brings God's words to the Corinthian Christians, 'In the time of my favour I heard you, and in the day of salvation I helped you. I tell you, now is the time of God's favour, now is the day of salvation' (2 Corinthians 6:2).

3 Leviticus - *The normal way of living is by holiness.*

*'The Lord said to Moses, "Speak to the entire assembly of Israel and say to them: **Be holy because I, the Lord your God, am holy.** Each of you must respect your mother and father, and you must observe my Sabbaths. I am the Lord your God. Do not turn to idols or make metal gods for yourselves. I am the Lord your God."'*

(Leviticus 19:1-4)

I have looked carefully into the beliefs and practices of the main world religions and life stances, generally considered to be: Agnosticism, Atheism, Baha'i, Buddhism, Christianity, Humanism, Hinduism, Islam, Jainism, Sikhism, and Zoroastrianism.[15] I found that most of them fixed their own human designed moral standards for their followers, and holy days and holy men are common features in religious groups, but only Christianity emphasises and holds centrally the need for holy behaviour with high moral standards set by God, applicable to all its believing followers.

Only Christianity claims to have the solution to sin set by a holy God who requires personal holiness. Hebrews tells us, 'Make every effort to live in peace with everyone and to be holy; without holiness no-one will see the Lord' (Hebrews 12:14). Peter writes, 'But just as he who called you is holy, so be holy in all you do' (1 Peter 1:15).

Only Christianity claims to have a founder and Saviour who lived, died, rose again and is alive for ever. John records

Jesus' actual words, 'I am the Living One; I was dead, and now look, I am alive for ever and ever!' (Revelation 1:18)

The OT has many references to the holiness of God. God was found to be so holy that when he was on Mt Sinai, for instance, no one was allowed to approach the mountain's base and if they did they would die (Exodus 19:12). In fact with the smoke, fire and violent trembling of the mountain, no one *wanted* to touch it (v18). Moses was aware of God's requirements, 'Moses said to the Lord, "The people cannot come up Mount Sinai, because you yourself warned us, 'Put limits around the mountain and set it apart as holy'" (v23).

The Rev Dr David Instone-Brewer is an honorary senior research fellow at Tyndale House, Cambridge, UK. He observes: 'The Israelites, like worshippers of other deities, knew from earliest times that God was holy and his presence was dangerous (Genesis 32:30)'[16]. He further adds, 'The Bible doesn't teach us that God wants us to be separate because of his holiness. It says the opposite: *God wants us to be close to him.*'[17] God is holy and requires holiness in his people. God says, "...out of all nations you will be my treasured possession. Although the whole earth is mine, you will be for me a kingdom of priests and a holy nation" (Exodus 19:5-6). This includes a right attitude towards and in the use of the cooking pots, and they should also be 'holy' (Zechariah 14:20). In other words our actions and even our equipment should be touched by God in which case they will be holy.

So we find in Leviticus, such as in the selected passage chosen from chapter 19 above, as one example, that holiness is not an option but a requirement to be separate from and above the standards of the world. In the NT, Jesus spoke about being sanctified (John 17:17), and Paul wrote to Titus to tell him that Jesus would '…purify for himself a people that are his very own…' (Titus 2:14). This action was not new since Malachi about 450 years earlier pointed out that God was a father who required honour and a master who expected respect because it was 'due' to him (Malachi 1:6). In other words, the people were to be holy, their relationships holy, their practices holy and their Sabbaths holy. As Matthew Henry[18] in his commentary concludes this chapter: 'Turn not from the true God to false ones, from the mighty God to impotent ones, from the God that will make you holy and happy to those that will deceive you, debauch you, ruin you, and make you for ever miserable. Turn not your eye to them, much less your heart.'

Unlike other world religions, and in this respect Christianity is unique, even **strange**! The normal life which the Lord our God expects of the Israelites of old, the Jews as they became known, and of Christians in NT days and now, is to live a life of holiness. In modern parlance God has 'set the bar high' and because he is holy we must be holy.

4 Numbers - *A donkey speaks to its owner.*

'Balaam got up in the morning, saddled his donkey and went with the Moabite officials. But God was very angry when he went, and the angel of the Lord stood in the road to oppose him. Balaam was riding on his donkey, and his two servants were with him. When the donkey saw the angel of the Lord standing in the road with a drawn sword in his hand, it turned off the road into a field. Balaam beat it to get it back on the road.

Then the angel of the Lord stood in a narrow path through the vineyards, with walls on both sides. When the donkey saw the angel of the Lord, it pressed close to the wall, crushing Balaam's foot against it. So he beat the donkey again.

Then the angel of the Lord moved on ahead and stood in a narrow place where there was no room to turn, either to the right or to the left. When the donkey saw the angel of the Lord, it lay down under Balaam, and he was angry and beat it with his staff.

Then the Lord opened the donkey's mouth, and it said to Balaam, "What have I done to you to make you beat me these three times?"

Balaam answered the donkey, "You have made a fool of me! If only I had a sword in my hand, I would kill you here and now." The donkey said to Balaam, "Am I not your own donkey, which you have always ridden, to this day? Have I been in the habit of doing this to you?" "No," he said.

Then the Lord opened Balaam's eyes, and he saw the angel of the Lord standing in the road with his sword drawn. So he bowed low and fell face down. The angel of the Lord asked him, "Why have you beaten your donkey these three times? I have come here to oppose you because your path is a reckless one before me. The donkey saw me and turned away from me these three times. If it had not turned away, I would certainly have killed you by now, but I would have spared it."

Balaam said to the angel of the Lord, "I have sinned. I did not realise you were standing in the road to oppose me. Now if you are displeased, I will go back."

The angel of the Lord said to Balaam, "Go with the men, but speak only what I tell you." So Balaam went with Balak's officials.'

(Numbers 22:21-35)

Some may doubt that a donkey could speak, but as with God's use of a bush on fire that didn't burn for Moses (Exodus 3:2-5), and in contrast to that the rock-shattering wind, earthquake and fire before a gentle whisper of God's voice for Elijah (1 Kings 19:12), God is showing he can use whatever means he chooses to get a person's attention. So here he uses a donkey. The Apostle Peter is aware of the account in Numbers and writes to his Christian friends, '…the unrighteous…' (2 Peter 2:9) '… have left the straight way and wandered off to follow the way of Balaam son of Bezer, who loved the wages of wickedness. But he was rebuked for his wrongdoing by a donkey – an animal without speech – who spoke with a human voice and restrained the prophet's madness' (v15-16). Peter didn't doubt this as a true and totally believable story.

The context of this story is important. Balaam, the son of Beor (Numbers 22:5), lived in Pethor near the river Euphrates. He professed obedience to God as his Lord but he struggled with greed with money and self-centredness. He was into magic arts (Joshua 13:22) and was a prophet and a Gentile (Numbers 24:2-9). He was able to speak with real power and bless or curse by his words. When the Israelites moved forward to attack Moab, Balak, their king summoned Balaam to put a curse on them. However, Balaam is told not to curse God's people: '… God said to Balaam, 'Do not go with (*the messengers*). You must not put a curse on those people, because they are blessed' (v12) (*Emphasis mine*).

Lia Martin, a Christian creative writer from Chicago, adds:

'Balak sweetens the offer, tempting Balaam with, "Do not let anything keep you from coming to me, because I will reward you handsomely and do whatever you say. Come and put a curse on these people for me." Then Balaam… goes back to God. He sees Balaam's heart. It's possible that God knew Balaam wanted the prize money more than God. But God allows him to go, giving Balaam a second chance, but warning him to "do only what I tell you."'[19]

We then see God's anger at Balaam going forward in his own strength and not relying on God. Off he went on his donkey. This humble creature was more spiritually aware and sensitive to God than the prophet. God then gave the donkey the ability to speak and challenge Balaam about what he was doing and what the donkey had seen: the presence of God in the angel. God then opened Balaam's eyes and he understood what was blocking the road physically and that he shouldn't be making the journey as he was not right with God spiritually. The angel also challenges him about cruelly treating his donkey!

'The angel of the Lord asked him, "Why have you beaten your donkey these three times? I have come here to oppose you because your path is a reckless one before me. The donkey saw me and turned away from me these three times. If it had not turned away, I would certainly have killed you by now, but I would have spared it"' (v32-33).

One feature of this whole story is that the Angel of the Lord may well be an OT appearance of Jesus because of the link with sin made by the angel. Lia Martin explains this as follows:

'Since this is the Angel of the Lord, and that the Angel of the Lord tells Balaam that his sin is against him personally (your way is perverse before Me), it indicates this is an Old Testament appearance of God the Son – the second member of the Trinity, Jesus, before his incarnation as a baby in Bethlehem. Jesus temporarily appeared in some sort of human form, for a specific Divine purpose.'[20]

I noted that God can use whatever means he chooses to get the attention of people. When his disciples, the twelve plus others, were so overjoyed because Jesus was coming into Jerusalem as King, and they thought it was God's time for the Romans occupying their nation to be overthrown, they praised God loudly. This didn't go down well with the solemn-faced religious people trapped in their traditions so they challenged Jesus about what they saw as unnecessary exuberance and inappropriate praise. The answer to this by Jesus was that if people were stopped in worship, in selfless, timely and uplifting worship, then his Father would cause the stones along the road in this triumphal procession to cry out in praise. He made it clear that God is pleased with worship and he could easily cause it and accept it from lifeless matter if people refused or were prevented from praising God.

> 'The whole crowd of disciples began joyfully to praise God in loud voices for all the miracles they had seen: "Blessed is the king who comes in the name of the Lord! Peace in heaven and glory in the highest!" Some of the Pharisees in the crowd said to Jesus, "Teacher, rebuke your disciples!" "I tell you," he replied, "if they keep quiet, the stones will cry out"' (Luke 19:37b-40).

I believe the same thing happened in this account of Balaam in Numbers 22. A prophet failed to respond to God and his angel, so God looked beyond him and accepted the spiritual sight of an animal. It is as simple as that. God being God gave the animal the **strange** ability to speak and be understood.

5 Deuteronomy - *Moses had a face to face relationship with God.*

> *'No prophet has risen in Israel like Moses, whom the Lord knew face to face, who did all those signs and wonders the Lord sent him to do in Egypt – to Pharaoh and to all his officials and to his whole land. For no-one has ever shown the mighty power or performed the awesome deeds that Moses did in the sight of all Israel.'*
>
> *(Deuteronomy 34:10-12)*

In these verses, according to the Christianity blog, a Christian web portal, providing articles on current topics, 'Moses is praised, and with good reason…He was indeed a very great man.'[21]

Moses was great because in his humility he was intimate with God who said of his servant Moses, ' With him I speak face to face, clearly and not in riddles; he sees the form of the Lord' (Numbers 12:8; repeated in Deuteronomy 34:10). God knew Moses face to face so Moses knew God face to face and saw more of the glory of God than anyone else up to that time. He was not spoken to in dreams and visions but fully awake and with a clear mind. He had a calm and personal relationship with God. It is not like this for everyone in the Bible. The people with Daniel reacted in panic when God revealed himself. We read, 'I, Daniel, was the only one who saw the vision; those who were with me did not see it, but such terror overwhelmed them that they fled and hid themselves' (Daniel 10:7).

Moses was great because of his understanding of God at work in his kingdom, including the natural world. God was tough

35

on Pharaoh when Moses was instrumental in bringing miracles and plagues to him. God was also very gracious and generous in providing for his people in the wilderness wanderings. Luke in Acts recorded Stephen's words giving a summary of Moses: 'He led them out of Egypt and performed wonders and signs in Egypt, at the Red Sea and for forty years in the wilderness' (Acts 7:36).

Moses was great compared to all the other OT prophets. All the prophets were great on Earth but none as great as Moses. God said through the last OT prophet, Malachi, "Remember the law of my servant Moses, the decrees and laws I gave him at Horeb for all Israel' (Malachi 4:4). The enemies of Israel feared him but God loved Moses. After his death the following was written, possibly by a scribe, under God's guidance, to round off the Torah,[22] attributed to Moses' authorship:

'The Israelites listened to him (*Joshua, Moses' successor*) and did what the Lord had commanded Moses. Since then, no prophet has risen in Israel like Moses, whom the Lord knew face to face, who did all those signs and wonders the Lord sent him to do in Egypt – to Pharaoh and to all his officials and to his whole land. For no-one has ever shown the mighty power or performed the awesome deeds that Moses did in the sight of all Israel' (Deuteronomy 34:9b-12) (*Emphasis mine*).

At the Transfiguration of Jesus, Moses appeared with Elijah: the two of them representing the law and the prophets respectively of the OT. God was pleased to raise them from their eternity to come back to Earth in their recognisable clothes and authority, and hold a conversation with Jesus about his imminent death and resurrection, referred to as his 'departure' (Luke 9:28-31). Moses was not only the law-giver under God's inspiration, he was also a prophet under God's direction foretelling the coming of the Messiah, who himself will be a prophet. God said through Moses, 'I will raise up for them a prophet like you from among their fellow Israelites, and I will put my words in his mouth. He will tell them everything I command him' (Deuteronomy 18:18).

Moses was such a close friend of God with an intimate 'face to face' relationship that at the end of his life, God took Moses to a vantage point from where he could see the Promised Land but told Moses he was not going to enter it.

'Then Moses climbed Mount Nebo from the plains of Moab to the top of Pisgah, opposite Jericho. There the Lord showed him the whole land – from Gilead to Dan, all of Naphtali, the territory of Ephraim and Manasseh, all the land of Judah as far as the Mediterranean Sea, the Negev and the whole region from the Valley of Jericho, the City of Palms, as far as Zoar. Then the Lord said to him, "This is the land I promised on oath to Abraham, Isaac and Jacob when I said, I will give it to your descendants. I have let you see it with your eyes, but you will not cross over into it." And Moses the servant of the Lord died there in Moab, as the Lord had said. He buried him in Moab, in the valley opposite Beth Peor, but to this day no-one knows where his grave is' (Deuteronomy 34:1-6).[23]

Moses died and God buried him in a secret grave in Moab. This amounted to a **strange,** impressive and close relationship. Such was the great love God had for Moses the humble leader of Israel, and a personal friend of God.

6 Joshua - *The day the sun stood still.*

'On the day the Lord gave the Amorites over to Israel, **Joshua said to the Lord in the presence of Israel: "Sun, stand still over Gibeon**, *and you, moon, over the Valley of Aijalon. So the sun stood still, and the moon stopped, till the nation avenged itself on its enemies, as it is written in the Book of Jashar.*[24] *The sun stopped in the middle of the sky and delayed going down about a full day. There has never been a day like it before or since, a day when the Lord listened to a human being. Surely the Lord was fighting for Israel! Then Joshua returned with all Israel to the camp at Gilgal.'*

(Joshua 10:12-15)

After the Pentateuch (the first five books of the Bible) establishing the beginnings of a relationship with a holy God and his laws, we come to the book of Joshua which tells the story of the early years of Israel as a nation and find that the Israelites are battling with warrior tribes in the Promised Land: land which God had given to his people. Joshua describes how the Israelites conquer and occupy the land of Canaan. The Bible's drama here moves to an important new stage – God's people are at last in their own land. But it also becomes clear that the road to living by faith and trusting God as his people will not be easy. We read how spies were sent into the land and report what they find, the river Jordan was miraculously crossed and the Israelites took the cities of Jericho and then Ai.

Chapter ten begins with Adoni-Zedek king of Jerusalem learning about Joshua's success, '…and that the people of Gibeon had made a treaty of peace with Israel and had become their allies' (Joshua 10:1b). Adoni-Zedek was not pleased with this and so he conspired with five local kings to attack and take back the important city of Gibeon.

Suddenly under attack, Gibeon appealed to Joshua. 'The Gibeonites… sent word to Joshua in the camp at Gilgal: "Do not abandon your servants. Come up to us quickly and save us! Help us, because all the Amorite kings from the hill country have joined forces against us" (v6). With God's promise of success, Joshua marched against them and was winning the battle when God, '…hurled large hailstones down on them, and more of them died from the hail than were killed by the swords of the Israelites' (v11b).

We then read the remarkable verse in which Joshua asks God for the sun and moon to stand still for a day. This was presumably to gain extra time so that he could totally defeat the enemy. As John Gill's Exposition of the Bible[25] puts it, '…and of the standing still of the sun, and of the moon, while vengeance was taken on them' (v12-14).[26]

This is an amazing story. The Oak Pointe Church in Michigan offers two explanations to interpret this action by Joshua:

1. 'God supernaturally slowed or stopped the rotation of the earth (for approximately a full day) to allow Israel to complete their conquest.
2. The section is poetic in nature and uses imagery to explain how God was fighting alongside of Israel because they sought his counsel and favour.'[27]

However, both explanations could be correct and are not exclusive, as God can easily work within natural laws, or to bypass laws to effect his will to fulfil his promises. This is fully within God's nature. Essentially, God fought alongside Israel to achieve a great victory.[28]

Matthew Henry points to the faith of Joshua, who gained much personal experience of faith and of God from his 'apprenticeship' to Moses:

'Notice the great faith of Joshua, and the power of God answering it by the miraculous staying of the sun, that the day of Israel's victories might be made longer. Joshua acted on this occasion by impulse on his mind from the Spirit of God. It was not necessary that Joshua should speak, or the miracle be recorded, according to the modern terms of astronomy. The sun appeared to the Israelites over Gibeon, and the moon over the valley of Aijalon, and there they appeared to be stopped on their course for one whole day.' [29]

We must note the thoughts of Dr. Mike Bagwell, Minister, First Baptist Church, Georgia who says:

'The Jews, their fighting men, are prevailing, routing the enemy. And (apparently) Joshua felt he needed more **time** to complete the assignment, to annihilate the wicked five-king coalition that so blatantly had attacked! So *he* (what faith) asked God to do something amazing, unheard of, almost unthinkable!'[30]

It was **strange** and amazing that the sun and moon stopped their normal circuits, and even more amazing that God listened to the voice of a man to effect this double miracle of stopping two heavenly bodies. 'There has never been a day like it before or since, a day when the Lord listened to a human being. Surely the Lord was fighting for Israel! (v14). We may well agree with Dr. Bagwell who adds, 'It certainly was a miracle, of almost "unbelievable" proportions! One of the most astounding in the entire Old Testament, maybe the entire Bible!'[31]

Paul summed up God's power to his Christian friends in Ephesus, 'Now to him who is able to do immeasurably more than all we ask or imagine, according to his power that is at work within us' (Ephesians 3:20). Matthew Henry concludes the story: 'I am the Lord, …Is anything too hard for me?' (Jeremiah 32:27)[32]

7 Judges - *The day Samson demolished a pagan temple.*

'Now the rulers of the Philistines assembled to offer a great sacrifice to Dagon their god and to celebrate, saying, 'Our god has delivered Samson, our enemy, into our hands.' When the people saw him, they praised their god, saying, "Our god has delivered our enemy into our hands, the one who laid waste our land and multiplied our slain." While they were in high spirits, they shouted, 'Bring out Samson to entertain us.' So they called Samson out of the prison, and he performed for them. When they stood him among the pillars, Samson said to the servant who held his hand, "Put me where I can feel the pillars that support the temple, so that I may lean against them." Now the temple was crowded with men and women; all the rulers of the Philistines were there, and on the roof were about three thousand men and women watching Samson perform. **Then Samson prayed to the Lord, 'Sovereign Lord, remember me.** *Please, God, strengthen me just once more, and let me with one blow get revenge on the Philistines for my two eyes.*

Then Samson reached towards the two central pillars on which the temple stood. Bracing himself against them, his right hand on the one and his left hand on the other, Samson said, "Let me die with the Philistines!" Then he pushed with all his might, and down came the temple on

the rulers and all the people in it. Thus he killed many
more when he died than while he lived.'

(*Judges 16:23-30*)

The book of Judges relates the cycle of Israel's repeated covenant breaking. They faced and often lost battles with foreign nations, in particular the Philistines, because, as a nation, they were not living in obedience to God and his laws and standards. Each time they became embroiled in serious warfare they cried out to God for help and he raised up Judges (military leaders and legal authorities) to lead them, fight for them and save them. But relief was temporary as each time they were delivered by God, they failed to keep his covenant and fell away into sin. In Jewish history numbers are significant. Israel was made up of 12 tribes and the book of Judges has 12 judges (and one other leader). The final two judges are Eli and Samuel who are in the First book of Samuel. Sadly, the people were rejecting their true Judge and Ruler and his theocratic leadership of the nation.

In chapter 13 we read of Samson's birth to Manoah and his wife. An angel delivered the message to them that they, as parents, must not drink alcoholic drinks or eat unclean food.[33] The angel said they were going to have a boy and he was to be a Nazarite. As such, he would never have a haircut, and be dedicated to the Lord from before birth. It was promised he would lead and deliver Israel. Samson was duly born and as he grew and was blessed by God, '…the Spirit of the Lord began to stir him…' (Judges 13:25). He had a spiritual awareness from an early age.

Samson unwisely married a Philistine (which was disobeying God), and had incredible supernatural strength linked to his hair, which showed itself when he killed a lion with his bare hands and gathered honey from an active swarm of bees without protection. Later he caught 300 foxes and tied them in pairs, tail to tail, fastened blazing torches to their tails and let them run through the cornfields of Philistia to destroy the crops of the Israelites' enemies. All this greatly annoyed the Philistines who wanted to defeat Samson, and an opportunity came through his latest Philistine partner, Delilah. He gave way to her deception and failed to see her continuing loyalty to her own people. Delilah was in a compromising position in life between Samson and her own people. But eventually, she gained manipulative control over Samson and his strength. His head was shaved, his strength was gone, his eyes were removed, and worst of all, '…he did not know the Lord had left him' (Judges 16:20c).

Samson was put in prison and was in a depressed and deeply sorry state. He had let his parents down; in disobedience to God, he had close liaisons with at least three Philistine women; and he let down his own people. He was at his lowest point. In contrast, the Philistines were triumphant believing their fish-shaped god, Dagon, (which had a human face and body of a fish), '…has delivered Samson, our enemy, into our hands' (v23). The Philistines used the capture of Samson as an excuse for a party at which he was to be the entertainment!

Bible Study Tools informs us of the scale of the celebration:

'The Syrians worshipped a fish, and … they will not eat any; and Gaza being a maritime city, a sea port, this might be their sea god in this form: the Philistine princes met together to sacrifice to him, not a common offering, but a great sacrifice. It is very probable that this was a public festival of the Philistines… an anniversary one; and perhaps was held in a grand manner on the present occasion.'[34]

The lords of the Philistines called for Samson to be brought out to amuse them so they could further humiliate him and his God. David Guzik, Pastor, Santa Barbara, California,[35] says the message on the lips of the followers of Dagon is clear, 'They said, "Our god is stronger than the God of Israel, because we have conquered Samson."'[36] However, Samson, aware of his fall from closeness to God, now shows a sensitive awareness of his sin and respectfully addresses God in prayer as his 'Sovereign Lord' (v28) and asks God to remember him and strengthen him one last time. In prison, his hair was starting to grow again. It seems he desires to stand up for his Lord and gain vengeance for all that is happening to him, typified by his enemies taking his sight. He is led to a central position in the arena where the on-lookers could make further fun of him, but he gains in his mind and physical position, control of his circumstances. He lost his strength from God through sin but re-gained it through prayer. His faith is again in place.

Samson showed repentance and respect in prayer towards God, pleaded for help, and trusted him for one last miracle in his life. He pushed with all his God-given renewed strength at the two pillars holding the temple roof in position and brought the whole structure down killing himself and thousands of the enemy. His twenty-year leadership as Judge of Israel had ended (v31). God answered Samson's prayer and this final victory in Samson's life was his greatest – but it cost him his life. However, he learned after his selfish and violent life to trust his life to God again just before he died.

Samson was a big man. On one occasion I met Frank Bruno (b1961), a former world champion (1995) heavyweight professional boxer with 40 wins from 45 contests 'under his belt,' standing 1.9m (6'2") high and 112Kg (17st. 6lbs) in weight. His handshake was amazing. His right hand wrapped around mine and looked and felt enormous. He was in retirement and at his country club, and my remit was to thank him for his financial generosity to my school pupils. I felt totally at ease and safe with him. This was not so with Samson. '…He performed…' (v25) for his enemies and had a servant 'lad' (v26 KJV) assigned to look after him, and in his blind state, he had to be led about. Such was his 'fall from grace!' Even so, because of his faith, he is mentioned in God's Hall of Fame (Hebrews 11:32) although his end was not glorious. Lou Nicholes, Evangelist and Missionary, sums up the life and death of Samson:

> Samson, the judge, paid with his own life for his greatest victory over the enemies of Israel. He is remembered more for what he destroyed than for what he built up. He failed to check the impulse that began early in his career and twenty years later they killed him.'[37]

Satan was behind this end-of-life story, and his work then as now, was to '… kill and destroy… (John 10:10a); this certainly happened for many Philistines and for Samson himself.

Pastor David Guzik[38] says of Samson's early life, 'Instead of putting himself in tempting situations, he should have fled from youthful lusts (2 Timothy 2:22) like Joseph did (Genesis

39:12). Samson was the great conqueror who never allowed God to properly conquer him.' Until the end of his life, Samson chose to rely on his own strength and his own resources.

Charles Haddon Spurgeon, (1834-1892), Pastor of Metropolitan Tabernacle, London for 38 years, renowned preacher and author, said in his sermon on Samson, quoted by David Guzik:

"The Old Testament biographies were never written for our imitation, but they were written for our instruction. Upon this one matter, what a volume of force there is in such lessons! 'See,' says God, 'what faith can do. Here is a man, full of infirmities, a sorry fool; yet, through his childlike faith, he lives. 'The just shall live by faith.' He has many sad flaws and failings, but his heart is right towards his God; he does trust in the Lord, and he does give himself up as a man consecrated to his Lord's service, and, therefore, he is saved.' I look upon Samson's case as a great wonder, put in Scripture for the encouragement of great sinners."[39]

Matthew Henry's Commentary on Judges 16:23-30 brings attention to Samson's change of relationship with God:

'Samson's afflictions were the means of bringing him to deep repentance. By the loss of his bodily sight the eyes of his understanding were opened; and by depriving him of bodily strength, the Lord was pleased to renew his spiritual strength.' He sought not his own death, but Israel's deliverance, and the destruction of their enemies. 'Great as was the sin of Samson, and justly as he deserved the judgments he brought upon himself, he found mercy of the Lord at last.'[40]

It is **strange** that Samson's supernatural strength is linked to his hair, but this gift he misused. In his sorrow for sin, Samson found God's forgiveness and mercy.

8 Ruth - A Gentile makes the God of the Jews her own God.

'In the days when the judges ruled, there was a famine in the land. So a man from Bethlehem in Judah, together with his wife and two sons, went to live for a while in the country of Moab. The man's name was Elimelek, his wife's name was Naomi, and the names of his two sons were Mahlon and Kilion. They were Ephrathites from Bethlehem, Judah. And they went to Moab and lived there. Now Elimelek, Naomi's husband, died, and she was left with her two sons. They married Moabite women, one named Orpah and the other Ruth. After they had lived there about ten years both Mahlon and Kilion also died, and Naomi was left without her two sons and her husband.

Then Naomi said to her two daughters-in-law, "Go back, each of you, to your mother's home. May the Lord show you kindness, as you have shown kindness to your dead husbands and to me. May the Lord grant that each of you will find rest in the home of another husband."

Then she kissed them goodbye and they wept aloud and said to her, "We will go back with you to your people." But Naomi said, "Return home, my daughters. Why would you come with me? Am I going to have any more sons, who could become your husbands?"

*At this they wept aloud again. Then Orpah kissed her mother-in-law goodbye, but Ruth clung to her. "Look," said Naomi, "your sister-in-law is going back to her people and her gods. Go back with her." But Ruth replied, **"Don't urge me to leave you or to turn back from you. Where you go I will go, and where you stay I will stay. Your people will be my people and your God my God. Where you die I will die, and there I will be buried.** May the Lord deal with me, be it ever so severely, if even death separates you and me." When Naomi realised that Ruth was determined to go with her, she stopped urging her.*
(Ruth 1:1-5; v8-11; v14-18)

The account of Ruth begins in the closing days of the period of Judges. That was a period of general unrest and of the Israelites failure to honour God and keep his covenant through a 400 year period culminating in the death of Samuel about 1035 BC. Samuel died eight years after the start of the monarchy with King Saul as the first king, from about 1043 BC.[41] The days of the judges were dark days for Israel and the phrase in Judges repeated a number of times is, ' In those days Israel had no king; everyone did *as they saw fit*' (Judges 21:25), (*Emphasis mine*).

There was a severe famine in the land of Israel so Elimelech with Naomi and their two sons went from the fertile area of Bethlehem[42] to the pagan country of Moab because life was so tough. Iain Gordon in his church blog, 'Living Waters': Jesus Plus Nothing, adds: 'Elimelech and Naomi were in such a situation and faced with running or trusting God, they chose the former and worse of the two options. It was a decision that would ultimately cost Elimelech and his two sons their lives. For we read that they left Bethlehem (which means 'the place of bread') in Judah ('praise') to go to Moab (which means 'from father: what father?')[43] As God had promised prosperity and plenty if the people obeyed him, a famine indicated that they were disobedient and so brought the famine and its consequences upon themselves (Deuteronomy 11:11-17). Their brief stay in Moab became ten tragedy-filled years, after which only Naomi returned to Israel. Matthew Henry's commentary on Ruth chapter 1 is also scathing about the decision to go to Moab instead of remaining in Israel and trusting God to provide. He writes: 'Elimelech's care to provide for his family, was not to be blamed; but his removal into the country of Moab could not be justified. And the removal ended in the wasting of his family.'[44]

The two sons married Moabite women, which was disobeying God, and eventually all three men died leaving three widows and the daughters had no children.[45] David Guzik, Pastor, Santa Barbara, California; Commentary on Ruth 1, remarks about this, 'To be a childless widow was to be among the lowest, most disadvantaged classes in the ancient world. There was no one to support you, and you had to live on the generosity of strangers. Naomi had no family in Moab, and no one else to help her. It was a desperate situation.'[46] However, she heard that God was at work in Israel, so she planned to return there and live in Judah. She was in a foreign land and needed to return to where she felt secure and would have support. She had been stripped of all that in Moab.

Naomi tried to persuade her daughters-in-law to stay with their own people in Moab which would have made good sense as they would be dependent on the charity of others as widows who were not, within their culture, allowed to work. She believed

God would provide for them and they would have a good new home life. She told them: 'May the Lord grant that each of you will find rest in the home of another husband' (Ruth 1:9). 'Rest' meant happiness and it indicated Naomi had real loving concern for Ruth and Orpah, as verses 10 and 11 show.

Orpah stayed in Moab, however, since she was not convinced about following Naomi's God, but Ruth insisted on travelling back with Naomi, since she liked what she heard of Israel and what she saw of the faith of Naomi and the love of her God. Both girls loved Naomi but Ruth 'clung' (v14) to Naomi and said she would never be separated from Naomi until death. Ruth insisted she would go or stay with Naomi and her people and God would be her own. This was a strange and amazing statement to make which she made very sincerely. David Guzik adds, 'This was more than change of address. Ruth was willing to forsake the Moabite gods she grew up with and embrace the God of Israel. She was deciding to follow the Lord. This Gentile woman, once far from God, had drawn near to him.'[47]

Naomi tried hard to discourage Ruth from coming with her back to Israel. She might have felt Ruth would be unsupported there and unprotected. Naomi may also have felt she was to blame for the tragedies in Moab because of not trusting God in Israel with her husband Elimelech and leaving for a foreign country. But, for ten years, Ruth had seen Naomi's values and she had been made very aware of Naomi's God and she didn't want any alternative, certainly not Moab's paganism! Ruth knew that the God of Israel was the true God. This was absolute commitment. The Lord of Naomi, the God of Israel, was fair, just and loving and could be trusted with her future. Ruth really was a Gentile convert, but when it came to leaving Moab behind, Orpah decided Israel was not for her, she was more comfortable in Moab.[48] We see with Matthew Henry, 'Those that go in religious ways without a steadfast mind, stand like a door half open, which invites a thief; but resolution shuts and bolts the door, resists the devil and forces him to flee.'[49]

Ruth had resolved to go with Naomi and face the future with her mother-in-law. She had complete confidence in Naomi and the Lord God who was now her Lord and God. This was a **strange** turn-around from idol worship and conversion of heart and mind.

9 1 Samuel - *An old man is deaf to God but a boy hears his voice.*

'The boy Samuel ministered before the Lord under Eli. In those days the word of the Lord was rare; there were not many visions. One night Eli, whose eyes were becoming so weak that he could barely see, was lying down in his usual place. The lamp of God had not yet gone out, and Samuel was lying down in the house of the Lord, where the ark of God was.

Then the Lord called Samuel. Samuel answered, "Here I am." And he ran to Eli and said, "Here I am; you called me." But Eli said, "I did not call; go back and lie down." So he went and lay down. Again the Lord called, "Samuel!" And Samuel got up and went to Eli and said, "Here I am; you called me." "My son," Eli said, "I did not call; go back and lie down." Now Samuel did not yet know the Lord: the word of the Lord had not yet been revealed to him.

A third time the Lord called, "Samuel!" And Samuel got up and went to Eli and said, "Here I am; you called me." Then Eli realised that the Lord was calling the boy. So Eli told Samuel, "Go and lie down, and if he calls you, say, 'Speak, Lord, for your servant is listening.'" So Samuel went and lay down in his place. The Lord came and stood there, calling as at the other times, "Samuel! Samuel!" Then Samuel said, **"Speak, for your servant is listening**.'"

(1 Samuel 3:1-10)

Eli the High Priest had become the thirteenth judge in Israel and would be followed by Samuel as the last one.[50] In this role he was also the chief administrator and his two sons collaborated with him conducting the sacrifices and ceremonies, as Eli, aged 98, was blind and frail but a large man. He was tired physically, emotionally and spiritually, especially from his parenting challenges. People came to consult him in disputes and he sat by the entrance to the house of God where he was easily accessible. 'Now Eli the priest was sitting on his chair by the doorpost of the Lord's house' (1 Samuel 1:9b); 'When (*the messenger*) mentioned the ark of God (*which had been captured by the enemy*), Eli fell backwards off his chair by the side of the gate. His neck was broken and he died, for he was an old man, and he was heavy. He had led Israel for forty years' (1 Samuel 4:18) (*Emphasis mine*).

According to the Levitical law, sacrifices had to be offered according to God's instructions and Eli's sons showed an arrogance and complete disrespect towards God and what he required (Leviticus 3:1-5). A summary of Eli's sons is found in a single verse which says they were, '…scoundrels; they had no regard for the Lord' (1 Samuel 2:12).

All was going well with Elkanah and Hannah's family life and God was blessing them and their support of Samuel in the temple (v18-21). In contrast, things were not going well for Eli who didn't discipline his sons but overlooked their greed and immorality (v22-25). God was preparing Samuel to be Eli's successor, instead of Eli's sons, 'And the boy Samuel continued to grow in stature and in favour with the Lord and with people' (v26).

After some years, when Samuel was probably twelve,[51] God revealed to Samuel what he had previously made known to Eli about judgment to come. In spite of his many weaknesses, Eli was humble enough to accept God's coming judgment as a just punishment for his failures (1 Samuel 3:15-18). Because Eli had become lukewarm in his faith and stopped listening to God, God bypassed him and so spoke to Samuel.

This failure to hear, or being selective in hearing, is the reason why Jesus spoke to people in parables, bypassing the learned Jewish leaders and speaking to the hearts of those in tune with him, who were often the common people.[52]

Don Fleming (b1949), writer of the Bridgeway Bible Commentary, evangelist, church planter and Bible teacher in Australia, gives us the background picture of life in Israel at the time of Eli's leadership, 'In those days the word of the Lord was rare; there were not many visions' (1 Samuel 3:1). Fleming explains, 'The word of the Lord was rare because of the hardness of heart among the people of Israel and the corruption of the priesthood. God will speak, and guide, when his people seek him, and when his ministers seek to serve him diligently.'[53]

Physically and spiritually, Eli had lost his sight and with his advanced age he was a very ineffective judge and leader of Israel. He was weak towards the end of his life as Isaac was (Genesis 27:1), but not as with Moses (Deuteronomy 34:7) who remained strong to the end. One morning before dawn, God spoke to Samuel in a clear audible voice, and Eli, who himself couldn't hear God speaking, encouraged Samuel at God's third attempt to get Samuel to listen to God.[54] Samuel was called by God because of the poor state the nation was in. He didn't understand that the voice speaking to him *was* God because we read, 'Now Samuel did not *yet* know the Lord: the word of the Lord had not yet been revealed to him' (1 Samuel

3:7) (*Italic mine*). Samuel would come to know the Lord at the right time. Using similar words of response over the years, God has spoken to individuals who have all similarly responded with the words, 'Here I am.'[55]

The Knowing Jesus blog helpfully suggests, 'It must have been overwhelming yet wonderful for such a young boy to hear God talking to him in the early hours of the morning and discover that he was to be used as a prophetic voice to the people of God. Samuel was ready and willing to hear the Word of the Lord and responded with words that many others have uttered down through centuries of time, 'Speak, for your servant is listening' (v10).[56]

In relation to verse 10, Fleming says Samuel is directed by Eli to say to God: '"Speak". We must hear from God. The preacher may speak, our parents may speak, our friends may speak, our teachers may speak, those on the radio or television may speak. That is all fine, but their voices mean nothing for eternity unless God speaks through them.'[57] The fact that it says the Lord stood alongside Samuel suggests it is a pre-incarnate appearing of Jesus before he was born as a baby at Bethlehem.

Roger Nam, Professor of Hebrew, Candler School of Theology, Georgia, adds: 'Remember, the Word of the Lord had been rare and precious. Samuel's eagerness is commendable, 'And he ran to Eli' (v5a), but an overzealous human spirit needs to take a backseat to God's sovereignty,'[58] such as when David wanted to build God a house, but God had been occupying a tent (2 Samuel 7:5) and the time was not yet right.

Nam also identifies the changes taking place in Samuel as he matures. In 1 Samuel 3, he 'undergoes eagerness, confusion, maturity, growth, realisation, knowledge, panic, and affirmation.'[59] As time passes, Samuel becomes a mature prophet (v20; 4:1), judge, military leader (1 Samuel 7:5, v15) and intercessor for the Israelites when they fail (1 Samuel 15:10-11). Sadly, at the end of his life when Samuel appointed his sons to take over the leadership of Israel after him, '…his sons did not follow his ways. They turned aside after dishonest gain and accepted bribes and perverted justice' (1 Samuel 8:1-3). Samuel's sons were no better than Eli's.

Nam concludes, 'The Lord is no respecter of persons and the eyes of the Lord continue to travel to and fro, looking for a person who has a listening ear, a trusting heart, and a willing spirit that is ready to say, 'speak Lord, your servant is listening' (1 Samuel 3:9b). The Lord is ready to use anyone who is willing to become an instrument to be used in the furtherance of his truth.'[60]

Dr. Ralph F. Wilson is a pastor, author, artist, publisher and director of Joyful Heart Ministries. He comments on this chapter, 'Our goal must be knowing God himself, not just experiencing the supposed novelty of hearing his voice. Hearing his voice is not a gimmick or spiritual token to attain so you can brag about it. Hearing his voice is part of a conversational relationship. Indeed, it adds greatly to the receiving part of communication.'[61]

Hearing and following instructions or orders are particularly important. Eli had lost touch with his God but despite his youthful age, Samuel was spiritually awake and receptive. It is sad that Eli could no longer hear God but also **strange** that Samuel could and was keen to obey. In the armed forces, the importance of hearing and following orders is drilled into service personnel. Alfred Lord Tennyson (1809 -1892), was an

English poet and the Poet Laureate during much of Queen Victoria's reign. He wrote in his poem, 'Charge of the Light Brigade' (1854), the immortal words:

> 'Theirs not to make reply,
> Theirs not to reason why,
> Theirs but to do and die.'[62]

Psalms has much to say about seeking God and listening to and obeying him, such as in Psalm 27:

> 'My heart says of you, "Seek his face!"
> "Your face, Lord, I will seek."'
> (v8)

> 'Wait for the Lord;
> be strong and take heart
> and wait for the Lord.'
> (v14)

At least Eli knew to tell Samuel to listen to God and wait for instructions.

10 2 Samuel - *God moved through the treetops sounding like marching soldiers.*

> *'Once more the Philistines came up and spread out in the Valley of Rephaim; so David enquired of the Lord, and he answered, "Do not go straight up, but circle round behind them and attack them in front of the poplar trees.* **As soon as you hear the sound of marching in the tops of the poplar trees, move quickly**, *because that will mean the Lord has gone out in front of you to strike the Philistine army." So David did as the Lord commanded him, and he struck down the Philistines all the way from Gibeon to Gezer.'*
>
> *(2 Samuel 5:22-25)*

David was anointed king over Israel (2 Samuel 5:3). Chronicles tells us a large fighting force of 340,800 volunteered to serve in the army under his leadership, but the rest of the nation Were 'fully determined' and 'of one mind to make David king' (1 Chronicles 12:38). There was a tremendous three-day party and celebration with 'plentiful supplies' …and 'joy in Israel' (v40b). David was victorious in battle, popular amongst his people, and in total reigned for 40 years (2 Samuel 5:4-5).

God had commanded Israel to take Jerusalem but 400 years later it was still in Jebusite hands until David and some of the army conquered the small Canaanite city in the centre of Israel. He '…took up residence in the fortress there and called it the City of David' (2 Samuel 5:9a). God was truly blessing David and he extended the city, 'And he became more and more powerful, because the Lord God Almighty was with him' (v10). Master craftspeople came and built David a fine house to further establish him as king, '...for the sake of (*God's*) people Israel' (v12). The kingdom was firmly established but David knew it belonged to God. (*Insertion mine*)

As David Guzik, Pastor at Santa Barbara, California, reminds us: 'David knew God wanted to use him as a channel to bless his people. It was not for David's sake that he was lifted up, but for the sake of his people Israel.'[63]

David took wives and concubines from Jerusalem who were undoubtedly Canaanites and with them he had many children. This was in contradiction to the law of Moses, 'He must not take many wives, or his heart will be led astray. He must not accumulate large amounts of silver and gold' (Deuteronomy 17:17). He should not have married outside his own people. For David, at a time of success and prosperity, he was laying a foundation for the future which would lead to problems.

The Philistines heard of David's success and anointing as king so they went in vast numbers to search for him and overcome him in battle at a town called Baal Perazim. David, who was raised up as leader specifically to save Israel,[64] wisely consulted God about what to do and God promised him success against them. So David went to battle, gained the promised victory, and said, 'As waters break out, the Lord has broken out against my enemies before me' (2 Samuel 5:20). David won the battle but gave God the glory. The Philistine soldiers were defeated, but more than that their idols carried into battle to help defeat the Israelites, were abandoned by the Philistines as they retreated, and carried off the battlefield by David and his men indicating the Lord was victorious over enemy gods.

Because David inquired of God and obeyed God, he had learned to listen to him and conduct his wishes.

The Philistines were unhappy to be beaten by Israel and so gathered their forces and prepared to attack a second time in the Valley of Rephaim. Again, David asked God what to do and God told him not to attack directly but to employ the strategy of attacking from behind after he had heard God moving into position, '…in front of the poplar trees' (v23b). It was the same enemy but not the same way to defeat them.

Bryce Morgan, Pastor of The Way of Grace Church, Buckeye, Arizona, adds: 'David was a seasoned warrior. If there was a tactical advantage to be gained, David would have found it. No, as God makes clear to David, this strategic placement was only strategic because David would be given a supernatural advantage.'[65]

David was not to move forward until God had struck the enemy first. The **strange** sign to David was '…the sound of marching in the tops of the poplar trees…' (NIVUK) '…when thou hearest the sound of a going in the tops of the mulberry trees, that then thou shalt bestir thyself…' (KJV) (v24a). At that point David was to move quickly. In the second battle, God ensured he had the glory because *he* led the people to victory.

Guzik quotes Spurgeon as saying, 'As the Rabbis have it, and it is a very pretty conceit if it be true, the footsteps of angels walking along the tops of the mulberry trees make them rustle; that was the sign for them to fight, when God's cherubim were going with them, when they should come, who can walk through the clouds and fly through the air, led by the great Captain himself, walking along the mulberry trees, and so make a rustle by their celestial footsteps.'[66]

Matthew Henry in his commentary on 2 Samuel 5 says, 'Two great victories obtained over the Philistines we have here an account of, by which David not only balanced the disgrace and retrieved the loss Israel had sustained in the battle wherein Saul was slain but went far towards the total subduing of those vexatious neighbours, the last remains of the devoted nations.'[67]

The bigger picture is that the nations of the world through Satan and the powers of evil were attempting to overthrow God's people and his kingdom. This is a constant battle as the Psalmist declares, 'Why do the nations conspire and the peoples plot in vain? The kings of the earth rise up and the rulers band together against the Lord and against his anointed, saying, "Let us break their chains and throw off their shackles"' (Psalm 2:1-3). The Philistines wanted Jerusalem for themselves. They were angry they lost the first battle and humiliated when they lost the second to Israel.[68]

It appears that God organised an army of angels to march over the tops of the poplar trees. At the sound of their marching David was to go forward by faith and follow the invisible army with his physical army to secure victory. It didn't mean that David was to sit back and do nothing. He was called to listen for the marching and wait to go forward.[69]

When God chooses to, he can use the wind and its sound moving to achieve his will. Compare the following three references:

1 'As for those of you who are left, I will make their hearts so fearful in the lands of their enemies that the sound of a wind-blown leaf will put them to flight' (Leviticus 26:36).

2 'As soon as you hear the sound of marching in the tops of the poplar trees, move quickly, because that will mean the Lord has gone out in front of you' (2 Samuel 5:24).

3 'Suddenly a sound like the blowing of a violent wind came from heaven and filled the whole house where they were sitting' (Acts 2:2).

In relation to the tree tops, Bryce Morgan concludes, 'We don't know what this sound was that David heard. Some think it was it simply God's way of describing the sound of a strong wind rustling the tops of the trees. Is this what God used to cover the sound of the attacking Israelites and give them the element of surprise?'[70] What we do know is that God was on the move ahead of Israel's army and David was to listen and follow God's leading as he was commanded to write out the law of the Lord, read it and live by it every day, when taking on the reign as king (Deuteronomy 17:18-20).

11 1 Kings - *A queen is overwhelmed by the wealth and lifestyle of a king.*

'When the queen of Sheba heard about the fame of Solomon and his relationship to the Lord, she came to test Solomon with hard questions. Arriving at Jerusalem with a very great caravan – with camels carrying spices, large quantities of gold, and precious stones – she came to Solomon and talked with him about all that she had on her mind. Solomon answered all her questions; nothing was too hard for the king to explain to her.

When the queen of Sheba saw all the wisdom of Solomon and the palace he had built, the food on his table, the seating of his officials, the attending servants in their robes, his cupbearers, and the burnt offerings he made at the temple of the Lord, she was overwhelmed. She said to the king, "The report I heard in my own country about your achievements and your wisdom is true. But I did not believe these things until I came and saw with my own eyes. Indeed, **not even half was told me**; in wisdom and wealth you have far exceeded the report I heard. How happy your people must be! How happy your officials, who continually stand before you and hear your wisdom!"'

(1 Kings 10:1-8)

The Queen of Sheba made a visit to see King Solomon at the height of his intellectual fame and prosperity. She recognised his authority unlike in Jesus day when the Pharisees asked Jesus for a sign of his authority for his teaching.

Jesus referred them to two people whose lives and actions of faith would condemn them: Jonah and the Queen of Sheba, as seen in our present passage being studied. Jesus calls the latter the Queen of the South, because it was South of Canaan, and says: 'The Queen of the South will rise at the judgment with this generation and condemn it; for she came from the ends of the earth to listen to Solomon's wisdom, and now something greater than Solomon is here' (Matthew 12:42; Luke 11:31).

Sheba may have been in Africa (Josephus says she was from Ethiopia). It is also possible she came from the South of Arabia. Rev Charles Ellicott (1819-1905), a vicar in Rutland then Bishop of Bristol, UK., believed she came from Ethiopia and that Sheba and Seba are both in that country.[71] Ellicott also affirmed, that one of her successors was Candace (KJV) or Kandake (NIVUK)[72] who gave the treasurer of Ethiopia permission to worship in Jerusalem (Acts 8:27). Geoff Fox, business executive and free church elder adds: 'The Queen, with her huge retinue, may have travelled up to 1500 miles to meet with Solomon.'[73] This would have taken her about 150 days, that is about five months, for a return journey and was quite an undertaking.

Clearly, she wanted to satisfy her curiosity about his fame, faith and knowledge (1 Kings 10:1), and 'she had heard reports of the connection between Solomon's fame and the Lord's name.'[74] She came to ask questions of him and to listen to his wisdom, as Jesus said. Word had got to her about his achievements and especially about '…his relationship to the Lord…' (v1). She had spiritual leanings and wanted to be better informed and, perhaps, become better acquainted with Solomon's God.

She came and shared with Solomon everything on her mind. Before and during her long journey to see Solomon, the Queen was determined to listen well and came respectfully as one monarch to another, not to buy any favours but in generosity to thank him for his time, answers to her questions and for his wisdom. Solomon received her with courtesy, gave her time and all his attention and answered everything to her complete satisfaction. He anticipated this sort of visit because he believed God would answer his prayer when initially he asked for exceptional wisdom:

'As for the foreigner who does not belong to your people Israel but has come from a distant land because of your name ... Do whatever the foreigner asks of you, so that all the peoples of the earth may know your name and fear you, as do your own people Israel, and may know that this house I have built bears your Name.'

(1 Kings 8: 41, v43)

Solomon is proud of the temple he has built, his prosperity and wisdom and is especially protective of his God and his Name. He wanted his visitors to come to know and love his God. The Queen was naturally impressed and affected by all she heard and by all she saw: the buildings, the furniture, the provisions, the working relationships of the servants, the professionalism of his staff, his wisdom and his humble and sincere worship of the Lord, his God. All of this 'overwhelmed' her (1 Kings 10:5). Her curiosity was satisfied and her doubts squashed. She found that *'seeing is believing.'* She then says something very **strange**,

'…not even half was told me; in wisdom and wealth you have far exceeded the report I heard' (v7b).

The Queen remarked on how happy both common people and officials must be. She praises God and acknowledges his love for Israel. She was so 'overwhelmed' she bestowed on Solomon great riches (v10-11) and she received from him gifts from his stores. She reminds Solomon that blessing and prosperity from God are by his grace and are not automatic (Ecclesiastes 9:11).[75] Good judgment and justice are also necessary (Jeremiah 22:15) to please God.

In discussing this chapter, Bible Study Tools tells us, 'Thus giving of thanks must be made for kings, for good kings, for such kings; they are what God makes them to be.'[76]

Solomon prayed sincerely and God answered his prayer super-abundantly and kept his promise to Solomon who had asked:

'…give your servant a discerning heart to govern your people and to distinguish between right and wrong. For who is able to govern this great people of yours?' The Lord was pleased that Solomon had asked for this. So God said to him, "Since you have asked for this and not for long life or wealth for yourself, nor have asked for the death of your enemies but for discernment in administering justice, I will do what you have asked. I will give you a wise and discerning heart, so that there will never have been anyone like you, nor will there ever be. Moreover, I will give you what you have not asked for – both wealth and honour – so that in your lifetime you will have no equal among kings."'

(1 Kings 3:9-13)

The visit of the Queen provides an example of answered prayer. This is what God can do. In his very extensive commentary, Rev. Joseph S. Exell (1849-1909) who was a Minister, editor and writer, wrote on 1 Kings 10:

> 'In this history, there are various points of view wherein the Queen of Sheba appears as a type and representation of the Church, as we know that Solomon is in many respects a striking type of Christ. We have illustrations of God's dealings with His people, and of the workings of Divine grace, in the following particulars relating to the Queen of Sheba.'[77]

In God's sovereignty and by his grace, God can and does choose to call people from a variety of places and backgrounds to achieve his will. For instance, he called the Queen from Sheba, Rahab from Jericho, Ruth from Moab, Nebuchadnezzar from Babylon, and the king of Nineveh. The Queen, raised up by God found Solomon had no equal among monarchs: kings *or* queens! This is a reminder of what God does for a person who comes to him by faith and becomes a Christian: a citizen of his kingdom,[78] and comes to receive eternal life and a home in heaven. As Paul told the Corinthian Christians: "What no eye has seen, what no ear has heard, and what no human mind has conceived' – the things God has prepared for those who love him – these are the things God has revealed to us by his Spirit' (1 Corinthians 2:9-10a). Despite the greatness of Solomon as discovered by the Queen of Sheba, Jesus is a much greater king. Geoff Fox concludes: 'Jesus Christ is the greatest! But the half has not been told!'[79]

12 2 Kings - *Elisha and the floating iron axe head.*

'The company of the prophets said to Elisha, "Look, the place where we meet with you is too small for us. Let us go to the Jordan, where each of us can get a pole; and let us build a place there for us to meet." And he said, "Go." Then one of them said, "Won't you please come with your servants?" "I will," Elisha replied. And he went with them. They went to the Jordan and began to cut down trees.

As one of them was cutting down a tree, the iron axe-head fell into the water. "Oh no, my lord!" he cried out. "It was borrowed!" The man of God asked, "Where did it fall?" When he showed him the place, **Elisha cut a stick and threw it there, and made the iron float**. "Lift it out," he said. Then the man reached out his hand and took it.'

(2 Kings 6:1-7)

As they increased in number, the company of the prophets with Elisha (2 Kings 2:5), who were in training with their master, were too crowded in their accommodation (2 Kings 6:1), so they went to the River Jordan to build a larger house. Josephus tells us that along the river there were large numbers of trees and shrubs, including willows, poplars and tamarisks. There didn't seem to be an owner of this land. Anyone could cut timber here, and so we read the whole group were involved: '...every man a beam...' (2 Kings 6:2 KJV). All were encouraged to do the cutting, shaping and carrying. Elisha, in charge of the project, when asked by the prophetic company should they start, gave it his blessing, '…And he said, "Go"' (v2).

One assistant prophet requested Elisha to go with them. Elisha agreed. Rev. Joseph S. Exell (1849-1909) who was a Minister, editor and writer, wrote on 2 Kings 6: 'He, therefore, raised no difficulty, but at once, in the simplest manner, acceded to the request. There is a remarkable directness, simplicity, and absence of fuss in all that Elisha says and does.[80]

So the workforce got to the banks of the Jordan and each started to cut down and prepare their own tree and shape it into a beam. This is when for one man disaster struck. The iron axe head he was using came off and fell into deep water. In the time of Moses, iron was already in use for axe heads (Deuteronomy 19:5). Axe heads were apparently prone to do this, so Moses issued regulations to cover that sort of occurrence. However, to the user, this loss was a particular problem. The head had disappeared and the axe was a borrowed one and so couldn't be returned to the owner.

This reminds me of an occasion when I thought the garden fork I was using to release and then lift a large boulder in my garden was a loan from a friend. I manged to lift the rock but snapped off a prong. This weighed heavily on my conscience as it couldn't be repaired. I therefore approached the owner and explained what had happened, apologised and offered to replace it. The old gentleman, owner of the fork, smiled reassuringly and said it was a gift and not a loan so I must not worry. I had damaged what was mine! This was not the case of the axe in 2 Kings 6.

The Theology of Work blog shows the prophet's dilemma as follows: 'He had borrowed the axe from a lumberjack. The price of such a substantial piece of iron in the bronze age would have meant financial ruin for the owner, and the prophet who borrowed it is distraught. Elisha takes the economic loss as a matter of immediate, personal concern and causes the iron to float on top of the water, where it can be retrieved and returned to its owner.'[81] The head just needed to be put back on the shaft.

Elisha realised the prophet felt the embarrassing loss very keenly so performed a miracle in spearing the head under the water and causing the iron to float. He turned to the assistant prophet, '"Lift it out," he said. Then the man reached out his hand and took it' (2 Kings 6:7).

To cause the iron to float even with the help of the small stick would have been a remarkable and **strange** sight but was one way he was able to help the assistant prophet to cope with his challenge! The miracle was simply that: God's intervention through God's man. That is why it appears in the Scriptures. Had it been luck or the skill of Elisha, it would not have been recorded. Elisha asked the prophet to retrieve it to fix in his mind for ever that this happened and that he lifted it out of the water, strengthening his own faith and being involved in this small and simple miraculous event.

The story teaches us of God's concern for a simple need (v5a). It was important for the prophet to share his need with Elisha and to see God at work in this situation and learn that if God can be at work in minute details he can take control of the bigger picture of the life and future of his people, Israel. Nothing escapes God's gaze, as the Psalmist shows us, 'You have searched me, Lord, and you know me. You know when I sit and when I rise; you perceive my thoughts from afar ' (Psalms 139:1-2). God sees and engages in insignificant things.

The story also shows us God's concern for his people in the work they do and enables success to those who work hard and trust him in the details as the Bible Outlines blog shows: 'It shows us the divine approval and value for God's people to work hard and do things for themselves when they can. We always need to work in the strength which He supplies, but we must put our hands to the axe and even reach into the water to pull out the floating axe head when God does work above the natural order of creation.'[82] Matthew Henry in his commentary on 2 Kings 6, also expresses things succinctly, 'This man was so respecting the axe-head. And to those who have an honest mind, the sorest grievance of poverty is, not so much their own want and disgrace, as being rendered unable to pay just debts. But the Lord cares for his people in their smallest concerns.'[83] The assistant prophet as borrower was in debt to the lender. God was concerned about the debt and he was concerned the assistant prophet should learn a valuable lesson.

The work and role of a prophet is not only to bring God's messages to people but also to restore to a pre-Fall condition the created order of things where possible and put right what 'the Fall' had disrupted on Earth. Paul wrote to the vibrant but challenging Christians at Corinth, 'And God has placed in the church first of all apostles, second prophets, third teachers, then miracles, then gifts of healing, of helping, of guidance, and of different kinds of tongues' (1 Corinthians 12:28).We also read that prophets are given, 'To equip his people for works of service…' (Ephesians 4:12a). This is exactly what Elisha was doing and showing his trainee prophets the principles of trust in God and that if God should choose to do so, he can work outside of his own created laws of nature when needed.

13 1 Chronicles - *The leaders consider it a privilege to give offerings to God.*

'Then King David said to the whole assembly: "My son Solomon, the one whom God has chosen, is young and inexperienced. The task is great, because this palatial structure is not for man but for the Lord God. With all my resources I have provided for the temple of my God – gold for the gold work, silver for the silver, bronze for the bronze, iron for the iron and wood for the wood, as well as onyx for the settings, turquoise, stones of various colours, and all kinds of fine stone and marble – all of these in large quantities. Besides, in my devotion to the temple of my God I now give my personal treasures of gold and silver for the temple of my God, over and above everything I have provided for this holy temple: three thousand talents of gold (gold of Ophir) and seven thousand talents of refined silver, for the overlaying of the walls of the buildings, for the gold work and the silver work, and for all the work to be done by the craftsmen. Now, who is willing to consecrate themselves to the Lord today?"

Then the leaders of families, the officers of the tribes of Israel, the commanders of thousands and commanders of hundreds, and the officials in charge of the king's work gave willingly. They gave towards the work on the temple of God five thousand talents and ten thousand darics of gold, ten thousand talents of silver, eighteen thousand talents of bronze and a hundred thousand talents of iron. Anyone *who had precious stones gave them to the treasury of the temple of the Lord in the custody of Jehiel the Gershonite.*

***The people rejoiced at the willing response of their leaders**, for they had given freely and wholeheartedly to the Lord. David the king also rejoiced greatly.'*
(1 Chronicles 29:1-9)

David is coming towards the end of his life and so he endorses his son, Solomon, as the next king and the one who should build for God an elaborate temple, worthy of the Lord his God. He worked hard to get together the materials as it was seen by him to be a task too great for Solomon to achieve on his own. The work is described as 'great' because, firstly, it was a vast project and secondly it was '…not for man but for the Lord God' (1 Chronicles 29:1). As Paul said to the Colossian Christians, '…Whatever you do, work at it with all your heart, as working for the Lord not for human masters' (Colossians 3:23). David said, '…with all my resources I have provided for the temple of my God' (1 Chronicles 29:2a). David Guzik, Pastor at Santa Barbara, California tells us, 'This was certainly true. When we consider all that David did to provide security, a location, the land, money, materials, supervisory staff, workers, plans, and an organized team to run the temple, it is evident that David gave this work of preparation all of his might.'[84] David gave all he could because he loved his Lord God and he considered it an honour to be involved in the building of a temple for his worship. It was David's treasure, and as Jesus said, 'For where your treasure is, there your heart will be also' (Matthew 6:21). God was personally his God so he says, '…my

God…' (1 Chronicles 29:2a). David gave personal treasures '… over and above everything I have provided…' (v3). He knew he was in a position to give a lot, and in his correctly directed heart he did so, but he also challenged the ordinary people to give what they could and give from a heart right with God. He said, '…Now, who is willing to consecrate themselves to the Lord today?' (v5b) This elevated their actions, as Guzik says, to the equivalent of 'ordination to the priesthood.'[85]

Then we read that the leaders of families, the officers of the tribes, the commanders and the officials, '…gave willingly' (v6b). The people saw the example of the generosity of the king and leaders of the nation, '(Who) gave towards the work on the temple of God…' (v7a). Precious stones, presumably jewellery, were given to the treasury and Jehiel the Gershonite kept these in safe custody. We then read some amazing and **strange** words, 'The people rejoiced at the willing response of their leaders, for they had given freely and wholeheartedly to the Lord. David the king also rejoiced greatly' (v9). The leaders found it easy to give when they saw the value of the project and good examples of the 'over and above' giving of King David. It gave them joy to give. As the NT teaches, 'Each of you should give what you have decided in your heart to give, not reluctantly or under compulsion, for God loves a cheerful giver' (2 Corinthians 9:7).

As Bible Study Tools blog tells us, 'They were not only glad that they had it to offer, but that they had hearts to do it; they found themselves quite free to do the work, and saw it was so with others, which gave them extreme pleasure: because with perfect heart they offered willingly to the Lord; not grudgingly, but cheerfully; not pressed and urged.'[86] Their giving honoured God and they gave to his glory. This is why David was able to rejoice because he saw excellent work going forward which he was about to leave behind, even though he knew he was about to die.

As Study Light blog reports: David, '…gladly acknowledged that everything that people possess comes from God; therefore, in making offerings to him, the Israelites had only given back what he had already given them. They had done this joyfully and willingly, and David prayed that they would maintain such devotion to God always (v10-20).[87]

14 2 Chronicles - *Praise is joined by fire and glory at the dedication of the temple.*

'When Solomon finished praying, fire came down from heaven and consumed the burnt offering and the sacrifices, and the glory of the Lord filled the temple. **The priests could not enter the temple of the Lord because the glory of the Lord filled it.**

When all the Israelites saw the fire coming down and the glory of the Lord above the temple, they knelt on the pavement with their faces to the ground, and they worshipped and gave thanks to the Lord.'

(2 Chronicles 7:1-3)

In chapter six, we read that Solomon blessed the people,'… the whole assembly…' (2 Chronicles 6:3). He stood and then knelt and with arms outstretched towards heaven (v12-13), he praised and worshipped God and prayed a heart-felt prayer dedicating the temple to God and for his worship. He had built what his father David wanted to do but wasn't allowed by God to do (1 Chronicles 17:4). He built the temple to proclaim the 'Name of the Lord' (2 Chronicles 6:10), just by its existence, size and splendour and he organised the ark containing the covenant commandments to be placed in it (v11).

So he could be clearly seen and heard Solomon stood on a platform and then in public view, knelt in humility before God and all the assembled people. The temple was in Jerusalem, which is where God chose to be, and from there he ruled his people. He states great truths to God in the hearing of the people and pleads their cause such as if and when they lose in battle and become discouraged:

> 'When your people Israel have been defeated by an enemy because they have sinned against you and when they turn back and give praise to your name, praying and making supplication before you in this temple, then hear from heaven and forgive the sin of your people Israel and bring them back to the land you gave to them and their ancestors.'
>
> (2 Chronicles 6:24-25)

Solomon continues to plead before God on behalf of the people and a number of times asks God to forgive sin, concluding with the words: '...Remember the great love promised to David your servant' (v42b). This was a mighty and truly sincere prayer.

We then move into chapter seven and have God's answer to Solomon's prayer. The first thing God did was send fire from heaven to burn up '...the burnt offering and the sacrifices...' (v1). Charles Ward Smith (1927-2013), an American pastor who founded the Calvary Chapel movement observes:

> 'It's a reminder of the dedication of the tabernacle in the wilderness where the fire of God came down and kindled the coals upon the altar and consumed the sacrifices. And the glory of God filled the tabernacle in the wilderness. And now the same thing happened as God's glory fills the temple.'[88]

In the Bible, fire is linked with coming from God on a number of occasions. It is mentioned coming to Earth from heaven in 627 Bible references, others indicate fire seen in heaven.[89] The following are just a selection:

- 'Fire came out from the presence of the Lord and consumed the burnt offering…'
  (Leviticus 9:24)
- '…fire from the Lord burned among them and consumed some of the outskirts of the camp.
  (Numbers 11:1)
- 'Fire flared from the rock, consuming the meat and the bread.'
  (Judges 6:21b)
- 'Then the fire of the Lord fell and burned up the sacrifice, the wood, the stones and the soil, and also licked up the water in the trench.'
  (1 Kings 18:38)
- '…the Lord answered him with fire from heaven on the altar of burnt offering.'
  (1 Chronicles 21:26b)
- 'When Solomon finished praying, fire came down from heaven and consumed the burnt offering and the sacrifices…'
  (2 Chronicles 7:1)
- 'I will rain upon him, and upon his bands, and upon the many people that are with him, an overflowing rain, and great hailstones, fire, and brimstone.'
  (Ezekiel 38:22bKJV)

- 'When the disciples James and John saw this, they asked, "Lord, do you want us to call fire down from heaven to destroy them?"'[90]
  (Luke 9:54)
- 'They saw what seemed to be tongues of fire that separated and came to rest on each of them.'
  (Acts 2:3)
- '…fire came down from heaven and devoured them.'
  (Revelation 20:9)

The second thing God did was to allow his glory to fill the temple (2 Chronicles 7:1). Fire and glory must have been a very **strange** sight. The glory in the temple stopped the priests entering and the fire descending and the glory in the sky over the temple, caused the people to fall on their faces in worship. We are told '…they knelt on the pavement with their faces to the ground, and they worshipped and gave thanks to the Lord…' (v3). The fire and glory were an impressive sight which affected everyone present.

The Worthy Bible Commentary produced on-line by Worthy Ministries, Nashville, Tennessee, on these verses tell us, 'By that token of God's acceptance they were encouraged to continue the solemnities of the feast for fourteen days, and Solomon was encouraged to pursue all his designs for the honour of God' (v4-11).[91]

The fire and the glory were a response from God in answer to the prayer of Solomon and because the hearts of the people were right with God. The writer to Hebrews writes: 'Our God is a consuming fire.' (Hebrews 12:29; based on: Deuteronomy 4:24). Isaiah asks a searching question:

'Who of us can dwell with the consuming fire?
Who of us can dwell with everlasting burning?'
(Isaiah 33:14b)

Fire from God in the Scriptures caused people to be very afraid, and they were thankful when it burned up a sacrifice indicating that God had accepted the sacrifice and turned his anger from the people. In 2 Chronicles 7, the people saw the fire and the glory and on this occasion were not afraid but knelt and worshipped and thanked God for his goodness and love. They were very aware of his holiness and of their own unworthiness. The king and all the people offered many sacrifices (2 Chronicles 7:4-5), as their response in worship to the immediate presence of God and the way that had touched them. The king's example made a deep impression on the people, and it shows that when a leader leads well, people follow. The scene is as follows: the priests assumed their positions and blew their trumpets, the Levites assumed their instruments intended for occasions of praise, and all the people stood in respectful reverence and awe. David not only appointed his choir leader and choir to remain in place after his death to serve Solomon, he also wrote the celebratory hymn of praise ready for the king and his people to use at the dedication of the temple (1 Chronicles 16:1-11). Solomon followed the example of David with the singers and musicians, and exuberant praise and worship. The people followed their king and '…gave thanks to the Lord, saying, "He is good; his love endures for ever"' (2 Chronicles 7:3b).

The celebrations went on for fourteen days altogether (seven for the dedication followed by seven for the festival), until Solomon sent the people home, '…joyful and glad in heart for the good things the Lord had done for David and Solomon and for his people Israel' (v10). The people had to be encouraged to return to their normal lives and Solomon completed the temple and his own royal palace, and as time passed, he continued living his life close to God. This was noted by God and we read, 'The Lord appeared to him…' (v12), and it was then that God was saying, in effect, despite all the fire and glory, despite all the praise and worship, despite all the promises to keep true to the Lord God on the part of King and people, he made it clear to Solomon that he knew he and the people would all fail and fall into sin. A new need for repentance and humility from people would emerge, and there would be a new need for forgiveness from God. I can almost imagine Solomon saying 'I won't let it happen. I will never let you down.' The Apostle Peter said the same thing years later when he said though everyone else fails, he would never let Jesus down (Matthew 26:33). But then the 'cock crowed!' And so we read that God said, 'If my people, who are called by my name, will humble themselves and pray and seek my face and turn from their wicked ways, then I will hear from heaven, and I will forgive their sin and will heal their land' (2 Chronicles 7:14).

15 Ezra - *God touches the hearts of Israelites and they rebuild the temple.*

'In the first year of Cyrus king of Persia, in order to fulfil the word of the Lord spoken by Jeremiah, the Lord moved the heart of Cyrus king of Persia to make a proclamation throughout his realm and also to put it in writing: "This is what Cyrus king of Persia says: The Lord, the God of heaven, has given me all the kingdoms of the earth and he has appointed me to build a temple for him at Jerusalem in Judah. Any of his people among you may go up to Jerusalem in Judah and build the temple of the Lord, the God of Israel, the God who is in Jerusalem, and may their God be with them. And in any locality where survivors may now be living, the people are to provide them with silver and gold, with goods and livestock, and with freewill offerings for the temple of God in Jerusalem."

*Then the family heads of Judah and Benjamin, and the priests and Levites – **everyone whose heart God had moved – prepared to go up and build the house of the Lord** in Jerusalem. All their neighbours assisted them with articles of silver and gold, with goods and livestock, and with valuable gifts, in addition to all the freewill offerings.'*
(Ezra 1:1-6)

When King Cyrus came to the throne of Persia God prompted him to let the Jews, who were in exile there, go back to their own land and rebuild the temple in Jerusalem. This happened about 536-8 BC (Ezra 1:1-4; 5:13). As Bill Pratt, a member of the leadership team of Cornerstone Baptist Church, North Carolina, explains in his commentary on these verses, 'The Book of Ezra is a history of the early days of the return of the Jewish people from their 70 years of captivity in Babylon. The book spans 538 BC to around 456 BC. Ezra 1-6 describes the return from Babylon under the leadership of Sheshbazzar (*Ezra 1:11*), and Zerubbabel (*Ezra 2:2*), and the rebuilding of the Jerusalem temple.' (*Insertions mine*).[92]

This was in accordance with Jeremiah's prophecies:

'This is what the Lord says: "When seventy years are completed for Babylon, I will come to you and fulfil my good promise to bring you back to this place. For I know the plans I have for you," declares the Lord, "plans to prosper you and not to harm you, plans to give you hope and a future"' (Jeremiah 29:10-11).

Babylon was to be punished for taking the Jews into captivity and Cyrus was being blessed and used by God to release them. There is also a link with Isaiah's prophesy where he: '...says of Cyrus, "He is my shepherd and will accomplish all that I please"' (Isaiah 44:28). Cyrus is mentioned by name 150 years before he was born! The authority for taking the initiative and for getting this information right is God's who says, 'I am the Lord, and there is no other; apart from me there is no God' (Isaiah 45:5).

The return of the Jews is also found on the 'Cyrus cylinder' discovered by archaeologists showing inscriptions by King Cyrus himself. The release of the captives was confirmed by a written decree (Ezra 1:1; 5:13), and this written decree was alluded to by King Darius of Persia some 20 or so years later. On it was written: 'Memorandum: In the first year of King Cyrus, the king issued a decree concerning the temple of God in Jerusalem: Let the temple be rebuilt...' (Ezra 6:2b-3a).

To summarise the situation: It was in King David's heart to build the temple and God said, not yet. Then his son, King Solomon, received the go-ahead from God to build it and it was built. As time passed, the Jews fell into sin and lost their close walk with God. This, linked with the unstable political situation, led to King Nebuchadnezzar II and the Babylonians capturing and transporting the Jews to exile in Assyria, and the temple in Jerusalem being destroyed. The Jews had been away from their own land of Israel for 70 years. At the start of the exile Jeremiah prophesied their return, 'This is what the Lord says: 'When seventy years are completed for Babylon, I will come to you and fulfil my good promise to bring you back to this place' (Jeremiah 29:10). Now, with a return from exile looming with the intervention of Cyrus, the temple was about to be re-built. That was the first step in re-building their nation. Sadly, only a remnant of the Jews returned initially, but this was in accordance with prophesy, 'Though your people be like the sand by the sea, Israel, only a remnant will return' (Isaiah 10:22a).

We then arrive at some remarkable and **strange** words in Ezra 1:5 which shows the prompting of God, the Holy Spirit, where family heads, the priests, the Levites, and 'everyone whose heart God had *moved*' (NIVUK) (*Emphasis mine*), were suddenly prepared to go up to Jerusalem to start the re-building. The way God spoke to people or touched them in some way has different shades of meaning brought out by different Bible translations. NIVUK has 'moved,' KJV has 'raised' based on the spelling 'raysed' in the C16[th] translations: Coverdale Bible (1535); Bishop's Bible (1568); and Geneva Bible (1587). Other versions have: 'roused,' 'stirred up,' 'motivated,' 'moved,' 'inspired,' 'prompted' and 'motivated.' All may be correct and all taken together shows God was wonderfully at work and the people responded to him and some were ready to go!

David Guzik gives his summary of the challenges facing the returning Jews and says, 'It was essential that God *move* the spirits of these returning exiles because they faced many difficulties:

- The journey itself was long, dangerous, and expensive.
- They returned to a city in ruins with no proper homes, roads, or city institutions.
- They didn't have all the material resources they needed.
- They didn't all return to Jerusalem but spread out over the province of Judea.
- They had many enemies.
- Their land was actually the possession of another empire.'[93]

The Study Light Christian information blog gives a useful explanation of the release of the Jews from Babylon:

'Cyrus had been ruler of Persia for some time before he conquered Babylon in 539 BC. His policy was, when he conquered a nation, to allow any people held captive by that nation to return to their homeland. Therefore, soon after he conquered Babylon, that is, in his first year as the Jews' new ruler, he gave permission for the Jews to return to Jerusalem.'[94]

Not only were the people able to go freely back to Israel, but the proclamation from King Cyrus respected and reverenced 'The Lord, the God of heaven…,' and said, 'Any of his people among you may go … and may their God be with them. And in any locality where survivors may now be living, the people are to provide them with silver and gold, with goods and livestock, and with freewill offerings for the temple of God in Jerusalem' (Ezra 1:2-4). This was wonderful freedom, wonderful provision. The leaders were to go and lead volunteers. And so, '…everyone whose heart God had moved – prepared to go…'(v5). Such was the presence of God that those who were 'moved' by him left for Jerusalem.

For a number of years, one of my favourite Christian songs has been, 'Just One Touch From The King' (and the first line continues…'changes everything'), written played and sung by Godfrey Birtill. I have been 'moved' by the song and prayed many times over people requesting prayer in services at an Anglican Church pleading with God to touch them. The words are powerful and God's touch, prompting, leading or moving makes an amazing difference in the heart of a person who is ready to hear and obey his 'small voice,' as Elijah was on Mt. Carmel.[95]

16 Nehemiah - *A sad wine-waiter asks a king if he can return home.*

'In the month of Nisan in the twentieth year of King Artaxerxes, when wine was brought for him, I took the wine and gave it to the king. I had not been sad in his presence before, so the king asked me, "Why does your face look so sad when you are not ill? This can be nothing but sadness of heart." I was very much afraid, but I said to the king, "May the king live for ever! Why should my face not look sad when the city where my ancestors are buried lies in ruins, and its gates have been destroyed by fire?" The king said to me, "What is it you want?"

*Then I prayed to the God of heaven, and I answered the king, "If it pleases the king and if your servant has found favour in his sight, let him send me to the city in Judah where my ancestors are buried so that I can rebuild it." Then the king, with the queen sitting beside him, asked me, "How long will your journey take, and when will you get back?" **It pleased the king to send me**; so I set a time.*
(Nehemiah 2:1-6)

Nehemiah is working in royal service in a significant position as cup-bearer or wine taster and waiter to the king, but, as a loyal Jew, he is keen to know how things are in Jerusalem.[96] He is told by his brother and friends that the re-building of Jerusalem and especially the temple is not going well and the remnant who returned are discouraged and in trouble. The main city wall has been severely damaged and the city gates burned down, by enemies sabotaging the work (Nehemiah 1:3). To Nehemiah this was dreadful news and we see his response in five active verbs telling us that he sat, wept, mourned, fasted and prayed – in that order (v4). Then he confessed his own and his people's sins and reminds God of his promise to bring his people to the promised land. This was his dream but was not the present reality. At the moment they are in Babylon which had been over-run by Persia. For four months he prayed and would not act in haste until one day when he knew he must bring the plight of the Jews to the king so he prays for the opportunity, '…Give your servant success today by granting him favour in the presence of this man' (v11b). The king was now Artaxerxes who was on the throne about 70 years after Cyrus. Nehemiah served him and respected him but knew he was just a 'man', and a man who was not more powerful than his God.

This is the background to chapter two where we find that the king notices the demeanour of one of his palace staff. Nehemiah is normally cheerful in front of the king but on this occasion, he couldn't hide the intensity of his sorrow and grief and so he writes, 'I had not been sad in his presence before, so the king asked me, "Why does your face look so sad when you are not ill? This can be nothing but sadness of heart. I was very much afraid."' (Nehemiah 2:1b-2).

Nehemiah was in a very central position in the court. He would be responsible for choosing the food and drink for the court on a daily basis so on this particular historically-identified day the king's adviser and confidante looked different. Normally he had the joy of the Lord as his strength (Nehemiah 8:10), but not today!

On the question of sadness, David Guzik, Pastor, Santa Barbara, California; tells us:

'As was true in the courts of many ancient kings, it was forbidden to be sad in the presence of the king. The idea was that the king was such a wonderful person that merely being in his presence was supposed to make you forget all of your problems. When Nehemiah looked sad, it could have been taken as a terrible insult to the king.'[97]

Though he was nervous, Nehemiah used his usual greeting to the king. He naturally had tasted the wine, and probably the food, and wished the king a long safe life,[98] but gave the king his reasons for sadness. His home city was still in ruins whereas it should by now have been re-built as the re-building started about 458 BC (Ezra 1:5). It was now some 12 years later, 446 BC. Nehemiah set the scene and the king was intrigued. Nehemiah recalled the conversation, 'The king said to me, "What is it you want?" Then I prayed to the God of heaven, and I answered the king…' (Nehemiah 2:4-5a). Matthew Henry (writing in 1706) tells us at this point, 'The king encouraged Nehemiah to tell his mind. This gave him boldness to speak; Nehemiah prayed to the God of heaven, as infinitely above even this mighty monarch.'[99] We see Nehemiah's graciousness, tact and wisdom linked to his faith and prayer before he answered the king. As the Pulpit Commentary (published 1909)[100] tells us, he used a subject dear to the heart of the king: tombs. 'The Persians, like the Jews, had a great respect for the tomb, and regarded its violation with horror. Artaxerxes would naturally sympathise with the wish of his follower to give security to the city where his ancestors were interred.'[101] Nehemiah simply asked for permission to inspect Jerusalem, sort out the problems, and kick-start the re-building work again, then return. We see Nehemiah's honesty in a very delicate situation.

Nehemiah was actually asking for an important thing of the king. He was saying in effect, according to Dr. Constable's Expository Notes, 'to Artaxerxes, to revise his official policy toward Jerusalem.'[102] In the absence of the Jews from their land, others had moved in who petitioned King Artaxerxes telling him the Jews should not be allowed to return.

'The king sent this reply:

To Rehum the commanding officer, Shimshai the secretary and the rest of their associates living in Samaria and elsewhere in Trans-Euphrates:

Greetings. The letter you sent us has been read and translated in my presence. I issued an order and a search was made, and it was found that this city has a long history of revolt against kings and has been a place of rebellion and sedition. Jerusalem has had powerful kings ruling over the whole of Trans-Euphrates, and taxes, tribute and duty were paid to them. Now issue an order to these men to stop work, so that this city will not be rebuilt until I so order. Be careful not to neglect this matter. Why let this threat grow, to the detriment of the royal interests? As soon as the copy of the letter of King Artaxerxes was read to Rehum and Shimshai the secretary and their associates, they went immediately to the Jews in Jerusalem and compelled them by force to stop.'

(Ezra 4:17-23)

Despite the letter received from Trans-Euphrates, and Artaxerxes' reply, the king now over-looked his earlier reply and was compassionate towards Nehemiah. He enquired how long Nehemiah would be away, and showed he valued Nehemiah and wanted him to get safely there and back. For his part, Nehemiah planned his absence and gave the king his word and promise to return within a certain time. Nehemiah worked with a plan and he knew his God worked with a plan believing the principles that, 'the plans of the Lord stand firm for ever, the purposes of his heart through all generations' (Psalms 33:11). Nehemiah's plans were as Solomon taught through Proverbs, 'The plans of the diligent lead to profit as surely as haste leads to poverty' (Proverbs 21:5).

Nehemiah knew what he was doing because he had pondered and prayed over the situation for four months,[103] talking to God and listening to him. He knew the journey would be dangerous through enemy territory and he knew what basic materials he needed when he got there, so he gave the king a time for his return based on his calculations.[104] And so Artaxerxes gave him permission and all the resources and protection he needed for his journey and the repair project. John Gill's Exposition of the Bible (1763), chapter two, makes it clear that once permission was granted Nehemiah set out but his reception in Jerusalem was resented because he found himself amongst enemies; he 'came to Jerusalem, to the great grief of the enemies of Israel.'[105] The king had provided Nehemiah with officers and mounted soldiers and letters of authority for his journey. Nehemiah acknowledged it was all granted '…because the gracious hand of my God was on me…' (Nehemiah 2:8b). However, ultimately, the walls were re-built despite the scoffing and taunting of the enemies (v19).

From the king's point of view, Nehemiah was special and so Artaxerxes was enthusiastically supporting him in this venture. Here we encounter those **strange** words from Nehemiah, 'It pleased the king to send me' (v6b). Strange, because the king needed him, but God was behind him going back to the land of Israel! As the on-line English Bible Notes group expresses it, 'Like Ezra, Nehemiah was sent with the Lord's approval,'[106] and this made his going right and worthwhile.

17 Esther - *A Jew becomes queen to a Persian king and saves her own people.*

*'The king and Haman went to Queen Esther's banquet, and as they were drinking wine on the second day, the king again asked, "Queen Esther, what is your petition? It will be given you. What is your request? Even up to half the kingdom, it will be granted." Then Queen Esther answered, "If I have found favour with you, Your Majesty, and if it pleases you, grant me my life – this is my petition. And **spare my people** – this is my request."'*

(Esther 7:1-3)

The book of Esther is unusual because it has no mention of God. Neither does it mention Jerusalem, the law, prophets, the Promised Land or exile. It doesn't include formal prayers or miracles, though it does mention fasting. However, it does link with the rest of the Bible and is held in particularly high esteem by present day Jews, and by Jews through the ages because it involves the survival of the Jewish nation. This is celebrated world-wide in the annual festival of Purim.

The book addresses several key themes through the story of Esther's life, as Amy G. Oden, Professor of Early Church History and Spirituality, Oklahoma, writes, that Esther is:

'...part of a religious minority living within the dominant Persian culture, and ultimately even in the heart of power, the Persian court at Susa. She, like the Hebrew people in exile, is an orphan as the book opens.

She is taken in by her uncle Mordecai, an advisor at the royal court and, later, a hero who saves the king from an assassination plot. Esther eventually finds herself as part of the king's harem, hiding her Jewish identity in order to manoeuvre into the king's favour with access to his ear. Her uncle's nemesis, Haman, has convinced the king to decree that all Jews be killed, including special plans to hang Mordecai.'[107]

The book is fascinating in its intrigues, where Esther maintains her nearness to the powerful king, Artaxerxes, but called Xerxes in this book. When she knows her own people are in a dangerous position and about to be killed, she acts to cause them to be delivered by her great people skills and tact. She reveals Haman's treachery, and in so doing reveals her own Jewish heritage to the king as she appeals for her life and the lives of her people. The king grants her requests, reverses the decree to kill Jews and gives them permission to defend themselves against anyone who treats them badly. This included his own people.

As a Jewish woman in a Persian court in Susa, a city conquered by Artaxerxes, but which gained much importance as a regional centre, she successfully navigated both cultures: Jewish and Persian. She eventually takes a courageous stand with the king in order to deliver and preserve her own people. As the story unfolds, we see the powerful are brought low, and those in servitude are exalted and honoured. The plot of the evil Haman to destroy the Jews is overturned, and Haman himself is killed. Through these **strange** events and this amazing reversal of circumstances, we see God at work defending and providing for his people.

The book of Esther therefore explains the importance to the Jews of Purim as the Jews are delivered by the actions of Queen Esther, and '…the month of Adar as the time when the Jews got relief from their enemies, and as the month when their sorrow was turned into joy and their mourning into a day of celebration' (Esther 9:21b-22a).

Having considered the overall situation, we must now consider the detail. Chapter seven begins with a second banquet being organised by the new queen Esther.[108] King Xerxes is the principal guest but another important guest was Haman whom the king had promoted to being a senior official, '…elevating him and giving him a seat of honour higher than that of all the other nobles. All the royal officials at the king's gate knelt down and paid honour to Haman, for the king had commanded this concerning him' (Esther 3:1-2). All the nobles bowed down to Haman, but not the Jewish Mordecai, who was a noble and court adviser. He refused as a Jew to bow down to a Persian. Hadassah, an orphan, also known as Esther, was his beautiful young cousin (Esther 2:7), and from this point comes into prominence. Haman was furious with Mordecai and decided to kill him and all his people. This would have included Esther.

Meanwhile, the kings wife, Vashti, was disrespectful to him and lost her position. There was a beauty contest to replace her and Esther won and became queen, but to be tactful, she kept her nationality secret (v10). Esther knew the truth as Solomon expressed it that there is, '…a time to be silent and a time to speak' (Ecclesiastes 3:7b). David Guzik, Pastor at Santa Barbara tells us, 'Esther, even when she finally made her request, showed great tact. She did not immediately identify herself as a Jew, targeted for massacre – even as Haman also hid the identity of the group he targeted when he made his request' (Esther 3:8).[109] He didn't make it clear to the king he was aiming to kill all the Jews.

Queen Esther greatly pleased the king who wanted to reward her and Mordecai for being faithful to him and to grant her a wish. Esther was very restrained but then opened up to the king, as the Pulpit Commentary explains, 'When the king for the third time put the question, "What is thy petition, queen Esther? and what is thy request? It shall be performed, even to the half of the kingdom," she opened all her mind.'[110]

The king asked a two part question, 'Now what is your petition?' and 'What is your request?' (Esther 5:6). Esther answered in a two part answer, '…grant me my life' '…And spare my people…' (Esther 7:3). Sadly, Mordecai had pointed out to Esther that Haman was determined to kill all the Jews including Esther herself, but he felt Esther was in the right place to plead for them to be spared. Iain Gordon in his Jesus Plus Nothing church blog concludes that, 'Exposing Haman… was no small event! … Esther got to the point where she was totally abandoned to her own will and self-preservation saying only "if I perish I perish." But the beauty of what was unfolding is that it all was done in accordance to the perfect precision of God's timetable.'[111] Mordecai sent a particularly challenging message to Esther:

> 'Do not think that because you are in the king's house you alone of all the Jews will escape. For if you remain silent at this time, relief and deliverance for the Jews will arise from another place, but you and your father's family will perish. And who knows but that you have come to your royal position for such a time as this?'
>
> (Esther 4:13-14)

With great courage she, therefore, asked for her life and that of her people. She appealed to the king on a personal basis knowing she had never displeased him. The king agreed to her request. She pointed out to him that Haman was working against her and the Jews. The king was furious that even his own wife's life was in the balance.

Before the king knew Haman's motive, he had been persuaded to allow him to erect a pole 23 metres high and to agree to impale on it anyone who did not honour him in his newly promoted position. He was anticipating making a public spectacle of Mordecai. However, things went badly wrong for Haman. Mordecai was honoured and Haman was executed for his treachery and impaled on his own pole (Esther 5:14; 7:9).

The end result is that God's own people were saved and secure and in that God receives the glory and honour, respect and reverence, even without the book of Esther saying so!

18 Job - *Satan has a conversation with God.*

*'In the land of Uz there lived a man whose name was Job.
This man was blameless and upright; he feared God and
shunned evil. He had seven sons and three daughters, and
he owned seven thousand sheep, three thousand camels, five
hundred yoke of oxen and five hundred donkeys, and had a
large number of servants. He was the greatest man among
all the people of the East. His sons used to hold feasts in
their homes on their birthdays, and they would invite their
three sisters to eat and drink with them.*

*When a period of feasting had run its course, Job would
make arrangements for them to be purified. Early in the
morning he would sacrifice a burnt offering for each of
them, thinking, "Perhaps my children have sinned and
cursed God in their hearts." This was Job's regular custom.
One day the angels came to present themselves before the
Lord, and Satan also came with them. The Lord said to
Satan, "**Where have you come from**?" Satan answered
the Lord, "From roaming throughout the earth, going to
and fro on it." Then the Lord said to Satan, "Have you
considered my servant Job? There is no-one on earth like
him; he is blameless and upright, a man who fears God
and shuns evil." "Does Job fear God for nothing?" Satan
replied. "Have you not put a hedge around him and his
household and everything he has? You have blessed the
work of his hands, so that his flocks and herds are spread
throughout the land. But now stretch out your hand and*

*strike everything he has, and he will surely curse you to your
face." The Lord said to Satan, "Very well, then, everything
he has is in your power, but on the man himself do not lay a
finger." Then Satan went out from the presence of the Lord.*
(Job 1:1-12)

The book of Job explores how righteous people sometimes suffer.
It uses a common literary device from ancient wisdom literature,
that of an extended conversation using poetic speeches. Job is
introduced as a good man but he has an adversary: Satan. He
is determined to point out a failing in God's moral oversight of
the universe and has decided that God is unduly protecting Job
and so his earthly success is a reward from God for goodness.
He argues that if that protection is taken away, Job will not be
successful, nor morally upright and will turn away from God.
This is then put to the test by God allowing Satan to test Job
with suffering.

Job comes from the land of Uz.[112] and he may well be the
author of this book bearing his name, writing about his own
experiences, and though the date of writing is uncertain, it is
commonly thought that it is the first book of the Bible to be
written using an ancient style of Hebrew, and is a masterpiece
of Hebrew poetic literature. It therefore represents the earliest
written record of a relationship between a person and God.

The book is not just about suffering and pain but also
explores theology. Job is grappling with his understanding of
God and why God doesn't function as he expects him to and
so the book relates his conversation with and experience of
God. God himself endorses Job's life and values when he links
Job with Noah and Daniel who could save only themselves by

their righteousness as revealed through Ezekiel in his prophecy (Ezekiel 14:14). They could not save the nation. Job is further endorsed by James, step-brother of Jesus, writing to people who knew their nation's history, 'As you know, we count as blessed those who have persevered. You have heard of Job's perseverance and have seen what the Lord finally brought about. The Lord is full of compassion and mercy' (James 5:11).

In the first verse we are told how Job is morally upright and has a close relationship with God. He is described as being 'blameless' but not sinless. In other words he had a very good relationship with people. He was righteous with an impeccable reputation and treated others well but he was still a sinner in God's eyes (Job 1:1). With present-day thinking, we would consider it remarkable that he worshipped the one true God without the benefit of other believers, literature or traditions springing from faith. In that sense, he was like Melchizedek who simply appeared on the world's stage without background or credentials (Genesis 14:18-20).[113]

The size of Job's family of ten children and the thousands of his livestock indicate he was a man of wealth and status. He was the greatest man in the East, but was also a godly man who managed his money time and energy well. He cared for the needy, disabled and dying; he rescued orphans and he defended the under-privileged, and Matthew Henry suggests this indicates he was a magistrate (Job 29:12-17; 31:16-21).

To get the whole picture of Job and his family, David Guzik, Pastor at Santa Barbara, California, points out that the family enjoyed life and especially celebrations in their happy and close relationships which is commendable, (Psalms 133:1).[114] Guzik says 'Spurgeon saw in Job 1:4-5 a permission for feasting and celebration among believers; he preached a Christmas sermon upon this very text and used it as proof that God allows and enjoys such celebrations among his people.' Job as a mature man of faith and a family man shows great responsibility for his children and covers them by his prayers and worship, as he acted as a priest for his family. After each celebratory feast we read, '…This was Job's regular custom' (Job 1:5b). The scene is now set for the battle to come. The place where it begins is heaven itself.

The day came when the angels came for an audience with God and Satan was there. This shows that even *fallen* angels are subject to God. Note, the fallen angel who was the lying spirit which entered some of Ahab's prophets (1 Kings 22:21), and Satan, who on one occasion, stood alongside Joshua the High Priest to accuse him (Zechariah 3:1). Satan is often seen as a powerful archangel as Michael and Gabriel, but he is a created being and not as powerful as God, although he wanted to be. This is why God expelled him from heaven partially and will expel him totally in the future (Isaiah 14:12-13; Revelation 12:9), and he has been trying to undermine God and his faithful people from his kingdom of Earth ever since. We read: 'How you have fallen from heaven, morning star, son of the dawn! You have been cast down to the earth, you who once laid low the nations! You said in your heart, "I will ascend to the heavens; I will raise my throne above the stars of God…"' (Isaiah 14:12-13a). The devil is given various names including: 'morning star,' and 'son of the dawn' but here we have, 'in Hebrew "the Satan." The adversary. He's Job's adversary – but even more foundationally – he's God's adversary.'[115]

In a personal conversation, God says some **strange** and unexpected words to Satan, 'Where have you come from?' (Job 1:7a) God made it clear that angels only operate in heaven and earth with God's express permission, so he wanted to know what Satan's business was. God, as omniscient, knew where Satan had been but he wanted Satan to say for himself. As Kirsten, from Georgia says in her blog for women: 'God doesn't ask because he doesn't know. He asks to give the opportunity to be honest and forthcoming.'[116] Job replies, '... 'From roaming throughout the earth, going to and fro on it' (Job 1:7b). This continued to be the situation and the Apostle Peter encouraged young Christians in the first century, 'Be alert and of sober mind. Your enemy the devil prowls around like a roaring lion looking for someone to devour' (1 Peter 5:8).[117]

God brings up the subject of Job with his godly character for discussion with Satan (Job 1:8). God points out he is upright and of impeccable character. He really is special to God, but later in the book we find he has his accusers, as well as Satan, against him. Satan starts to attack Job in his audience with God, accusing God of moral failures and Job as not having personal integrity, but saying it only exists because God is especially protecting him (v9-11). However, Satan's power is limited as it was before his expulsion from heaven and ultimate future as we read in Revelation, 'Now have come the salvation and the power and the kingdom of our God, and the authority of his Messiah. For the accuser of our brothers and sisters, who accuses them before our God day and night, has been hurled down' (Revelation 12:10).

In his tempting of Peter, as the trial and crucifixion of Jesus approached, it seems that Satan wanted almost to destroy Peter but Jesus limited Satan's activity there as with Job, 'Simon, Simon, Satan has asked to sift all of you as wheat. But I have prayed for you, Simon, that your faith may not fail. And when you have turned back, strengthen your brothers' (Luke 22:31-32). God's protection of Peter is like a hedge around him as Satan recognises with God's protection of Job as he argues, 'Have you not put a hedge around him and his household and everything he has?' (Job 1:10) It is then not clear who is causing Job's suffering: Satan or God, as we read the words of Satan to God, 'But now stretch out your hand and strike everything he has, and he will surely curse you to your face' (v11). *Explaining the book blog* includes the following: 'I think it goes like this – Satan can't do anything apart from the Lord's permission. And sometimes the Lord permits Satan to harm people. And when he does, God himself takes some responsibility for the results.'[118]

The battle lines are being drawn and still are. The battle for Job's soul, for Peter's and for believers everywhere is raging and so the Apostle Paul encourages the Ephesians and all of us to, '…stand your ground, and after you have done everything, to stand, (Ephesians 6:13b). David Guzik reminds his readers, 'In response to Satan's accusation, God gave him great – though limited – permission to attack Job. God would let down the hedge without completely removing it.'[119]

Satan is now given the opportunity to attack Job but within limits! Paul said to the Early Church, '…put on the full armour of God (v11-18a). God's words through Paul are just as relevant to Job, '…be alert and always keep on praying…' (v18b). Satan had a mandate. He had the power to attack Job and his family, possessions and health, and cause much suffering but could not kill Job. 'Then Satan went out from the presence of the Lord' (Job 1:12b). Christianity blog, a Christian web portal, providing articles on current topics, said in relation to the power of Satan on the Earth, 'The Scripture speaks thus to teach us that God directs the affairs of the world.'[120] (Revelation 20:1-2)

19 Psalms - *God is everywhere including hell.*

'Whither shall I go from thy spirit?
Or whither shall I flee from thy presence?
If I ascend up into heaven, thou art there:
If I make my bed in hell, behold, thou art there.'
If I take the wings of the morning,
And dwell in the uttermost parts of the sea;
Even there shall thy hand lead me,
And thy right hand shall hold me.
If I say, Surely the darkness shall cover me;
Even the night shall be light about me.
Yea, the darkness hideth not from thee; But the night
shineth as the day:
The darkness and the light are both alike to thee.'
(Psalms 139:7-12 KJV)
'Is there any place I can go to avoid your Spirit?
to be out of your sight?
If I climb to the sky, you're there!
If I go underground, you're there!'
                    (Psalms 139:7-8 The Message)

Psalm 139 is an amazing Psalm written as a song by David for his chief musician to use in worship, and it is one of my favourites. I have used the oldest Bible version in common use, KJV of 1611, and one of the newest, MSG of 2002,[121] with its contemporary language to give a comparison. The verses I have chosen to concentrate on are verses seven to eight but the whole section is being considered from verse seven to verse 12 because this gives the context and other aspects of God's omniscience;[122] from verse seven the focus is on his omnipresence: his ability to be everywhere at once.[123] David mentions some of the places he might go, only to discover God is already there, and this brought him some comfort.

If David wanted to escape from God, it was impossible to achieve as others before him found. Elijah ran to the desert beyond Judah to escape King Ahab's wife, Jezebel, and her anger but God met him there after earth-shattering events, in a small whisper (1 Kings 19:9-18). There was also Jonah whom God told to go East, and he disobeyed and left for a destination in the West as far as he could in the known world, but on his journey God met him in the stomach of a great fish directed by God to swallow him (Jonah 1:1-3, v17).

For a Christian the omniscience of God is a great comfort. Jesus said, '…I'll be with you… day after day after day, right up to the end of the age' (Matthew 28:20 MSG); the writer to the Hebrews said, '… Never will I leave you; never will I forsake you' (Hebrews 13:5b).

Psalm 139 shows David enthralled with God's personality: he knows David's movements, his thoughts and his conduct. Before that he knew all about his conception and development in the womb. He not only *knew about* David, he also actually *knew him* at those stages. David learns of God's immense power and knowledge and that he is as much present on earth as in heaven and, to introduce a **strange** word and concept, in *'hell'* (KJV), *'Sheol'* (ESV),[124] or *'the depths'* (NIVUK).

Pastor David Guzik[125] says at this point on this psalm, 'David did not describe what we normally think of as *hell* – Gehenna (Matthew 10:28; 18:9), *(and)* the lake of fire (Revelation 20:

14-15). The Hebrew word here is *Sheol,* which normally has the sense of *the grave* or by implication *the afterlife* (Psalms 139:8).

Most people accept God is present on Earth, and know him in nature, know him through their conscience, or know him personally through Jesus Christ; less people seem to know they will live with him one day in heaven; even less accept that God is also present in hell. In fact, many question the very existence of hell.[126] This indicates they don't fully understand the teaching of the Psalm being examined: 'If I make my bed in hell, behold, thou art there,' (KJV), 'If I go underground, you're there!' (MSG).

Hell, Sheol, or *the Depths* are all describing the same thing, that God is everywhere including the place reserved for those who reject him and his love. God is everywhere and sees everywhere and so we read wise words from Solomon in the following two versions of the same verse:

'Death and Destruction lie open before the Lord – how much more do human hearts!'
(Proverbs 15:11 NIVUK)
'Hell and destruction are before the Lord: How much more then the hearts of the children of men?'
(Proverbs 15:11 KJV)

Death holds no fear for the righteous,[127] but the fact of God in hell should grip those who are not righteous, who are not Christians, with fear.

The prophet Amos also describes God's omnipresence and judgment of everyone equally and fairly when he says, 'Though they dig down to the depths below, from there my hand will take them. Though they climb up to the heavens above, from there I will bring them down' (Amos 9:2).

It is sadly a fact that torment in hell is not caused by Satan or fire but from the presence of a truly holy God in his wrath against sin and unforgiven angels and sinners.

These are those who have known the truth and rejected Christ as Saviour. The Bible describes God as loving and merciful on the one hand and just and fair on the other. This is covered thoroughly in my book, Two Destinies.[128]

Shawn E. Thomas; Pastor of the First Baptist Church of Angleton, Texas, sums this up with great passion concisely:

> 'We sometimes talk about being "separated" from God in hell, but that is not quite true. Those who go to hell are indeed separated from the glorious presence of the Lord, but there is a real sense in which they are not "separated" from God – the sad fact is that they will experience the awesome, fiery presence of God in his wrath. Jonathan Edwards said, "The saints are in his glorious presence, and the wicked in hell are in his dreadful presence"[129]

Steven Cole, retired pastor of Flagstaff Christian Fellowship, California, tells us, 'The first Soviet cosmonauts[130] irreverently joked that they didn't see God from their spaceship. But God saw them! He is there!'[131]

This Psalm 139 is a psalm of praise and a prayer which David's chief musician put to music as explained in the first paragraph. David pours out his heart to God and clearly states what he has come to understand that because of who God is and because of his character, we are always loved and never alone. Meg Bucher, freelance writer, blogger and author, indicates she closely links this psalm with prayer, 'When we seek to learn, when we look for help or healing, when we express gratitude or anxiety, and when we celebrate blessings … we pray. Prayer is conversation with God, layered with all of these intricate levels which contribute to our relationship with God our Father.'[132]

20 Proverbs - *Foolish people are considered wise if they keep quiet.*

'Even fools are thought wise if they keep silent,
and discerning if they hold their tongues.'

(Proverbs 17:28)

The book of Proverbs is a collection of wise sayings from one of the wisest men who ever lived: Solomon. We are not told in the Scriptures that Solomon was perfect and without sin or obvious failings, rather the opposite he was a normal human being. Though he was ordinary, we shall find he had a gift which was extraordinary. We are told, 'Solomon loved the Lord, walking in the statutes of David his father...' (1 Kings 3:3a) sadly, as the verse continues, '...only he sacrificed and burnt incense in high places' (v3b). God had clearly said through Moses that the Israelites were to resist and reject any aspect of idolatry and the Lord was to be their only God. They were not to have any idols. Once in the Promised Land, they were to eradicate idol worship and break down the altars they would find there, smash sacred stones, burn Asherah poles, cut down any idols and wipe out the names of any false gods (Deuteronomy 12:2-3). Solomon had a sincere faith but had not lived up to the high expectations of the Lord God. He continued in some aspects of idolatry and had some character failings in relation to women in his life, nevertheless, God blessed him and used him. God in his grace still answered Solomon's prayer when he asked for wisdom one night as he was asleep and dreaming (1 Kings 3:5). This greatly pleased God who gave him wisdom and '...a wise and discerning heart…' and much more than he had asked for including '…wealth and honour…' so that he would be the greatest king of his day and, in terms of wisdom and wealth, the greatest king in Israel's history (v12-13).

We therefore have many **strange** and remarkable sayings in Proverbs, none more so than our chosen verse in Proverbs 17. There are several important themes in this chapter. Bible Reference blog, a ministry of Got Questions, a Christian resource group, tells us, 'Among them are the importance of controlling one's words: hasty or spiteful language can do great harm…wisdom and foolishness tend to be self-perpetuating. Wise people seek wisdom, foolish people seem immune to it.'[133]

Words are powerful and important, and controlling them is difficult as James reminds us (James 3:2-5). One of our main challenges as human beings is inappropriate or poorly thought out speech. I know I tend to react and speak instead of thinking then speaking. On the other hand, choosing to remain silent gives the impression we are wise but keeping our counsel for the right moment. With effort, I do this as well. This gives the impression of wisdom. Got Question Ministries adds, 'Even if someone is wallowing in stupidity and ignorance, those flaws are disguised by their silence. Before Peter allowed Jesus to change his life he was seriously lacking in self-control, particularly with speech. He just seemed to blurt out what came into his mind such as telling Jesus, '…I will lay down my life for you' (John 13:37b). This statement fits into a whole brief conversation with Jesus in which Peter protests loyalty. The outcome was quite different from what he promised (John 13:36-38). When Jesus was warning the disciples about his forthcoming death and resurrection, Peter burst out with the words: 'Never, Lord!...This shall never happen to you!' (Matthew 16:22b), Jesus then rebuked him for his ignorant response and addressed Satan at the same time who was motivating Peter to speak out (Matthew 16:21-23).

There is something about speech which indicates character. It might show knowledge or folly (Proverbs 15:2); it might be cares which spring from a dream or too much talking which mark out the fool (Ecclesiastes 5:3). Learning doesn't come through talking but through listening, and it is easy to hurt people through speech (James 3:5-6). In fact, James who writes from experience says, 'The tongue also is a fire, a world of evil among the parts of the body. It corrupts the whole body, sets the whole course of one's life on fire, and is itself set on fire by hell' (v6). These are strong words!

The blog, Let God be True, includes the following interesting contribution, 'President Abraham Lincoln, nearly 3000 years after King Solomon wrote his proverbs, agreed with this inspired rule of wisdom and public decorum by his well-known words from a different angle, "It is better to remain silent and be thought a fool, than to speak out and remove all doubt."'[134] This is why Paul spoke firmly to the Christians in Ephesus, 'Nor should there be obscenity, foolish talk or coarse joking, which are out of place, but rather thanksgiving' (Ephesians 5:4). So many people on so many occasions make light of very serious matters. Solomon describes the superficiality of many people, and I have been in many social situations where this is an apt description of what happens, 'It is better to heed the rebuke of a wise person than to listen to the song of fools. Like the crackling of thorns under the pot, so is the laughter of fools. This too is meaningless' (Ecclesiastes 7:5-6). It is a very sobering thought that God hears our words and more than that, he knows our thoughts and motives, 'Nothing in all creation is hidden from God's sight. Everything is uncovered and laid bare before the eyes of him to whom we must give account' (Hebrews 4:13).

Nothing changes very much as the centuries pass. Speech remains important and can indicate wisdom or folly. Note how words are used on the following occasions:

- Adam, about the C40th BC[135]: 'The Lord God called to the man, 'Where are you?'
He answered, 'I heard you in the garden, and I was afraid…' (Genesis 3:9-10a).
- Solomon; third king of Israel; about the C10th BC[136]: 'Now, Lord my God… I am only a little child and do not know how to carry out my duties' (1 Kings 3:7).
- Jesus Christ; C1st AD; the Word: 'I tell you that everyone will have to give account on the day of judgment for every empty word they have spoken. For by your words you will be acquitted, and by your words you will be condemned.' (Matthew 12:36-37).
- Matthew Henry, theologian, C18th AD[137]: 'A man… is careful when he does speak, to speak to the purpose.'

Matthew Henry (1662-1714), non-conformist minister, author and theologian, writes on our verse: 'A man may show himself to be a wise man, by the good temper of his mind, and by the good government of his tongue. He is careful when he does speak, to speak to the purpose. God knows his heart, and the folly that is bound there; therefore he cannot be deceived in his judgment as men may be.'[138]

John Gill (1697-1771), English Baptist pastor, biblical scholar and theologian, writes on our verse: 'Not only one that is sparing of his words, and is really a man of knowledge and understanding; but even a fool, if he is but silent, and does not betray his folly by his words, will be reckoned a wise man by those that do not know him; and, whatever fool he may be in other respects, yet in this he acts the wise part, that he holds his peace and says nothing.'[139]

Calvary Chapel at Jonesborough, Tennessee, have written on their blog in 2012, in application of this verse, 'God can do more with a few words that we can do with an entire novel of our own. When He speaks - things happen! Therefore we need to restrain our words - to be the ones that He desires for us to speak. Then we can know that the words we speak will contain real power - real comfort - real conviction - and real love.'[140]

Travis D. Smith, Pastor of Hillsdale Baptist Church, South Carolina, concludes his study of this verse in 2015 with, 'For those who always have to say something, remember biting your tongue and saying nothing is not only wise, but in effect leads others to believe you might well be the wiser! Finally, should you need one more prod to encourage you to hold your tongue, consider this old Arab proverb, *Silence is the covering of the stupid.*'[141]

21 Ecclesiastes - *People have an in-built sense of eternity.*

*'What do workers gain from their toil? I have seen the burden God has laid on the human race. He has made everything beautiful in its time. **He has also set eternity in the human heart**; yet no-one can fathom what God has done from beginning to end.*

I know that there is nothing better for people than to be happy and to do good while they live. That each of them may eat and drink, and find satisfaction in all their toil — this is the gift of God. I know that everything God does will endure for ever; nothing can be added to it and nothing taken from it. God does it so that people will fear him.'

(Ecclesiastes 3:9-14)

Living as I do in a holiday destination for many people, I don't always realise how beautiful the coast of Cornwall is. In fact I don't always realise how beautiful this country is until I fly over it returning from overseas ready to land at a major airport. If I extend my thinking further, countries of the world I have visited all have a special, and I believe, God-given beauty.

John writes at the beginning of his gospel, 'Through him all things were made; without him nothing was made that has been made' (John 1:3). Paul the Apostle tells us why, 'Christ is all, and is in all' (Colossians 3:11b), in both people and the physical creation. God is behind how things are and how they are going to be ultimately. Genesis is clear that creation came about in stages, that is, progressively, even though in total we would say a week is a truly brief time.[142] It is reassuring to read that as each day progressed, God assessed his own work and concluded that it was good at the end of each day (Genesis 1:4). And so we read that Solomon assessed the stages of God's creation as being 'beautiful in its time' (Ecclesiastes 3:11a).

Adam Clarke, in his commentary of 1832, compares the beauty of nature with the best works of art of talented artists, 'God's works are well done; there are order, harmony, and beauty in them all. Even the *caterpillar* is a finished beauty in all the *changes* through which it passes, when its structure is properly examined, and the *end* kept in view in which each change is to issue. Nothing of this kind can be said of the works of man.'[143]

Another consideration is that God has perfect timing. He never does things early and never arrives late. The Got Questions blog[144] reminds us that, 'In 1965, the folk rock band The Byrds recorded a song, "Turn! Turn! Turn!" that used a portion of this passage and helped contribute to its recognition in pop culture.'[145] After stating that there is a time for everything at the beginning of our chapter being studied, Solomon lists a range of human experience and concludes that the comfortable and the challenging are both 'beautiful' and are from him and are designed to achieve his purpose.

In the Hope Reflected blog, concerning Christian living and encouragement, we read:

'It's very easy to forget that God's perfect timing for our lives can turn out to be completely different from what we imagine as being right. In Isaiah 55:8-9, we're told, "For my thoughts are not your thoughts, neither are your ways my ways, saith the Lord. For as the heavens are higher than the earth, so are my ways higher than your ways, and my thoughts than your thoughts." Our thoughts and ways are usually very different from our Lord's, aren't they?'[146]

God's time for things to happen is the right time. Jesus knew it was when he started his ministry with the words: '"The time has come," he said. "The kingdom of God has come near. Repent and believe the good news!"' (Mark 1:15) Paul said in his letter to young Christians at Ephesus that God's will was, 'to be put into effect when the times reach their fulfilment – to bring unity to all things in heaven and on earth under Christ' (Ephesians 1:10). We all, including Abraham so long ago, find it hard to wait for things to happen. Abraham was waiting for God's blessing on his life and for his circumstances to change for the better, 'And so after waiting patiently, Abraham received what was promised' (Hebrews 6:15). Peter informs his readers of how God views time, 'But do not forget this one thing, dear friends: with the Lord a day is like a thousand years, and a thousand years are like a day' (2 Peter 3:8).

Matthew Henry says on Ecclesiastes 3:11: 'Everything is as God made it; not as it appears to us. We have the world so much in our hearts, are so taken up with thoughts and cares of worldly things, that we have neither time nor spirit to see God's hand in them. The world has not only gained possession of the heart, but has formed thoughts against the beauty of God's works.'[147]

Having established that we don't dictate to God what he must do but rather wait for him to act at the right time with his own and not our agenda, we reach the wonderful but **strange** words that, '…He has also set eternity in the human heart…' (Ecclesiastes 3:11b).

This verse Is one of my favourites in the Bible and assures me that all human beings who are aware of, and listen to their conscience, know that there is life beyond this life. As the Bible indicates, it goes on into eternity and this deep truth has been put into hearts by God himself. So, it is a God-given awareness. The awareness is as true a fact as knowing right from wrong because of knowing deep down that there is a God. 'In the human heart' is a term which includes the mind, soul, or spirit of each person. God places eternity into that heart.

The third part of the verse tells us, '…yet no-one can fathom what God has done from beginning to end' (Ecclesiastes 3:11c). It might be that human ignorance is being contrasted by Solomon with God's perfect wisdom, or probably, that God has placed in each human heart a longing for eternity. This, then, sets people apart from all other creatures who can think of and deal with life now but not with the future and certainly no other life forms have an understanding of eternity. This reminds us that for people there is a time for everything and a season for every activity on earth (Ecclesiastes 3:1), and this is built into the human framework. By God's grace we might live 70 years, or even 80 if we are in good health (Psalm 90:10), which gives time for everything God wants us to experience and we know in the Northern and Southern temperate hemispheres of the world about seasons coming and going, although I have found when I have been in Kenya that for those on the equator there are no seasons!

Adam Clarke has a view on *eternity*: '… eternity hath he placed in their heart, without which man could not find out the work which God hath made from the commencement to the end.'[148]

The editor of Connect Us Fund blog points us to the fact that God is mysterious and yet he knows what he is doing, telling us '…we don't always understand what God is actually doing and why. Sometimes he reveals himself, but often he is content to leave us with this fact: he does everything for his glory and for our good' (Isaiah 48:9; Romans 8:28).[149]

Having said there is time and there are seasons, from God's perspective, life is little more than a temporary mist, as in James' summary of his general letter principally to scattered Christian Jews, 'Why, you do not even know what will happen tomorrow. What is your life? You are a mist that appears for a little while and then vanishes' (James 4:14).

There is more than this life and we pass on through it and on to eternity. For the Christian this is an exciting thought but for those who don't yet have a relationship with God, it can be a worrying thought, and an uncertain future which needs to be put right.

22 Song of Songs - *The banner of love is seen over two relationships: The king and his bride; Christ and the church.*

(The woman speaks of the man):

*'Like an apple tree among the trees of the forest is my beloved among the young men. I delight to sit in his shade, and his fruit is sweet to my taste. Let him lead me to the banquet hall, and **let his banner over me be love.**'*
(Song of songs 2:3-4)[150]

Song of Songs, or Song of Solomon, is a beautiful love story celebrating the love between groom and bride and explains the current situation between King Solomon and his bride. There is also a future application which many Christian theologians see: a picture of the relationship between Christ and the church.

The apple tree is cultivated and productive and would be in a garden or orchard, compared to the trees of the forest which may be larger but not bearing choice fruit. The fruit would be ripe and luscious. I can identify with this because an old, gnarled apple tree in my garden is so full of fruit the lower branches are weighed down towards the ground and I have to duck to get under them! The apples are in beautiful condition and in this July moment, almost ready to be picked, and being Bramley cookers, will be made into jam and crumbles. Solomon painted this sort of picture in Proverbs in relation to wise words of a judge, 'Like apples of gold in settings of silver is a ruling rightly given' (Proverbs 25:11). The analogy is that the groom is in choice condition and far superior to any other suitor. He had brought his bride into his banquet room, literally, a 'wine house,' or the Hebrew can also be translated as underground 'wine store' or garden 'vineyard' to celebrate the marriage. They are finally together and about to begin a life-long relationship. The groom is not a poor peasant but the king! The king is greater than all alternatives, as Jesus is to any other in heaven or on Earth, as the book of Hebrews tells us, 'So he became as much superior to the angels as the name he has inherited is superior to theirs' (Hebrews 1:4). The psalmist gives us an amazing insight into Jesus, 'You are the most excellent of men and your lips have been anointed with grace, since God has blessed you for ever' (Psalms 45:2). The same may be said of King Solomon, since he has been specially chosen, honoured, gifted and blessed by God.

The king owns the magnificent banquet house containing the very best wine, food and the finest accommodation available. He has every luxury and money is no object, and he offers it all to his bride. Sitting under the shade of the tree is the picture of contentment and the apple was a symbol of love in the ancient world. Living in the shade means it is a place of safety and security. As Hosea explains, 'People will dwell again in his shade; they will flourish like the corn, they will blossom like the vine – Israel's fame will be like the wine of Lebanon' (Hosea 14:7). The psalmist gives further re-assurance, 'Whoever dwells in the shelter of the Most High will rest in the shadow of the Almighty' (Psalms 91:1). Wonderful comfort is being offered by Solomon to his bride and by Christ to his church!

The woman in overwhelming thankfulness responds '…let his banner over me be love' (Song of Songs 2:4b). We therefore have a courting couple under an apple tree and a **strange** symbol of a banner overhead, but for the presence of the banner, whether it is a metaphor or reality, there is an explanation. Craig Harris, journalist, author and youth Minister in Texas, informs us:

'When Israel was in the desert, the people would use (their banners) to find their homes among all of the tents. Later, royal families would fly them above their homes to signify their identities. True, banners were used as a rallying point for troops in battle, but this is not a battle scene, this is a love scene. His love is covering her like a banner. His love *is* his banner. It is showing her who she belongs to and that she is safe under his care. It gives her the identity of his name and all of the wealth that goes with that.'[151]

The immediate picture may be of Solomon and his bride, but it also foretells how Jesus will relate to his bride, the church. Jesus said he was the bridegroom of the church, 'How can the guests of the bridegroom mourn while he is with them? The time will come when the bridegroom will be taken from them; then they will fast' (Matthew 9:15). Paul speaks about physical marriage, and says it is a picture of '...Christ and the church' (Ephesians 5:31-32). John sees into the future and gives a picture of the end days, 'Let us rejoice and be glad and give him glory! For the wedding of the Lamb has come, and his bride has made herself ready' (Revelation 19:7).

Craig Harris concludes:

'The good news is that Jesus is our very rich groom. He will take us to his banquet table and feast with us.

And his banner over us is love. We are safe beneath it and we can find our identity by it. We belong to him and he belongs to us. And others will know that we are Christians because God's love covers us and flows through us now and for all eternity.'[152]

John Gill, in his detailed commentary on the Bible, is quite intent to apply this banner inscribed with the word, 'love,' to our position as Christians and therefore our position in Christ. He says,

'The allusion may be to the names of generals being inscribed on the banners of their armies; so Vespasian's name was inscribed on the banners throughout his armies. Christ's name, inscribed on his, was 'love,' his church's love; and by which his company or band was distinguished from all others, even by electing, redeeming, calling love. It may signify the security and protection of the saints, while in the house of God, and enjoying communion with him, being under the banner of love, with which they are encompassed as a shield; and it may denote the very manifest and visible displays of it, which the church now experienced.'[153]

David Guzik; Pastor, Santa Barbara, California, commenting on this verse in Song of Songs 2, adds to the debate about the reason for the banner, 'Taken more poetically, the maiden rejoices that her beloved publicly and openly proclaimed his love for her, as if he had set up a banner or flag to say it'.[154] The woman is not afraid of the public seeing the great love the king has for her, in fact she is so proud of it she wants everyone to know and the banner will make it very obvious to all. Love is at the very heart of *her* relationship with the king and is the centre of attention. He also is unashamed to acknowledge *her* publicly. She can sit at his side without fear knowing that she is safe: his bride of choice.

In conclusion, I refer you to Matthew Henry who finds a worthy comparison between the banner in Song of Songs 2, verse 4, and the gospel message, 'The gospel is compared to a banner or ensign (Isaiah 11:12),[155] and that which is represented in the banner, written in it in letters of gold, letters of blood, is love, love; and this is the entertainment in the banqueting-house.'[156]

23 Isaiah - *God proclaims the Earth to be a sphere long before the scientists.*

'Do you not know? Have you not heard? Has it not been told you from the beginning?

Have you not understood since the earth was founded?

*He sits enthroned above **the circle of the earth**, and its people are like grasshoppers. He stretches out the heavens like a canopy, and spreads them out like a tent to live in.'*
(Isaiah 40:21-22)

Before and after the birth of Christ, I refer to in the traditional way of BC and AD (or left without the suffix to indicate AD), and not BCE and CE, which are used by some, meaning before common/current era and current era. The study of the size and shape of the Earth has fascinated people and for centuries there has been disagreement between theologians and scientists. Theologians in the Western world, many of whom believe in creation by God, are supported by their understanding of the Bible and specifically by their reference to Genesis. There are also scientists who believe in abstract matter coming together and then developing in some inexplicable way. For centuries, faith and science have been in conflict. As Encyclopaedia Britannica tells us:

Pythagoras (570-490 BC) a Greek philosopher who made important developments in mathematics, astronomy and the theory of music, first proposed a spherical Earth around 500 BC, mainly on aesthetic grounds rather than on any physical evidence. Like many Greeks, he believed the sphere was the most perfect shape.

Anaxagoras (500-428 BC) a Greek philosopher of nature remembered for his cosmology and for his discovery of the true cause of eclipses, argued for the spherical nature of the Earth. During a lunar eclipse, when the Earth is between the sun and the moon, he identified the shadow of the Earth as it moved across the moon, and found it was round.

Aristotle (384-322 BC) a Greek philosopher, mathematician and student of Plato, was among the first to recognize the fact of our planet being a round sphere. He observed lunar eclipses and noticed that a round sphere could cause a circular shadow. He proved the work of Pythagoras.

Despite the earlier work of philosophers, particularly the Greeks, and the development of scientific advances in the Middle Ages,[157] there was still a strong belief that the Earth was flat and not round. This is a challenge scientists like Galileo and Isaac Newton wrestled with. In their days, some believed the Earth to be round, but most still believed it to be flat right up to the C19th.

Galileo (1564-1642) an Italian natural philosopher, astronomer and mathematician, observed that the celestial bodies (Sun, Mercury, Venus, Mars, Jupiter, Saturn) do not revolve around the Earth in spherical paths which was believed for over 2000 years since Aristotle.

Isaac Newton (1642-1727) an English physicist and mathematician, first proposed that Earth was not perfectly round. Instead, he suggested it was an oblate spheroid. That is, a sphere that is squashed at its poles and swollen at the equator.[158]

Charles Darwin (1809-1882) an English naturalist, geologist and biologist promoted his theory of evolution and natural selection, a relatively recent discovery, in 1859, and published his Origin of Species.[159] With this book he shocked Victorian society, particularly the religious scholars and ministers of his day. From his particular upbringing, he tried to link *faith* and *science*. This had a real impact on the scientific community. To Darwin and colleagues, the Earth was spherical and the 'flat earth' theory was no longer believed.[160]

Having looked at our summary of those who commented on the shape of the Earth and saw the thinking firstly of philosophers and later that of scientists, it may come as a shock to realise that Isaiah (born about 720 BC, and ministered as a prophet 740-695 BC), was given by God the understanding that the Earth was a sphere, not just round, some 200 years before Pythagoras! God is making a proclamation and so we arrive at the **strange** and surprising words: '(*God*) sits enthroned above the circle of the earth, and its people are like grasshoppers. He stretches out the heavens like a canopy, and spreads them out like a tent to live in' (Isaiah 40:22) (*Insertion mine).*

As this statement was long before philosophers and scientists, it is encouraging to find their discoveries confirm the Bible's teaching. As the Got Questions research blog says, It is important to see that Isaiah didn't invent these words or develop the idea as a theory but he tells us that it is God who surrounds the Earth, and this fact is given as a comfort for God's people (Isaiah 40:1). 'The comfort is found in the content of Isaiah 40 and the subsequent chapters.'[161] Job says God, '…marks out the horizon on the face of the waters for a boundary between light and darkness' (Job 26:10). Solomon tells us of wisdom, 'I was there when he set the heavens in place, when he marked out the horizon on the face of the deep' (Proverbs 8:27).[162] From a very high vantage point, the horizon appears to be a circle around a person surveying it.

A number of commentators such as **Albert Barnes** (1798-1870) an American theologian, clergyman, abolitionist, temperance advocate and author, explain the Hebrew word for 'circle' as used in '…the circle of the earth…' Barnes explains that to be correct it means, '"above" the circle of the earth. The word rendered 'circle' (Hebrew: chûg) denotes "a circle, sphere, or arch"; and is applied to the arch or vault of the heavens, "Thick clouds veil him, so he does not see us as he goes about in the vaulted heavens"' (Job 22:14).[163] In other words, the heavens appear as a vault or curve, over the earth. This is the view of Tony Chan, an expert in Biblical hermeneutics on the use of 'circle' in Isaiah 40:22. He tells us, the Hebrew: chûg, used in this verse in Isaiah, is also translated as 'vault' in Job

22:14, and 'the horizon' in Proverbs 8:27. It is used as a noun in a special sense in, 'The carpenter measures with a line and makes an outline with a marker; he roughs it out with chisels and marks it with *compasses*' (Isaiah 44:13) *(Emphasis mine).*[164] Compasses are used to make a circle. It is used here describing the carpenter marking out a circle with an instrument, as Denis Bratcher, Professor of OT, Virginia, of the Christian Resources Institute, informs.[165]

While most modern Bible versions translate *chûg* as 'circle,' a good case can be made that 'sphere' was the sense intended by the original Hebrew. Historically, scholars have often taken this view, preferring the Latin words *sphaera, globus* and *orbis.*

Dominic Statham, a Christian Chartered Engineer, Loughborough University, UK, also makes the point, '...a sphere *appears* as a circle when seen from above—and indeed from whatever direction it is viewed. Moreover, there is good reason to believe that the word translated 'circle' might be better translated *sphere.*'[166] *(Emphasis mine)*

The point Isaiah is making of 'the circle of the earth' is that God is far above all the affairs of people. He is located in heaven above and surrounding the earth and supports, comforts, protects and strengthens his people constantly. We are also told by the psalmist that God is worthy of our praise all day long from the time the sun is seen in the morning, to the time it appears to disappear in the evening, 'From the rising of the sun to the place where it sets, the name of the Lord is to be praised' (Psalms 113:3).

If I go to the top of high cliffs here in Cornwall and I look out at a great expanse of sea, perhaps ten miles to left and right, then the horizon is clearly curved. And if I could put a 1 Km long straightedge on the sea I am told the ends would be 8 cm above the water because of the curvature of the Earth.[167]

The amazing truth in Isaiah 40:22, is that God is 'enthroned' and therefore this is a reference to him being king, and he encircles the Earth. From his perspective, from wherever he looks at the Earth, it is a circle, and although people are described by Isaiah as being as small as grasshoppers, if they are in his kingdom by faith they are safe.[168]

24 Jeremiah - *God organises the weather.*

'But the Lord is the true God; he is the living God, the eternal King. When he is angry, the earth trembles; the nations cannot endure his wrath. 'Tell them this: "These gods, who did not make the heavens and the earth, will perish from the earth and from under the heavens."'

But God made the earth by his power; he founded the world by his wisdom and stretched out the heavens by his understanding. When he thunders, the waters in the heavens roar; he makes clouds rise from the ends of the earth. **He sends lightning with the rain and brings out the wind from his storehouses.'**

(Jeremiah 10:10-13)

Having dismissed worthless pagan idol gods and making it clear to readers they did not create anything and will perish (v10), Jeremiah then arrives at a proclamation that the one and only God created everything through and by his wisdom and understanding (v12). As Job confidently said, the world is not only created by God, but is suspended on nothing in outer space (Job 26:7). The whole of creation including the world owes its origin to the Lord God and belongs to him (Psalms 24:1), above it, heaven also belongs to him (Psalms 19:1).

As Matthew Henry reports in his commentary on Jeremiah 10:13, '...It was a common saying even among the Greeks - *He that sets up to be another god ought first to make another world.*'[169] The Enduring Word Bible Commentary explains, 'In contrast to the pagan gods, 'Yahweh is a living, active God who made the earth and established the world, and who stretched out the heavens.'[170] Yahweh is the true and only living God (v8-10). Idols cannot do or make anything. Charles Ward Smith, American pastor, expresses it well, 'So he (*Jeremiah*) is talking to the people concerning these gods that they had made themselves. The indicates a vast difference. There is a God who has made man, and then there are men who make their gods, gods who are made by men. A God who carries men, and a god who must be carried by men.'[171] (*Insertion mine*) The idol gods are simply figures made by people. In contrast God made the universe and keeps it supported and in being.

As Charles Ward Smith further explains, 'The gods that have not made the heavens and the earth, even they shall perish from the earth, and from under these heavens. He hath made the earth by his power, he hath established the world by his wisdom, and hath stretched out the heavens by his discretion.'[172]

These are the things which are *constant* (v10-12) including creation and God's position in the government of the world, and control of the world, but Jeremiah also addresses things which are *changeable* (v13).

God gives or sends, by his voice, abundance of water from heaven. He is able to make the sound of roaring accompanied by thunder. As John Calvin (1509-1564) French theologian, statesman and reformer, says, '...for though it often rains without thunder, yet when God thunders from heaven, there is a sudden change, which not only disturbs the air, but also fills us with dread. As then in this sudden and unexpected change the power of God more strikingly appears.'[173] As Jeremiah expressed it, 'When he thunders, the waters in the heavens roar' (v13a).

Having established God's work in creation, we are given a summary of God's power and ability with the weather using **strange** words of bringing lightning, wind, and rain from his 'storehouses' (v13). Jeremiah, impressed by the physical and powerful things God can do, including using the weather to achieve his will, says the same thing again using almost the same wording towards the end of the book (Jeremiah 51:15-16).

As the water vapour rises upwards and makes clouds, God shows that he rules both heaven and earth. Even more dramatic seems to be the ability to create powerful storms with thunder, lightning and rain (Jeremiah 10:13),[174] but many people cannot see the power or glory of God in these events which point to an all-powerful God. Then we read of God choosing if and when he decides, to bring the wind out of his 'storehouses' (NIVUK) or ('treasures' KJV). These were hidden but ready to come out and obey God's command. Even weather experts are at a loss to tell us where the wind comes from and where it finally goes to, though they guess and try to explain the inexplicable. Meteorologists point to the sun, the rotation of the Earth, land masses, jet streams, water currents, temperature, air pressure changes and so on, but much of the weather remains a mystery, and God is the one who controls it. It is difficult to fully understand and impossible to replicate.

Today's experts have extraordinarily little extra understanding compared with Calvin 500 years ago who wrote that so-called experts do not, 'have regard to God, who brings the winds out of his treasures, for he keeps them hidden. We wonder that the wind rises suddenly when it is quite calm; who ought not to acknowledge that winds are formed, and are sent here and there at God's pleasure?'[175] We might maintain that wind and fire are natural phenomena, although no one can tell us who first caused or created them, but Psalms tells us otherwise: 'He makes winds his messengers, (or 'angels' NIVUK margin) flames of fire his servants.' 100 years after Calvin's birth, the following version was written: 'Who maketh his angels spirits; his ministers a flaming fire.' (KJV) (Psalms 104:4).

It is true to say the senses can be heightened by experience of the weather. Elijah was sure of his God and told the king, Ahab, that he could hear '…the sound of a heavy rain,' and this was said in faith and prophetically, when there was no rain in evidence and at first, not even a cloud in the sky. Elijah assured the king that rain was coming. After prayer, he sent his servant to the king with the message, 'Go and tell Ahab, "Hitch up your chariot and go down before the rain stops you." Meanwhile, the sky grew black with clouds, the wind rose, a heavy rainstorm came on and Ahab rode off to Jezreel' (1 Kings 18:44b-45). Elijah had prayed not just for rain but for heavy rain which could have impeded the king's progress in his heavy chariot. He was so sure that God would answer his prayer, he warned the king to leave the place where he was vulnerable.

We can be sure that God has all the power, he sees everything and he is present everywhere.[176] He has power over the weather, but those who know and love him know they are safe, whatever the weather is like. See Psalm 16, and especially these verses: 'Lord, you alone are my portion and my cup; you make my lot secure…I keep my eyes always on the Lord. With him at my right hand, I shall not be shaken (Psalms 16:5b, v8).

25 Lamentations - *Having life tough when you are young prepares you for the future.*

'The Lord is good to those whose hope is in him, to the one who seeks him; it is good to wait quietly for the salvation of the Lord. **It is good for a man to bear the yoke while he is young.**'

(Lamentations 3:25-27)

The pace of life in Cornwall, England, is slower than the busy urban areas of Great Britain. There is a slang word which people use when something doesn't happen straight away it is the word 'dreckly.' It is used as follows:

'Person 1: "Are you ever going to do the washing up?"
Person 2: "Yeah, dreckly."
It basically means that the said task will be happening in the not too distant future, but the Cornish are notorious for their slow-paced lifestyle so it could be a while.'[177]

The word 'dreckly' as used, means directly or soon. It covers the situation where the user will do something eventually!

Waiting can be tedious; it can be frustrating. It can feel like time is being wasted. Waiting for God to answer prayer in the way and with the answer hoped for can be a special challenge and needs special patience. Jeremiah, the writer of Lamentations knows all about unanswered prayer and the need for patience. The book name based on the word lament is particularly appropriate to use in the time between request and response; suffering and solution.

Mark Vroegop, lead pastor of College Park Church, Indianapolis, says his book, *Dark Clouds, Deep Mercy*, '… walks through the need for Christians to learn to lament.'[178] He then indicates an interesting aspect of translation of Lamentations 3:

> 'What you cannot see in your English translation is that verses 25–27 all begin with the Hebrew word "good." It could read:
> Good is the Lord to those who wait for him,
> Good it is that one should wait quietly for the salvation of the Lord,
> Good it is for a young man to bear the yoke in his youth.
> So there is obviously something good here. What is it? To wait on the Lord means to place your hope in him— to trust that God is the one who can deliver you. Your entire confidence rests on him. We wait upon the Lord because he is God and we are not.'[179]

If God is sovereign and has a plan for our lives, it is **strange** that it is so hard waiting for him to be active in the way we think he should. Yet, even though we can't see God working, he *is* working, and he watches to see how we act, learn, and maintain faith and trust in him. This is a valuable lesson to learn by individual people whilst they are still young and trainable. With God, time and experience are never wasted, but help shape us to what God wants us to be. I like one of Vroegop's conclusions, 'We wait upon the Lord because he is God and we are not.'

The final end of trials is not suffering but compassion, so great is God's love as Lamentations tells us, 'For no-one is cast off by the Lord for ever. Though he brings grief, he will show compassion, so great is his unfailing love'[180] (Lamentations 3:31-32). With God, there is always hope and encouragement. It is sometimes through the practice of lamenting that we arrive at a final victory. Pain, suffering and death are not the end for Jeremiah, or for the Christian; compassion, love and heaven are for those whose lives are right with God. As with Jeremiah, the Psalmist had great confidence in God and the future, 'I remain confident of this: I will see the goodness of the Lord in the land of the living' (Psalm 27:13).

We now need to look into these three verses to see what else they tell us. First of all in Lamentations 3:25, we find that it is not people but God who is good, and he is good to those who seek him, find him and put their trust or hope in him. The Pulpit Commentary on v25, explains how patience can lead to God's glory being unveiled. 'The Lord is actually good unto such as wait for him. He is pledged to this. His servants have ever found this to be the case. For the expectation honours him from whom the blessing is expected. The patient are delivered from their troubles, and to those who seek the Lord his glory is unveiled.'[181] Jeremiah said in his prophecy, 'You will seek me and find me when you seek me with all your heart' (Jeremiah 29:13). Jeremiah lived his life under pressure and being ridiculed but his faith remained stable and in God, whom he loved, and he knew God loved him and, in all he did, was good!

The Knowing Jesus blog tells us on this verse,

'Despite the mocking, ridicule and cruel treatment he received from his fellow-Israelites, Jeremiah had submitted to the Lord throughout his life and in this final distress and pain, he was able to call to mind the faithfulness of God. Jeremiah knew that despite the unfaithfulness of his people, the Lord would keep all His promises to Israel.'[182]

The writer to Hebrews summarised the hardships of some of the men and women of faith who served God faithfully in OT days and referred to in God's 'Hall of Fame' in Hebrews 11:36-38a where there is thought to be a veiled reference to Jeremiah and his death in the list of un-named people.[183]

Jeremiah is learning some positive lessons that despite circumstances, God is good and this is found to be so especially by those who find God, and who seek to please him by faith (Hebrews 11:6). That was a lesson Jeremiah was learning with a quiet, calm and patient approach.

We then read in Lamentations 3:26 that God will save, both from sin and from the circumstances which heap trouble on faithful believers. It all takes time and it is good not to fret but wait patiently. To wait quietly, literally, *and be in silence*, and in doing so, abstain from all complaining, is quite a challenge and one to aim for; however, it is not easily attained.

It must have been distressing for Jeremiah to see the Israelites shackled and led away to slavery, to see their homes destroyed, to see Jerusalem destroyed, and worst of all, to see the beautiful temple, with all its symbolism indicating God's presence amongst his people, raised to the ground. He knew God was disciplining rebellious people but it must all have made him weep. It was a hopeless situation, but like Moses and the Israelites grinding away at brick-making in Egypt, David being sought by the murderous Saul because he was a more successful soldier than Saul, and Elijah totally defeated and depressed on Carmel because Queen Jezebel despised him and wanted him dead, salvation comes eventually. Isaiah encouraged waiting for salvation, 'In that day they will say, "Surely this is our God; we trusted in him, and he saved us. This is the Lord, we trusted in him; let us rejoice and be glad in his salvation"' (Isaiah 25:9). Salvation includes eternal life, and the Apostle Paul wants the Christians in Rome to be sure of this as he writes, 'To those who by persistence in doing good seek glory, honour and immortality, he will give eternal life' (Romans 2:7).

We are told in Lamentations 3:27, it is good to bear the yoke, especially before we get too old to do so. By bearing a yoke in youth, we can learn the lesson of endurance, and so find it easier to be calm and patient in later years. This is how I feel about facing up to God and living for him whilst there is opportunity and not leaving it until it is too late and we are before God giving an answer to why we rejected his Son as our Saviour. Then, finding that it is too late to change one's mind.[184] As to what the 'yoke' is, it may be God's commandments, God's correction or God's moral law; possibly all three. It could well be a reference to living in faith before God with a clear conscience. We would now say in our day a number of centuries after the example of Jesus on Earth, that we understand what Jesus meant by the 'yoke,' as recorded by Matthew, 'Take my yoke upon you and learn from me, for I am gentle and humble in heart, and you will find rest for your souls. For my yoke is easy and my burden is light' (Matthew 11:29-30).

John Gill, Minister of the Metropolitan Tabernacle before Spurgeon, in his preaching and commentary makes the point,

'…as there is a close connection between a profession of faith in Christ, and submission to his ordinances, and suffering reproach and persecution for the same; it is good for a man to bear the one, as well as the other, "in his youth"; this will serve to keep him humble and hide pride from him.'[185]

26 Ezekiel - *God can perform heart operations.*

'I will take you out of the nations; I will gather you from all the countries and bring you back into your own land. I will sprinkle clean water on you, and you will be clean; I will cleanse you from all your impurities and from all your idols. **I will give you a new heart** *and put a new spirit in you; I will remove from you your heart of stone and give you a heart of flesh. And I will put my Spirit in you and move you to follow my decrees and be careful to keep my laws. Then you will live in the land I gave your ancestors; you will be my people, and I will be your God.'*

(Ezekiel 36:24-28)

In 1967 on December 3 the world's first heart transplant took place when 53-year-old Louis Washkansky received the first human heart at Groote Schuur Hospital in Cape Town, South Africa. Washkansky, a South African grocer dying from chronic heart disease, received the heart from a 25-year-old woman who was fatally injured in a car accident. The surgeon was Christiaan Barnard.[186] The operation was held to be a success because the heart beat unaided. However, the patient died 18 days later.

In 2011, when I went into heart failure and experienced the best of the British health service; I had part of my heart reconstructed, for which I am grateful. However, I then had an irregular heartbeat, so I had to undergo a second procedure several weeks later, called a cardioversion. 'An electrical cardioversion is a treatment which aims to get your abnormal heart rhythm (arrhythmia) back to a normal pattern. It's done by sending controlled electric signals to your heart through electrodes placed on the chest.'[187] Unlike Washkansky, I have my original heart.

We are now considering what God meant when he said through Ezekiel that he would give his people, in rather **strange** words, 'a new heart' (Ezekiel 36:26a).

Michal Elizabeth Hunt is a lecturer, author and director of Agape Bible Studies, who sees that God will act to restore Israel for the sole purpose of restoring his Name among the nations. In answer to the question of how will he do this she answers, 'He will gather them from among the nations and return them to their land (v24). He will pour clean water over them to spiritually cleanse them of their guilt and the contamination by false idols (v25, v33). He will give them a new heart and a new spirit. Their new hearts will give them the spiritual strength they need to demonstrate their obedience to God's judgments and commandments (v26-27). They will live in the land that is their ancestral heritage as God's covenant people (v28).'[188]

The situation was that the land of Israel was desolate and God's people were exiled when Ezekiel, a Hebrew captive in exile in Babylon for 70 years, delivered his prophecy. Ezekiel was very conscious of the sins and failings of his people and of the awful consequences. The Jews had a parable they quoted followed by the result of the parable:

'"The parents eat sour grapes,
and the children's teeth are set on edge"?'
(Ezekiel 18:2)

'The one who sins is the one who will die.'
(v4b).

It was a desperate and very unhappy situation but God gave Ezekiel a message of hope, renewal and restoration, and a promise they would go back to their own land (Ezekiel 11:16-17). There was not only going to be a restoration to the land of Israel from Babylon, but there was also going to be a spiritual restoration which would ultimately include the coming of the Messiah. The promise in chapter 11, is repeated in chapter 36:24, but followed by further blessings promised for the Jewish people. These blessings were the fulfilment of the covenant promise of land, God made to Abraham (Genesis 12:1-3), law, made to Moses (Exodus 19:4-6) and the promise of a Davidic dynasty, made to David from which the Messiah, the Saviour would come (2 Samuel 7:16).

Pastor David Guzik reminds us that throughout the Bible God reveals his plan of redemption through a series of covenants. After the extended story of the fall and ruin of humanity (Genesis 1-11), the story of the covenants begins.[189]

God was, therefore, embarking on a new covenant with his special and chosen people, and it was announced in various OT books including our present one being studied: (Deuteronomy 30:1-6), (Jeremiah 31:31-34), and (Ezekiel 36:24-28). The first covenant under Moses is replaced by this new one and what the old covenant couldn't achieve, the new one could.

God says that metaphorically speaking of traditional and ritualistic sprinkling with water; God's people are to be made clean by this outward sign. This was established in Exodus for ritual washing, (Exodus 30:17-21) but here in Ezekiel 36:25, and v17, it cleanses the people from sin and contamination from idols. It foreshadows the cleansing of mankind potentially by faith, achieved by Jesus on the cross and is linked with the baptism of believers in the NT and through the centuries to the present day. As the Ethiopian said to Philip in the chariot looking at the countryside they were passing, '…Look, here is water. What can stand in the way of my being baptised?' (Acts 8:36b) He had faith in Jesus as Saviour and a change of heart when he understood what he was reading in Isaiah's prophecy of a suffering Saviour to come (Isaiah 53:7-8).

Ezekiel was sure that God could forgive past sins, with a change of heart on the part of the people, and responding to God's initiative, God would remove all impurities and imperfections. This would be linked to a return from exile.

Outward washing is symbolic, a change of heart on the inside is a fresh start and is real change. This is a major promise addressed by Charles Spurgeon, who preached on Ezekiel 36:26,

> 'From all your actual filthiness, as well as from all your original filthiness, will I cleanse you. From all your secret filthiness, and from all your public filthiness; from everything that was wrong in the family; from everything that was wrong in the business; from everything that was wrong in your own heart – from all your filthiness will I cleanse you.'[190]

The work of the Holy Spirit in cleansing and renewal is crucial to receiving a new heart. God said through Joel about 250 years before Ezekiel:

> '…I will pour out my Spirit on all people. Your sons and daughters will prophesy, your old men will dream dreams, your young men will see visions. Even on my

servants, both men and women, I will pour out my Spirit in those days' (Joel 2:28-29).

Michal Hunt added to her earlier comment, 'Like life-giving water that makes the earth fertile, God's spiritual cleansing will nourish the fruits of holiness which will guarantee the favour and protection of God' (Ezekiel 37:24; 39:29).[191] God will be a shepherd to his people and pour out his Spirit upon them.

Wil Pounds, missionary and visiting professor of Bible and Theology at Peniel Theological Seminary in Riobamba, Ecuador, writes, 'There are twenty-five references to the Holy Spirit in the book of Ezekiel. A new heart and a new spirt are themes Ezekiel reflects on several times.' Pounds points out that Jesus may have had this in mind when he spoke to Nicodemus about being born again of water and the Spirit (John 3:3, v5, v7).[192]

As Ezekiel made it clear to the Jews of his day, the new covenant replaces the old; Paul said the same to Christians in his day, such as to the Corinthians, when he said that the newly created person who has come into Christ, replaces the old creation, the old life, 'Therefore, if anyone is in Christ, the new creation has come: the old has gone, the new is here!' (2 Corinthians 5:17).

As we go a little further into Ezekiel 36, we see in verse 27 spiritual transformation with God working on the inside of a person. This was the only way my physical heart could be re-constructed. It was impossible to do from the outside. My chest had to be opened up. The second procedure, the cardioversion was done from the outside. For the Jews, what was not achievable in the first covenant became possible in the second covenant as God worked his work of grace by the Holy Spirit.

As Spurgeon developed his sermon, he added,

> 'True religion begins, then, with the heart, and the heart is the ruling power of manhood. You may enlighten a man's understanding and you have done much, but as long as his heart is wrong, the enlightenment of the understanding only enables him to sin with a greater weight of responsibility resting upon him.'[193]

The Holy Spirit couldn't live in the old heart, he needed a new heart to effect a complete transformation and make a permanent change. As all this happens, God's people are promised that their own land will be given back to them and again they will be God's special people and he will be their God. The giving back of the land, and a return to this land is the sign and seal that the people had received new hearts.

The Eden Project opened in 2001 in Cornwall.[194] The project is located in a reclaimed china clay pit covering 30 acres. It attracts just less than one million visitors a year. It has world famous biomes containing natural gardens of the world and has been built on waste land. God has promised something similar to the whole land of Israel, far bigger than this tourist destination. He has said to the whole nation of Israel physically and to individual people of faith worldwide spiritually,

> 'This land that was laid waste has become like the garden of Eden; the cities that were lying in ruins, desolate

and destroyed, are now fortified and inhabited. Then the nations around you that remain will know that I the Lord have rebuilt what was destroyed and have replanted what was desolate. I the Lord have spoken, and I will do it'(Ezekiel 36:35-36).

27 Daniel - *Shadrach, Meshach and Abednego walk unharmed in fire.*

Then King Nebuchadnezzar leaped to his feet in amazement and asked his advisors, "Weren't there three men that we tied up and threw into the fire?"

They replied, "Certainly, Your Majesty."

*He said, "**Look! I see four men walking around in the fire**, unbound and unharmed, and the fourth looks like a son of the gods."*

(Daniel 3:24-25)

I feel I approach life with an uncomplicated, male, single-task-at-a-time logic. I don't mind being kept busy and I don't mind taking instructions from my wife, what I find difficult is being given too many instructions at once or being given part of a story and having to piece things together with Insufficient information so I can't understand the whole picture. I suppose I am doing that with giving part of the story of Shadrach, Meshach and Abednego. In fact, in some senses I am giving my selection of a passage which is the end of the story, so I am going to summarise the background and beginning of the story so the end makes sense perhaps for the benefit of those who, like me, need the whole picture! This amazing story really begins at verse eight of Daniel 3 and continues to the end of the chapter at verse 30, but includes parts of chapter one.

King Nebuchadnezzar of Babylonia ordered his chief court official to find suitable, handsome and intelligent young men from the nobility carried off from the tribe of Judah in Israel into exile, about 600 BC, to train to serve the king in his court (Daniel 1:3-4). In preparation, they had to learn the language and literature of the Babylonians. Daniel and three friends, outstanding in every area, were amongst those chosen and as time passed, these four Hebrew young men were given positions of authority within the kingdom of Babylon.

Nebuchadnezzar was a powerful dictator and set up a statue so that he would receive honour, praise, and worship as well. Yahweh-worshipping captives couldn't worship an idol. A group of astrologers, jealous of the Hebrew young men who had been given positions of authority at Daniel's request (Daniel 2:49), took exception to the three not honouring the customs of Babylon, so they reported this to the uncompromising King. As Dr J. Mike Minnix, founder and editor of PastorLife says, 'This presented a difficult problem for the King, for he simply couldn't allow someone anyone to skirt the law and get by without it appearing to be diminishing his authority and power.'[195]

The king responded angrily and ordered Shadrach, Meshach and Abednego, using their new Babylonian names,[196] to be brought to him to answer for their failure to worship his golden statue. The three were firm in their faith and convictions, and informed the king that their God was the one whom they worshipped and the one they could entrust with their lives. They stood their ground, kept their faith, and said they would not compromise and bow down to the golden image. Nebuchadnezzar couldn't force them to worship him and the statue so he was going to force them to die instead. In his anger the king had them tied up and thrown into a blazing furnace which killed the soldiers who threw the friends in because of the intense heat.[197]

The king, watching with indignation and delight seated on his throne, jumped up horrified; firstly, because the three were unbound and unharmed, and secondly, because he saw not three but four people in the flames. The sight of the fourth person troubled him and he said those **strange** words, 'Look! I see four men walking around in the fire' (Daniel 3:25), and decided it was '…a son of the gods' (v25), '…the Son of God' (KJV), or an angel (v28). It may well have been a pre-incarnate appearance of Jesus sent to protect the three friends.

Nebuchadnezzar immediately called for the three to come out of the furnace and saw the flames hadn't touched them. They didn't even smell of the fire. He pledged allegiance to Yahweh and decreed his nation should do the same and he would not allow anyone to speak against their God. Then he promoted Shadrach, Meshach and Abednego to high ranking positions of authority in his extensive kingdom.[198]

Mary Fairchild, Christian minister, writer and editor in Florida tells us,

'Through God's miraculous deliverance of Shadrach, Meshach, and Abednego that day, Nebuchadnezzar declared that the remaining Israelites in captivity were now protected from harm and were guaranteed freedom of worship. And Shadrach, Meshach, and Abednego received a royal promotion.'[199]

Daniel must have been involved in other duties that day because he was not involved, but was no doubt encouraged by the stand his friends took and by God's wonderful protection of them. Sarah Coleman, author and blogger, compares these youths with Abraham who, 'never wavered in believing God's promise. In fact, his faith grew stronger, and in this he brought glory to God. He was fully convinced that God is able to do whatever he promises' (Romans 4:20-21).[200]

She goes on to say, 'Nothing could make them bow to Nebuchadnezzar's statue - no threats, no consequence, no punishment. They were fully persuaded of the promises of God and in their obedience to him' (Daniel 3:16-18).[201] The young men may well have been aware of the words of Isaiah 100 or so years earlier,

> 'Do not fear, for I have redeemed you; I have summoned you by name; you are mine. When you pass through the waters, I will be with you; and when you pass through the rivers, they will not sweep over you. When you walk through the fire, you will not be burned; the flames will not set you ablaze' (Isaiah 43:1b-2).

And Job said, 'Though he slay me, yet will I hope in him' (Job 13:15a). They took these and similar words to heart and lived them out in their experience. Certainly, their trust was in God as Lord and their true Sovereign (Ephesians 3:20), although they were still very respectful to the king. In terms of the parallel for the Christian, Minnix wants to remove all doubt when he says, '...let me make this clear – a Christian cannot lose. If I live, Jesus is with me; if I die, I am with Jesus. He will deliver us one way or the other.'[202] Shadrach, Meshach and Abednego lived out their faith with the same assurance.

Charles Wesley (1707-1788) was a Vicar in the church of England and English leader of the Methodist movement. Wesley was a prolific hymnwriter,[203] who wrote in 1738 in the hymn, *And can it be*, 'My chains fell off my heart was free. I rose went forth and followed thee.' Though this may well be based on the prison release of Paul and Silas in Acts 16:26, it is parallel to the tied faithful men who were also released by God in the flames, '…unbound and unharmed…' (Daniel 3:25). The faith of Shadrach, Meshach and Abednego was unwavering and God honoured that.

28 Hosea - *God tells Hosea to love his unfaithful wife, even though she loves raisin cakes.*

*'The Lord said to me, "**Go, show your love to your wife again**, though she is loved by another man and is an adulteress. Love her as the Lord loves the Israelites, though they turn to other gods and love the sacred raisin cakes."*

So I bought her for fifteen shekels of silver and about a homer and a lethek of barley. Then I told her, "You are to live with me for many days; you must not be a prostitute or be intimate with any man, and I will behave the same way towards you."'

(Hosea 3:1-3)

Hosea prophesied to the Northern kingdom of Israel in the second half of the C8th BC. Following the death of Jeroboam II, Israel had six evil kings in about 20 years. Assyria was in its ascendency conquering surrounding nations including Israel. By 722 BC most of the Northern kingdom was in exile. Israel had drifted into Baal worship and Hosea denounces their worship and practice as being corrupt. He also took issue with their allegiance to foreign powers and rejection of the moral laws and their heartless greed. The people rejected Hosea's preaching and pleading and simply mocked him. What we shall see in chapter three is God instructing Hosea to take back his unfaithful wife, Gomer. This was a picture of the nation of Israel in the future being forgiven and shown great love by faithful Yahweh who brings them out of exile to give them a fresh start.

Hosea is commanded by God to find his wife, and as seen in the **strange** words of our passage, 'Go, show your love to your wife again' (v1a). She was living in an adulterous situation with another man and he was to take her back and show his love in a practical way as an act of will, not just by *chance*. He had to pay for her with about 195kg, 30st of grain and 15 shekels of silver, half the price of a slave (Leviticus 27:4), indicating her partner owned her and didn't really value her.[204] Hosea made it clear to her he expects her to live faithfully with him (Hosea 2:6-7), and he promises to live faithfully with her, (v19-20). Pastor David Guzik points out, 'In providing this way for his own wife, Hosea also showed her: "I can give you what the others can. You don't need them. Let me show you how I can provide for your needs."'[205]

The whole experience enacted will be seen by Israel as an example of what they should do in returning to the Lord. '(*After the exile*), the Israelites will return and seek the Lord their God and David their king. They will come trembling to the Lord and to his blessings in the last days' (Hosea 3:5) (*Insertion mine*). 'David' here refers to David's heir: '"The days are coming," declares the Lord, "when I will raise up for David a righteous Branch"'(Jeremiah 23:5). This refers to a God-honouring king in the near future, and also to Jesus as king in the distant future.

In verse one of chapter three, Hosea is to love his wife again, even though she seems to have become a prostitute (v3). The people have as a nation turned to other gods and preferred special foods traditionally for celebrations. The Israelites had come to love to eat raisin cakes, so often enjoyed on special occasions

(2 Sam. 6:19), but they were also offered to Baal in Eastern countries as part of a religious ceremony at this time (Jeremiah 44:19). A raisin cake seems to be the ancient equivalent of really nice chocolate: energy-rich, delicious, and luxurious.[206] They are referred to as a symbol of turning to other gods and the luxuries of the world without any spiritual consideration. In a sense it is a preference for rich living by the Israelites, as with Gomer seeking after riches and pleasure.

Bible Study Tools informs us that the nation, 'loved the delights of the world, and not the law and commandments of God; and in the feasts that were made in the temples of their idols they loved good eating and drinking, and that made them like idolatry the better for the sake of those things.'[207] An example of this sort of idolatry and indulgence is found in Exodus, at the giving of the Law to Moses and the making of the golden calf because of Moses' delay in returning to the camp. 'So the next day the people rose early and sacrificed burnt offerings and presented fellowship offerings. Afterwards they sat down to eat and drink and got up to indulge in revelry' (Exodus 32:6).

Gomer was seeking material pleasures: wool, linen and olive oil (Hosea 2:5), rings and jewellery (v13), but she was forgetting her husband. Similarly, the nation is forgetting the Lord. As her husband doesn't forget her, so the Lord doesn't forget his people, 'I will betroth you in faithfulness, and you will acknowledge the Lord' (v20).

In verse three of Hosea chapter three, just as Gomer, after her separation is to live with Hosea for a long time, so the Israelites, after their separation in exile (the Northern kingdom from 722 BC and the Southern kingdom from 586 BC) are to return to faith and trust in God for a long time. Bible.org explains, 'By analogy with the situation between Hosea and Gomer, unity and security can come to Israel only when they seek God.'[208] As Matthew Henry explains, God, '…is willing to show them kindness, and that the matter should be compromised; he deals not with them in strict justice, according to the rigour of the law, but according to the multitude of his mercies.'[209]

29 Joel - *The pouring out of the Holy Spirit will bring spiritual gifts to men and women.*

*'You will know that I am in Israel, that I am the Lord your God, and that there is no other… and afterwards, I will pour out my Spirit on all people. **Your sons and daughters will prophesy**, your old men will dream dreams, your young men will see visions. Even on my servants, both men and women, I will pour out my Spirit in those days.'*

(Joel 2:27-29)

Joel was raised up by God as a prophet and he preached about 830-820 BC according to Professor John C. Whitcomb (1924-2020).[210] The exact dates of his life and years of preaching are difficult to say for certain since they don't link up with particular kings. However, in his short ministry and book bearing his name, he packs a powerful message and as with most prophecy there is a local and future aspect and fulfilment.

Matthew Henry puts the date of local fulfilment about 100 years later than Whitcomb at 720 BC about the time of the departure of the Northern kingdom into exile under his heading of 'a time of mercy'.[211]

Whenever it was prophesied to the Israelites, 820 or 720 BC, it needed the following sequence of events before the eventual restoration and return to the Promised Land of Israel:

- constant sin and wayward living based on idolatry and the ignoring of Yahweh;

- captivity in Babylonia where the people would regret their sin and turn afresh to God;
- release and return to their own land by God's mercy and forgiveness; they would seek God afresh when released in 586 BC;
- realise that their experience of being overrun by a foreign army and taken away captive is metaphorically as described by Joel who writes in detail about the plague of destructive locusts.

The book includes a graphic description of a massive swarm of locusts which over-run the Southern kingdom of Judah and eat their way through everything edible in sight. After a call to repent, the people are then given a detailed description of the swarm which is likened to an invading army under the authority and leadership of God. Joel insists that the day of God's judgment has come and so pleads with people to repent and show their contrition through fasting, prayer and changed lifestyles. If they do that, Joel promises that God will drive the locusts away and restore to the people their losses. He gives the full picture that God will defeat Judah's enemies and pour out his Spirit on the surviving people. He makes it clear that if they return to God, their prosperity will be restored when the day of the Lord arrives as they are released from exile and return to Israel.

As chapter two of Joel unfolds, God promises, 'I will repay you for the years the locusts have eaten… my great army that I sent among you' (Joel 2:25). 'You will have plenty to eat, until you are full, and you will praise the name of the Lord your God…' (v26a). 'Then you will know that I am in Israel, that I am the Lord your God, and that there is no other…' (v27a).

After all this immediate fulfilment in the scene around them of devastation of the land caused by the army of locusts, and the eventual arrival and devastation of the people caused by the army of Babylon, we arrive at some key but **strange** words, 'Your sons and daughters will prophesy' (v28b). NIVUK adds a sub-heading at this point:

The day of the Lord
'And afterwards,
I will pour out my Spirit on all people.
Your sons and daughters will prophesy,
your old men will dream dreams,
your young men will see visions.
Even on my servants, both men and women,
I will pour out my Spirit in those days.'
(v28-29)

The question is, what are these verses talking about? It is not restoration from the agricultural disaster (caused by locusts). It is not restoration from the demographic disaster (caused by Babylonians). It must be much further into the future and a visitation by God the Holy Spirit to people who are right with him and ready for his intervention bringing a spiritual restoration in 'the Last Days' and so, we need to briefly look at that. Along the way we shall see how sons and daughters come into the picture.

Words in Joel, 'I will pour out my Spirit on all people,' are used by Peter in his preaching on the Day of Pentecost (Joel 2:28-29; Acts 2:17-18).[212] Peter is seeing the start of the church and from that point onwards, at the start of what Peter calls, 'the last days,' (Acts 2:17) the Holy Spirit comes into those who accept Christ as Saviour. This became 'the new normal' to quote a popular phrase, as compared with the occasional and transitory visits of the Holy Spirit in OT days, and right up to the Day of Pentecost.

Jesus said he would come to those ready for him and stay permanently, 'I will ask the Father, and he will give you another advocate to help you and be with you for ever – the Spirit of truth' (John 14:16).

Charles Ward Smith, American pastor, in his commentary, is sure that the prophecy in Joel 2:28, '...pertains to the nation of Israel when God restores to Israel his position of divine favour and blessing, and Israel will once be again the instrument of God to bring light into the world. "And it shall come to pass afterward," after Israel is restored...'[213]

The Got Questions blog points out, 'One of the surprising outcomes of Joel's prophecy was that even non-Jews were filled with the Spirit. In Acts 10:45 we read, "The believers from among the circumcised . . . were amazed, because the gift of the Holy Spirit was poured out *even on* the Gentiles."' (*Emphasis mine*)[214] I notice Luke, a Gentile, uses the words '*even on,*' he must have been very encouraged that there was real hope for Jews and Gentiles! This was, and always is, wonderful provision for Christian service.

To return to Joel, it is interesting to see the groups of people affected, with the children placed first, and as the summary by the Christian Student Group reports on Joel 2:28-29:

'God addresses different categories of the people of Israel: the sons and daughters (v28b), the old, and the young (v28c). This blessing of the Holy Spirit is for *all flesh:* all of God's people will receive his Spirit. We should also pay further attention to the people groups mentioned in this verse. From the youngest to the oldest, from the servants to those with more, God's Spirit will be poured out to all, without distinction of gender, class, educational levels, or wealth. All of his people will receive his Spirit.'[215]

30 Amos - *Faithful Bible preaching will become rare.*

*'"The days are coming," declares the Sovereign Lord, "when I will send a famine through the land – not a famine of food or a thirst for water, but **a famine of hearing the words of the Lord**. People will stagger from sea to sea and wander from north to east, searching for the word of the Lord, but they will not find it."'*

(Amos 8:11-12)

Life is often difficult in terms of political, economic, moral and spiritual challenges, and some people are over-confident and complacent, especially with spiritual things and so let things go unsolved and misunderstood. It is easy to say that things are not as good as they were, but I think in many respects this is true. I am reminded of a powerful verse, 'Righteousness exalts a nation, but sin condemns any people' (Proverbs 14:34). I rarely hear righteousness spoken of and certainly rarely hear of holiness being preached in churches.

In the eighth century BC this was the position in the northern kingdom of Israel. There was one evil king after another and the people were relaxing in their complacency waiting for God to deal with their enemies for them, and just living as they chose. Into this overconfident atmosphere came Amos, a shepherd and farmer from the Southern kingdom of Judah. He announces doom and defeat for Israel at the hands of their enemies. He said God was not impressed with the wealth and military might of Israel and called people to repent from their sin and turn from their self-indulgence and implement justice and care for the poor as the only way to avoid destruction. It was not necessarily an easy message to give to both Israel and the surrounding nations, but it was the one God gave him.

As expected, this message did not go down well with the people, and the faith leader, Amaziah, the High Priest at Bethel, threw Amos out of the country. However, the oracles, or sermon summaries, of Amos survive. In chapter eight, people were hardly willing to seek words from God and even if they did, by then God had withdrawn his words and his grace leaving a famine-like situation.

John Gill (1697-1771), in his commentary of this chapter eight, reminds us that the oracle of the basket of ripe fruit (Amos 8:2), was a picture of the people of the land who were ripe and ready for destruction. The poor were being oppressed by the rich and so they are, '…threatened with entire ruin, sudden calamities, and very mournful times, instead of light, joy, and gladness…and particularly with a famine of hearing the word of God.'[216]

The people were used to famines with fluctuating weather and consequent crop yield. History should have told them that disobedience to Yahweh was also a cause of judgment and God sometimes punished them through their enemies or famines, but verse 11 is different. Here we read the **strange** and unexpected words to warn the nation of what is coming: 'a famine of hearing the words of the Lord.' God was saying that he would withhold prophecy, since the people were deliberately not facing up to their responsibilities as his own chosen people and were preferring idol worship which he strongly objected to. An example is found in 1 Samuel where, because of the spiritual and moral failures of King Saul, God refused to communicate with him through prophets, 'He enquired of the Lord, but the Lord did not answer him by dreams or Urim or prophets' (1 Samuel 28:6). God refused to speak to them because they had abandoned him. Therefore, at the time of Amos, God would allow them to be punished by the Babylonians who would come and defeat them in battle and take them away as captives to be slaves.

We need to understand why 'a famine of hearing the words of the Lord' came. Israel had rejected God's Word. Holy living was opposed (Amos 2:11-12); Amos was ejected by Amaziah the High Priest (Amos 7:12-13). Because Israel had not listened when they had the opportunity, God was going to remove his Word, as explained by Dr. Justin Imel, Church of Christ, Texas.[217]

The lesson to learn from Amos 8:11 is clear. God's truths, laws and expectations have been proclaimed by prophets and handed down as Scriptures as the Apostle Jude tells us, '… contend for the faith that was *once for all* entrusted to God's holy people' (Jude v3) (*Emphasis mine*). There was a distinct lack of Scripture, or the Word of God to guide and bless then, and this can sometimes be the case now, as the Never Thirsty blog informs,

> 'Verse-by-verse expository teaching of the Word of God is difficult to find these days. Some pastors have been accused of teaching a seminary class because they are explaining the meaning of every chapter, verse and some words. Application is the norm today… As a result, there is a famine for hearing the words of God today.'[218]

Between the OT and NT there was a gap of 400 years when there were no prophets or prophesies until John the Baptist, the last of the OT prophets in OT style (Matthew 3:1-4), particularly like that of Elijah. Almost worse than having no word from God, the Jews had to suffer the indignity of opposition from the Greek king Antiochus Epiphanes who was cruel to the Jews and desecrated their temple in Jerusalem.[219]

Amos 8:12 of our passage tells us that people will be seeking[220] God's word 'from sea to sea,' that is from West to East, the Mediterranean to the Dead Sea. This gives the picture of people in a severe fog not knowing where to go, as happened at the collapse of the twin towers of the World Trade Centre when people staggered in clouds of dust. As the people there didn't know what to do or where to go, so it will be when God removes his Word.

The famine will be so severe that everyone will be affected including those who would be in the strongest position to resist its effect: the fit and well young women and men. Disaster will affect everyone equally (v13).

After punishment by God of his people is complete and the famine of a lack of God's word ends, God promises restoration and Amos ends on a positive note, '"I will plant Israel in their own land, never again to be uprooted from the land I have given them," says the Lord your God' (Amos 9:15).

31 Obadiah - *As you have treated others, you will be treated.*

*'The day of the Lord is near for all nations. **As you have done, it will be done to you;** your deeds will return upon your own head.'*

(Obadiah v15)

Obadiah, written about 840 BC is the shortest book in the OT at 19 verses long. Obadiah is the earliest writing prophet, a contemporary of Elisha. His background is unclear but his message is very pointedly directed at a foreign nation: Edom, which treated Judah particularly badly. He is writing about Jerusalem as being special to him, so it is thought he comes from near there. For historical reasons, Edom hated Israel and warred against them (v10-14), with the help of neighbouring countries. Edom descended from Esau, the brother of Jacob, later called Israel, after whom the country was named.

When the Babylonians completely devastated Israel, Edom joined in looting the city of Jerusalem, Israel's capital. They also lay in wait and intercepted fleeing inhabitants from Judah and handed them over to the Babylonians to be enslaved or killed.

This was the unhappy relationship between Israel and its neighbour and into this situation of tension and hatred Obadiah was called by God to address Edom in plain language for working hard against God's chosen people. Obadiah speaks against their cruel treatment of Israel promising their destruction. He goes on to re-assure the people of Judah that God would restore their fortunes and states that ultimately the kingdom would be the Lord's and under his control.

There are only a few of the prophets, often called minor prophets, who were called by God to addresses foreign nations. Others are Nahum, Habakkuk and Jonah. Whilst three speak against the nations and announce God's judgement and punishment, Jonah is called to Nineveh which is ready to repent and respond to God and his word (as our next chapter will show). Chuck Swindoll (b1934), an evangelical Christian pastor, author and educator in Texas, summarisers Obadiah's prophecy and tells us,

> 'Obadiah's singular focus points to a significant, albeit difficult, truth about humanity's relationship with God: when people remove themselves from or place themselves in opposition to God's people, they can expect judgment, rather than restoration, at the end of life.'[221]

Obadiah's name means *worshipper of Yahweh*. This is both his name and position as he humbly serves Yahweh faithfully. He challenges Edom's pride (v3), and God hates this pride, '"...I will bring you down," declares the Lord' (v4b). It was through Obadiah, that God spoke against Edom because of their poor treatment of his people (v12–14). Three times he tells Edom what they *should not* do and at the same time, promises redemption and restoration for Israel, referred to as Jacob and Joseph. Edom is referred to as Esau. As the years pass, Edom does not survive but disappears into history because of its unrepentant pride as we read in Proverbs, 'Pride goes before destruction, a haughty spirit before a fall' (Proverbs 16:18).

Pride is very destructive and the result of selfishness to the exclusion of others. It is right to be humbly under God's authority. As Peter says to his Christian audience, 'Humble yourselves, therefore, under God's mighty hand, that he may lift you up in due time' (1 Peter 5:6).

As we arrive at Obadiah verse 15, it is a verse in two halves. Firstly, we find from our current prophecy and several others that foreign, anti-Yahweh, heathen nations, including the Egyptians, Philistines, Tyrians, Ammonites, Moabites, Edomites and others will be punished by God for their sins and rebellion against God (Isaiah 34:2), and especially for opposing God's own people. This is God's judgment on both Judah and the foreign nations as he says 'The day of the Lord is near...' (Obadiah v15a); and the day *is* near!

Jeremiah writes: 'So I took the cup from the Lord's hand and made all the nations to whom he sent me drink it' (Jeremiah 25:17). But, secondly, this will not excuse God's people, as Bible Study Tools blog expresses it in relation to our chosen **strange** words, 'As you have done, it will be done to you' (Obadiah v15), '...this is particularly directed to Edom, upon whom the day of the Lord 's vengeance shall come; when he punished the heathens, then the Edomites should be (*punished*) in their own way' (*Emphasis mine*).[222]

This verse rather reminds me, and perhaps it did Charles Kingsley (1819-1875), vicar, university professor, social reformer, historian, novelist and poet, of the Water Babies children's story (1863), of Mrs. Do-as-you-would-be-done-by. This is worthy of consideration![223] It is certainly true that you reap what you sow (Proverbs 22:8). What the Edomites have done to Judah will be done to them.

Bible Reference blog put this in perspective:

'Edom looted (Obadiah v13), so they will be looted (Obadiah v6). Edom was violent and took Jews from their homeland (Obadiah v14), so they will experience violence (Obadiah v8) and be driven from their homes (Obadiah v7). Edom laughed while Israel was destroyed (Obadiah v12), so they will be shattered and put to shame' (Obadiah v10).[224]

The same thought is also taken up by Jesus when he said, 'Do to others as you would have them do to you' (Like 6:31). This is a very sobering thought but God is fiercely devoted to his chosen people: his family, and he is about to repay the Babylonians for what they have done to his family.

God's judgement against Edom was as promised to Abraham in Genesis, 'I will bless those who bless you, and whoever curses you I will curse' (Genesis 12:3). God is not to be trifled with. His judgments and actions are just and right.

32 Jonah - *A giant fish swallows a man.*

'The Lord provided a huge fish to swallow Jonah, and Jonah was in the belly of the fish three days and three nights.

From inside the fish Jonah prayed to the Lord his God. He said: "In my distress I called to the Lord, and he answered me. From deep in the realm of the dead I called for help, and you listened to my cry. You hurled me into the depths,

into the very heart of the seas, and the currents swirled about me; all your waves and breakers swept over me."'

(Jonah 1:17, 2:1-3)

At times, It may not be obvious I am a Christian, at least not by my witness in words, unless I feel prompted by God that the time is right. However, sometimes when I am called by God to speak, I don't. It's as if I am called to go East and I go West! I can therefore sympathise with Jonah in his reaction to God's calling to him as a lone person, a Hebrew, being sent to a heathen nation to tell them they are going to be destroyed unless they immediately repent. I can understand why he ran in the opposite direction! Superficially as a children's story or at depth, Jonah is an exciting story with a lot to teach us about faith and God's protection and provision, so it is worth getting into the details.

We are not told much about Jonah's background, except that his father was called Amittai, and he was a Hebrew of sincere faith (Jonah 1:1, v9). He is one of the twelve minor prophets of the Nevi'im (The 'prophets'), reverenced by God's people. The book is set in the reign of Jeroboam II (786-746 BC), King of the Northern Kingdom of Israel about 50 years before the Exile. Jeroboam was an evil but successful king.

Bible Study Tools Christian support group point out that 'Unlike most other prophetic parts of the OT, this book is a narrative account of a single prophetic mission.'[225] The story unfolds in a mere 40 verses full of action, plus eight more verses in Jonah's poetic prayer.

Jonah is the central figure of the book and God commands him to go East to Nineveh,[226] the Assyrian capital city of 120,000 people, Israel's greatest enemy at the time. He is told to preach against the wickedness there and to warn it of imminent danger of divine judgment. He is therefore unusual in the OT in prophesying only to a Gentile nation. Encyclopaedia Britannica informs us, 'Jonah, like the Jews of the day, abhors even the idea of salvation for the Gentiles. God chastises him for his attitude, and the book affirms that God's mercy extends even to the inhabitants of a hated foreign city.'[227]

To escape God's call to go East, Jonah hurries on to a boat going West, to the Western Mediterranean. Whilst on the boat, a huge and unexpected storm arose, sent by God (v4), and the sailors, who were God-fearing (v16), realising this was no ordinary storm but had a connection with someone on board the ship, discovered by lottery that Jonah was to blame. They linked Jonah's presence with his disobedience to God, '...the Lord, the God of heaven, who made the sea and the dry land... (*and it*) terrified them' (v9-10a) (*Insertion mine*).

When found out and awoken from his deep sleep, Jonah confirmed he was running away from God and felt so ashamed to be the cause of the storm he asked the sailors to throw him overboard. He was prepared to risk his own life in order to save the sailors. This was done and the storm calmed. As part of God's plan, Jonah doesn't die in the turbulent waters but is miraculously saved by God. And we read how by God's **strange** action: 'The Lord provided a huge fish to swallow Jonah…' (v17a), and so he was protected. This caused the raging storm to immediately become calm. God needed to teach Jonah a lesson in faith and obedience. The fish was especially large with a throat which could swallow Jonah whole, and God, all-powerful, directed the fish to the right spot to save him before he sank to the bottom of the sea and drowned. Whilst in the fish's stomach with all the food it had swallowed recently, and in complete darkness, Jonah prays earnestly and sincerely with thankfulness to God for his mercy and promising to serve him as he requested. He recognises his only means of escape is for God in his mercy to see his genuine humility and change of heart, and when God sees this he commands the fish to vomit Jonah on to dry land.

God then re-commissions Jonah a second time to travel to Nineveh and preach to the people there. Jonah obeys God and walks for a day from the outskirts towards the city centre and warns the people by his preaching, 'Forty more days and Nineveh will be overthrown' (Jonah 3:4). This cuts them to the heart; faith, fasting and repentance ensue. The endangered Ninevites, led by their king,[228] appeal to God for mercy; people show their sorrow for sin by wearing sackcloth and ashes. God sees this genuine remorse and forgives them and spares the city.

Jesus used the account of Jonah to answer the Pharisees and lawyers who wanted proof of who he was, so Jesus tells prophetically the parallel of him being dead for three days in the same way as Jonah was restricted in the fish for three days. He also said the positive response of the Ninevites shamed the Jews who were unwilling to repent, (Matthew 12:38-41; Luke 11:29-30, v32). He later repeats his use of the Jonah account this time to the Pharisees and Sadducees together, 'A wicked and adulterous generation looks for a sign, but none will be given it except the sign of Jonah' (Matthew 16:4). This story of Gentile conversions would have been particularly resented by the Jewish leaders, but Jesus used it because he knew it really happened!

33 Micah - *One day there will be no more war.*

'Many nations will come and say,
"Come, let us go up to the mountain of the Lord,
to the temple of the God of Jacob.
He will teach us his ways,
so that we may walk in his paths."
The law will go out from Zion,
the word of the Lord from Jerusalem.
He will judge between many peoples
and will settle disputes for strong nations far and wide.
They will beat their swords into ploughshares
and their spears into pruning hooks.
Nation will not take up sword against nation,
nor will they train for war anymore.'

(Micah 4:2-3)(and Isaiah 2:4; Joel 3:10)

The prophet Micah, a contemporary with Isaiah and Hosea, is raised up by God to prophesy principally to the Southern kingdom of Judah during the reigns of three kings: Jotham, Ahaz and Hezekiah. He foresees that Samaria, capital of Israel, and Jerusalem, capital of Judah, will be destroyed because of their injustice and disobedience towards God. The people have abandoned their side of the covenant with God, taking up the pagan religious practices of the Canaanites. The rich and powerful are ruthlessly exploiting the poor and are ignoring the laws given them by Moses. Micah warns that in punishment for their unfaithfulness and injustice, both kingdoms will be invaded, conquered and the people carried off into exile. This came about when Samaria fell to the Assyrians in 722 BC and Jerusalem fell to the Babylonians in 586 BC. From speaking of justice and judgment in chapter three, Micah now moves on to blessings for God's people in chapter four.

After punishment there will be restoration and a return to their own land in the near future. However, in the distant future, they will be ruled by a righteous king and become a light to the whole world, pointing all nations to the Lord.

The two long verses selected for this study give us a lot of information, and as the old English idiom says, *they are a peg to hang your hat on.*[229]

Micah 4:2. Jerusalem, the City of Zion, will ultimately be restored and exalted by God. We read in the Psalms, 'He has founded his city on the holy mountain' (Psalms 87:1), and, '"The glory of this present house will be greater than the glory of the former house," says the Lord Almighty. "And in this place I will grant peace," declares the Lord Almighty' (Haggai 2:9). Haggai delivers his prophecy soon after the return from exile, but the fulfilment of much of it is distant, even towards the end of the age. Some theologians tell us that at Christ's Second Coming, his Millennial Temple will be built in Jerusalem and assume great importance. Jesus will set up his government there and Israel will become the leading nation amongst all the nations of the world. The attitude of many who are against the Jews will be reversed and people will encourage each other to go up the mountain of the Lord to the temple of the one true God.

To answer the question will everyone have to travel to Jerusalem to find and worship God, Got Questions blog gives an answer, 'The fact that people from every nation come to Jerusalem does not mean that everyone *must* travel to Jerusalem during the millennial reign. Most likely, people will be able to worship the Lord from anywhere in the world. Isaiah re-assures us: "…the earth will be full of the knowledge of the Lord as the waters cover the sea" (Isaiah 11:9).'[230]

Micah knows this is a long time into the future and will not be fulfilled immediately; many people will flow back to the city from distant parts of the world. God will teach his ways and his word or law will go out from Jerusalem. The complete fulfilment of this is in the millennial reign of Christ. This is beyond the scope of this book, except that it is touched on in the last chapter: Revelation. However, when Christ returns to the Earth to start his reign as '…King of kings and Lord of lords' (Revelation 19:16b), there will be great blessing for those who love him as Saviour and honour him as Lord. There will also be justice and judgment for those who reject him. The Knowing Jesus blog tells us that in Micah's time there will be, '…the destruction of the Northern kingdom of Israel and the dispersion of the Southern kingdom of Judah.'[231] Knowing Jesus go on to say, 'How very different from the world in which we live today - and yet God has written the end from the beginning so that we who are Christ's Body and saints of all ages, may know that God's Word will one day be fulfilled... and we will all see it together.'[232] We must remember though, that just as Jesus will bring blessing for those who love him, so too for those who reject Jesus we are told, 'You will break them with a rod of iron; you will dash them to pieces like pottery' (Psalm 2:9).

Micah 4:3. Pastor David Guzik explains the judgement of Jesus and the absence of war, 'During the reign of the Messiah, there will be no more war. There will still be conflicts between nations and individuals, but they will be justly and decisively resolved by the Messiah and those who reign with him.'[233] But, Jesus will sit in judgment '...between many peoples...and will settle disputes for strong nations far and wide' (Micah 4:3a). Micah then proclaims the **strange** words: '...Nation will not take up the sword against nation...' (v3c). A number of world leaders have used the quotation which is found in Micah, Isaiah and Joel, in major speeches, and it is carved on the wall facing the UNHQ.[234] This is describing peace as a result of righteousness and will be so much valued when it happens. There will be no war, rumours of war, or need for war, because there will be a new ruler on Earth, the Lord Jesus Christ, and there will be no need for weapons. Those that do exist will be turned into peaceful things such as agricultural implements. The change is not just the re-working of weapons but the change of heart of the people.

Matthew Henry tells us, '...angry passionate men, that have been fierce and furious, shall be wonderfully sweetened, and made mild and meek.'[235] He points us to confirmation in Paul's letter to Titus, 'Remind the people to ...slander no-one, to be peaceable and considerate, and always to be gentle towards everyone' (Titus 3:1-2).

Before the monarchy was established in Israel, the Judges were in power but the people of Israel rejected them and God as their king. During his first coming and earthly ministry, Jesus was also rejected as king. However, at his Second Coming, Jesus will sit on David's throne and rule with justice and righteousness. Kings and mighty leaders of nations will then submit to him and his authority and bring their disputes for him to settle. All people will sit at peace in their own gardens and not be afraid because God will ensure this peace. (Micah 4:4)

Satan's rule through people, which has dominated the world since Adam and Eve sinned in the garden of Eden, will be replaced with God's kingdom and his rule. It will be established by Jesus and the world will finally understand the significance and centrality of Israel in God's eternal plan of salvation and redemption. However, this sits in contrast with human efforts and the Knowing Jesus blog concludes, 'Peace without God is the objective of the arrogant United Nations. But peace without God is impossible.'[236] A very sobering thought!

One day, Micah's prophecy will be totally fulfilled and the new world order will be clear for all to see. The Lord, himself will descend '… with power and great glory' (Luke 21:27), to '…comfort Zion…' and make '…her wastelands like the garden of the Lord' (Isaiah 51:3b), and this will bring in worldwide peace (Micah 4:3), because God's people will be able to say, '…he will be our peace…' (Micah 5:5).

These are exciting days which are worth waiting for.

34 Nahum - *God can split rocks by wrath alone.*

'The Lord is a jealous and avenging God;
the Lord takes vengeance and is filled with wrath.
The Lord takes vengeance on his foes
and vents his wrath against his enemies.
The Lord is slow to anger but great in power;
the Lord will not leave the guilty unpunished.
His way is in the whirlwind and the storm,
and clouds are the dust of his feet.
He rebukes the sea and dries it up;
he makes all the rivers run dry.
Bashan and Carmel wither
and the blossoms of Lebanon fade.
The mountains quake before him
and the hills melt away.
The earth trembles at his presence,
the world and all who live in it.
Who can withstand his indignation?
Who can endure his fierce anger?
His wrath is poured out like fire;
the rocks are shattered before him.

(Nahum 1:2-6)

When we consider the growth of a tree or something even smaller such as the annual growth of weeds in the garden, sometimes things seem to happen very slowly. A tree may last for many years before its life-span is over, but weeds seem to die back at the end of the growing season each year. The following year new weeds rise again. It was rather like that with the fall and rise of empires in the history of the Israelites or Jews as they became known after the exile. From 883 BC, and an extended period of dominance, the Assyrians were losing power and control of their empire and in 612 BC, the capital, Nineveh, and the empire of Assyria was about to fall to the combined forces of the Babylonian, Median and Scythian forces which were gradually linking together against their common enemy. Countries like Israel which had been cruelly treated by the Assyrians saw what was about to happen and felt the Assyrians were getting what they deserved. Into this situation, Nahum rises as a prophet of Judah proclaiming that God would rule over the kingdoms of the Earth. Nahum proclaimed that Assyria would be judged and punished, and in being sent by God to Nineveh, Nahum was the second prophet to address the nation; Jonah was the first.

When Jonah was called to prophesy between about 785-772 BC, his main task was to visit Nineveh and speak against its godlessness; he expected by faith that the people would repent and turn to Yahweh, the one true God: the God of the Israelites. Unexpectedly to Jonah, the people did repent and the city turned to God in vast numbers. For a century, the Ninevites experienced God's blessing and grace. A hundred years later, God again expected repentance as he sent a second prophet but this didn't happen so Nahum pronounced God's vengeance and wrath over the wickedness he saw there in a vision. Godly ways had been forgotten and evil idolatry in the city returned with the people plotting against Yahweh and the Israelite captives.

The Jews took comfort that the powerful Assyrian empire which troubled them so much was going to be destroyed. God is a jealous God (Nahum 1:2a); he is protective of his people and will punish those who oppose him and his special people. Those who set themselves up against God will end up reaping his vengeance. God is more patient than people and was awaiting his time before acting (v3b). God would not leave the guilty unpunished; neither would he just clear the guilt. Nahum tells us God's '...wrath is poured out like fire...' (v6a). As Full Of Eyes blog tells us, 'This is the wrath that Nahum so graphically portrays as divine fire that shrivels its adversaries, shakes the earth, melts the hills, and shatters the rocks' (v5-6).[237]

In his Enduring Word blog, David Guzik makes a particularly challenging statement about this verse, 'Every sin will be paid for – either in hell or at the cross.'[238] Exodus gives both aspects of God, his justice (wrath) and his mercy (love), as he is 'maintaining love to thousands, and forgiving wickedness, rebellion and sin. Yet he does not leave the guilty unpunished; he punishes the children and their children for the sin of the parents to the third and fourth generation' (Exodus 34:7).

We then read a key sentence in our passage being studied showing God's power over nature and the environment, 'His way is in the whirlwind and the storm, and clouds are the dust of his feet' (Nahum 1:3c, d). 'He parted the heavens and came down; dark clouds were under his feet' (Psalms 18:9). God is able to use the weather to do his bidding when he chooses to.[239]

God controls the mightiest forces known to people, but they are nothing to God who waits a long time before taking action but when he does it is very decisive. God is angry, but it is a controlled anger (Isaiah 27:4), as Matthew Henry points out in his commentary on Nahum 1 verse 6.[240]

In our passage there are **strange** words about God's power to split rocks:

'His wrath is poured out like fire; the rocks are shattered before him' (NIVUK), '…the rocks are thrown down by him' (KJV), '…his fury shatters boulders' (MSG)[241], '…the rocks are destroyed by him' (AMP)[242] (Nahum 1:6b).

Nahum 1:6 points to the power of God, but the verse also looks forward to the work of Jesus on the cross when he faced God's wrath as he carried the sins of the world. As the Knowing Jesus blog reports, we read that Jesus: '…stood before this, he endured this (*God's wrath*). And, just as the rocks of Calvary were split at his death (Matthew 27:51), so too Christ himself – the Rock (1 Corinthians 10:4) – was split under the rod of divine wrath such that water gushed out and gave life to a barren world' (*Insertion mine*).[243] (Isaiah 48:21; John 19:34).

35 Habakkuk - *Even when farming fails, God can still be praised.*

'Though the fig-tree does not bud and there are no grapes on the vines,
though the olive crop fails and the fields produce no food,
though there are no sheep in the sheepfold and no cattle in the stalls,
***yet I will rejoice in the Lord**, I will be joyful in God my Saviour.'*

(Habakkuk 3:17-18)

The historical setting of this prophecy is important. Habakkuk prophesied about 620-612 BC about the same time as Nahum and Zephaniah leading up to the Babylonian invasion of Judah, the Southern kingdom. The Northern kingdom of Israel had been conquered by Assyria in 722 BC and now, almost a century later, the Assyrian empire is waning, and Babylon is on the ascendancy.

Historical records tell us that in 612 BC the Babylonians conquered Nineveh, the capital of the Assyrian empire, which had ruled over God's exiled people for a century. In 609 BC, Judah's young, promising and godly king, Josiah, was killed in battle against Egypt. In 605 BC, the Assyrians were totally conquered by the Babylonians, and that year they marched on Jerusalem for the first of what became three invasions: 605, 597, and finally 586 BC. Each conquest gave the Babylonians more captives to take to exile.

God is not only watching the changing political situation, but he is also telling Habakkuk what he is going to do. At the time, Habakkuk is extremely low in his spirits and complaining to God about the injustice and wickedness in his enemies *and* amongst his own people. Much of the book of Habakkuk sees him in conversation with God and not addressing people, unlike other prophets.

David Mathis, Executive director of Desiring God, teacher and community leader at Cities Church, Minnesota, invites us to 'walk with Habakkuk on his pathway from fear to faith, from protest to praise, and see that in the midst of rampant wickedness, chaos, and upheaval, in trying times, trusting the God of unshakable justice enables his people to live with patience and joy.'[244] God's judgment on his enemies and trials for his own people caused Habakkuk to be anxious (Habakkuk 3:16), but in verses 17-18 chosen for this study, we see Habakkuk's clear-cut faith. It is seen in chapter 2 verse 4 '…the just shall live by his faith.' It is also seen in his proclamation: 'For the earth will be filled with the knowledge of the glory of the Lord as the waters cover the sea' (2:14), and in his assurance that all will be well (Habakkuk 3:17-18). He includes his own testimony with unexpected and **strange** words, 'Yet I will rejoice in the Lord, I will be joyful in God my Saviour' (v18), even though everything seems to be failing.

The fields, gardens, barns and animal pens were empty. Everything is void, dry and barren in Habakkuk's world. That is the picture, and then Habakkuk affirms that in the middle of the dryness, barrenness and the emptiness of everything, all we look to in this world and we long for in this world, all we need in this world, even food, amidst emptiness and barrenness, even so, Habakkuk rejoiced in the Lord. As David Platt, pastor at McLean Bible Church in Washington, D.C., tells us in his podcast, '…when we lose great things in this world, great people in this world, and it's not that the tears aren't many, they are, it's not that the suffering isn't real, it's real, but we have in God a treasure that is far better, far greater, far more wonderful than good health.'[245]

Habakkuk is a positive example to many and he humbly submits to the sovereign hand of God as he walks in patience and faith. The third and last chapter of this short book is both a prayer and a song of praise offered to God and is set to music by his director of music (Habakkuk 1:1, 3:19). The reason Habakkuk could cope with the challenges he was facing was because he could say, 'The Sovereign Lord is my strength…' (v19a). That was his position; that was his testimony!

Habakkuk 3 is quite a journey. As the theologian Matthew Henry says on this chapter, 'Thus the prophet, who began his prayer with fear and trembling, ends it with joy and triumph.'[246] He has a loss of harvest and livestock, but was still able to rejoice and find God as his strength, and who gives him a 'spring in his step' and a positive approach to life and living (v19).

David Mathis concludes, 'For God's people - for those who are righteous by faith - hardship is not the end of the story. It never ends in pain for the people of God. It never ends in darkness. It never ends in trouble. Devastation never has the last word.'[247]

36 Zephaniah - *God will look favourably on those who are disabled and marginalised.*

*"At that time I will deal with all who oppressed you. **I will rescue the lame**; I will gather the exiles. I will give them praise and honour in every land where they have suffered shame.*

At that time I will gather you; at that time I will bring you home. I will give you honour and praise among all the peoples of the earth when I restore your fortunes before your very eyes," says the Lord.'

(Zephaniah 3:19-20)

It is easy being a critic and easy summarising a leader as being good or bad, but this is what the Bible does as it assesses its kings after their reigns. Most leaders are a mixture of these two qualities but the Bible writers don't mince their words. After all, they are handling precious material which could affect lives to bring people close to God or not, depending on what is read in holy Scripture.

King Manasseh of Judah was a bad king in that he caused or allowed great corruption, injustice and idol worship. However, God raised up a good king in his grandson, Josiah who, guided the nation to faith and obedience to God, as well as independence from the neighbouring godless empires (2 Kings 22:2). Zephaniah ministered during Josiah's reign and he was fearless enough as a prophet to stand up and warn everyone around him of the dangers linked to the nation's breaking of the covenant with Yahweh leading to the nation being on the brink of destruction. Zephaniah was from a royal background, being the great-great-grandson of the good King Hezekiah who conducted spiritual reforms in Judah. His name means *Yahweh is hidden*. This is a link to both his background and message, and his parents probably gave him this name to indicate they were devout in their faith, and it expressed how they felt. Zephaniah may have been a Jerusalem resident since he knew its districts and was familiar with particular activities in the capital city. As with Joel and Amos, he is very conscious of the impending judgment of God and proclaimed that, '…the day of the Lord is near…' (Zephaniah 1:7).

Dr. Justin Imel, Sr., Minister of the Church of Christ, Deer Park, Texas, summarises God's judgment and indignation:

> 'In the midst of … righteous indignation, God offers great hope. Those who turn to the Lord in repentance have an opportunity to avoid the great disaster about to befall Judah.'[248]

Imel points us to an important verse: 'Seek the Lord, all you humble of the land, you who do what he commands. Seek righteousness, seek humility; perhaps you will be sheltered on the day of the Lord's anger' (Zephaniah 2:3).

In the third chapter of the prophecy Zephaniah brings a two-fold message: firstly a promise from God to the people of Judah to assure them of restoration and blessing if they humbly accept God as a Mighty Warrior amongst his people and secondly, he brought a message of judgment to the enemies of God, including any of his own Judean faithless people. On that day, Zephaniah warned the people of Judah to seek the Lord so they would be *hidden* from his anger when he says, 'I will sweep away everything from the face of the Earth' (Zephaniah 1:2). He names people, animals, birds, fish, idols and idol-worshippers (v3-6). We see more detail as the drama of chapter three unfolds.

Jerusalem includes the principal groups of people: officials, rulers, prophets and priests (v3-4). John Gill in his Bible Exposition tells us,

'The hardness, impenitence, and shamelessness of this people, are exposed and aggravated by the just Lord being among them; who, by his example and doctrine, taught them otherwise; yet they were not amended or made ashamed (Zephaniah 3:5), nor received instruction, nor took warning by the judgments of God on other nations' (v6-7).[249]

God had decided to bide his time before taking action against the assembled foreign nations, until Judah had observed judgments on the nations and they had learned to serve and worship God for themselves (Zephaniah 3:9-11). Then God would gather them to himself and protect them and deliver them from their enemies. This would cause Judah, called the '...daughter Zion...Israel...' (v14), to sing, shout and rejoice. The Lord had pardoned them and set them free and it was something to shout about.

Kathryn M Schifferdecker, assistant professor of OT and minister of the Evangelical Lutheran Church, Arkdale, Wisconsin, adds, '...not only is "daughter Zion" forgiven, but the Lord himself is with her. Therefore says the prophet, "Do not fear, Zion…" (v16a). It is the injunction spoken to everyone who encounters the near presence of the Lord.'[250] Israel will have no need of a king because the Lord is King and is amongst them and will not leave them. He is the promised '…Mighty Warrior who saves…' (v17a).

God will deal with Israel's enemies and then we read unexpected and **strange** words, that he would '…rescue the lame…' (v19), words which represent those with disabilities, and gather the exiles. Why? God says, '…I will bring you home' (v20a). What a wonderful thought! Especially so because God himself will be rejoicing and singing over his people (v17d). As the morning stars sang at the creation of the world, '…and all the angels shouted for joy' (Job 38:7), so God sings with elation over his beloved nation. As David danced in front of the Ark of the Covenant, in ecstatic praise and worship, so God rejoices over his people (2 Samuel 6:5). '…as a bridegroom rejoices over his bride, so will your God rejoice over you' (Isaiah 62:5). Despite great hardships he endured, the Apostle Paul encouraged churches, such as at Rome and Philippi to have and express their joy: 'Be joyful in hope…' (Romans 12:12). 'Rejoice in the Lord always. I will say it again: Rejoice!' (Philippians 4:4)

I have a heart for those with disabilities after working for decades with these very special children and adults and I am heartened that they have a special mention in Zephaniah and I note that it is God's initiative with inclusion, as he gives special mention of those with disabilities, as typified by reference to '*the lame*' (Zephaniah 3:19). This complete scenario is God entering into the life of the world, dealing with the bad and the good, restoring, renewing and redeeming his people and as he does so often, giving them a fresh start. Zephaniah's final words are very encouraging, '"I will gather you… I will bring you home. I will give you honour and praise… when I restore your fortunes before your very eyes," says the Lord' (v20). Over 50 years earlier, Isaiah was writing about restoration, 'The wolf will live with the lamb, the leopard will lie down with the goat, the calf and the lion and the yearling together; and a little child will lead them' (Isaiah 11:6). A picture of restoration; a picture of heaven on Earth![251]

37 Haggai - *God causes people to re-assess their priorities.*

'This is what the Lord Almighty says: "These people say, The time has not yet come to rebuild the Lord's house."

Then the word of the Lord came through the prophet Haggai: "Is it a time for you yourselves to be living in your panelled houses, while this house remains a ruin?"

Now this is what the Lord Almighty says: "Give careful thought to your ways. You have planted much, but harvested little. You eat, but never have enough. You drink, but never have your fill. You put on clothes, but are not warm. You earn wages, only to put them in a purse with holes in it."

*This is what the Lord Almighty says: "**Give careful thought to your ways**."'*

(Haggai 1:2-7)

Babylon fell to invaders, particularly the Persians under Cyrus their king, in 539 BC as they gained power and influence. Shortly after this, Cyrus allowed the Jews to return home in 536 BC, and a remnant of 50,000 did so and start to rebuild the temple. Haggai was writing about 520 BC and recording developments. God used Cyrus to allow this release which was clearly a miracle and which provided what the Jews desperately wanted: to go home. However, as we found in looking at Ezra and Nehemiah, neighbouring people, mainly Samaritans who had moved in to take control of the land whilst the Jews were away in exile, made life difficult for those re-building Jerusalem. The resentful neighbours had influence in the Persian court, and this they exploited. We read,

> 'Then the peoples around them set out to discourage the people of Judah and make them afraid to go on building. They bribed officials to work against them and frustrate their plans during the entire reign of Cyrus king of Persia and down to the reign of Darius king of Persia' (Ezra 4:4-5).

This caused the work to stop for 16 years before re-starting when King Darius became king in Persia. Darius listened less to the Samaritans than Cyrus did. Haggai urges the people to restart the work. His preaching is clear-cut and he calls specifically on Zerubbabel, the appointed governor, and Joshua, the high priest,[252] to lead the project forward. The historical context is given in Ezra 5.[253] The Jews had no king now but were under Gentile rulers which happened in their history from time to time and was even spoken of by Jesus who said, '...Jerusalem will be trampled on by the Gentiles until the times of the Gentiles are fulfilled' (Luke 21:24b). In 520 BC the construction of the temple resumed and was finally completed in 514 BC followed by the dedication ceremony during the annual Passover and Feast of Unleavened Bread (Ezra 6:15-22).

Haggai, in this the second shortest book in the OT, delivers several messages to the people with challenge, encouragement and promises from God that there will be new blessings if they obey him, because the Jews are back in their own land again.

Haggai's name is interesting because it comes from a word meaning *to keep the feast* or *festival* and this is what the people did with feasts being restored and observed. Ultimately, God in all his glory will fill the 'house (temple)' (Haggai 1:2 AMP).[254] This was so important and so impressive that the writer to Hebrews quotes Haggai in saying this (Haggai 2:7-8; Hebrews 12:26). However, the people had to be rebuked first for beautifying their own homes and not getting on with rebuilding God's house.

Bible Study Tools blog points out, '…this book (*Haggai*) is to reprove the Jews for their negligence in building the temple, after they had liberty granted them by Cyrus to do it, and to encourage them in this work; which he does by the promise of the Messiah, who should come into it, and give it a greater glory than the first temple had.' (*Insertion mine*).[255] Haggai is saying, *Make God first in your life*. Or, as Jesus put it, 'But seek first his kingdom and his righteousness, and all these things will be given to you as well' (Matthew 6:33).

The people were arguing that it was not the right time to rebuild the temple, but God had to correct them, it *was* the right time! They took a lazy view of the importance of Yahweh in the life of the nation. The Study Light blog points out quoting Dr Constable's Expository Notes, 'The need to rebuild is urgent, because temples in their world are the centre for administering the political, economic, judicial, social, and religious life of the nation.'[256]

'Twice God used the **strange** words of our passage above for study of this book, '…Give careful thought to your ways' (Haggai 1:5b, v7b). The people hadn't realised why things were going wrong for them, such as a poor harvest, hunger, thirst, inadequate clothes and being careless with wages. They expected much and it became little and what they did take home God says '...I blew away...' (v9a), because they were neglecting God's house, and became busy with their own houses (v9b). They had got their priorities wrong and didn't realise God had caused their circumstances! All had become 'vanity' (KJV) 'meaningless' (NIVUK) as Solomon declared (Ecclesiastes 1:1). 'The punishment for their neglect had been futility, they laboured much but produced little,' according to André van Belkum, Pastor of the Church of God, New Zealand and the Pacific region.[257]

Steven Cole, retired Pastor of Flagstaff Christian Fellowship, Lake Gregory Community Church, California, believes:

> '(*Haggai*) was written to people, like us, who would have told you that God must be first. They believed that; we believe that. But, they had drifted into a way of life where their intellectual belief in the supremacy of God was not reflected in the way they were living. They gave lip service to the priority of God, but in fact they lived with other priorities. God sent this prophet to help his people get their priorities in line with what they knew they should be.'[258]
>
> (*Insertion mine*).

We must note that the change of heart began with the leaders, Zerubbabel and Joshua (Haggai 1:12), who responded to Haggai's preaching. That took humility on their part. It would have been easy for them as the leading political and spiritual leaders to resist Haggai's message in order to preserve their reputation in the eyes of the community. The people then followed and worked hard with a clear focus. Haggai encouraged them to go to the mountains where there were lots of trees they could cut down, and bring cedar logs in by sea (Ezra 3:7) and to continue the re-building of the temple. The completed temple would please and glorify the Lord God. This is always the case when work for God is done willingly.

38 Zechariah - *Satan schemes to accuse God's servant.*

*'Then he showed me Joshua the high priest standing before the angel of the Lord, and Satan standing at his right side to accuse him. The Lord said to Satan, "**The Lord rebuke you, Satan**! The Lord, who has chosen Jerusalem, rebuke you! Is not this man a burning stick snatched from the fire?"*

Now Joshua was dressed in filthy clothes as he stood before the angel. The angel said to those who were standing before him, "Take off his filthy clothes."

Then he said to Joshua, "See, I have taken away your sin, and I will put fine garments on you."

Then I said, "Put a clean turban on his head." So they put a clean turban on his head and clothed him, while the angel of the Lord stood by.'

(Zechariah 3:1-5)

The prophet Zechariah was a contemporary of Haggai. They began together but Zechariah served for longer. He brought messages from God to the returned exiles of Judah beginning in the second year of King Darius of Persia in 520 BC, and continued prophesying to about 488 BC. The overall message of his book is that God has everything in place for the rebuilding project. After a number of prophecies and visions, the book's final one predicts that after the people have suffered under bad shepherds or leaders, God would send a righteous king, a descendent of David. He proclaims that the Lord will one day triumph over every enemy and be king over the whole earth.

Joshua is heading up the priesthood and his appearance is typical of that priesthood; the vision uses him as an example and visual aid. In judicial language he is being accused as he stands before the angel of the Lord. His clothes were very dirty so the angel dealt with that by asking his assistants to remove them. They were replaced by fine holy garments and a turban. (The turban was part of the High Priest's garments and on the front it had a gold plate inscribed with the phrase: 'HOLY TO THE LORD') (Exodus 28:36-38). This enactment typified the removal of sin. He was commanded to walk in obedience to God and as he did so he was promised a senior position in God's courtroom. Joshua and his colleagues, '… who are men symbolic of things to come…' (Zechariah 3:8a), and are promised they will see '…God's servant, the Branch' (v8b). This is a reference to the Messiah: Jesus. John Gill in his commentary, Exposition of the Bible, quoted by Bible Study Tools blog says, '…the chapter is closed with an account of the prosperity, peace, and safety of the saints under the Gospel dispensation,'[259] (Zechariah 3:10). This takes us at the close of this ten-verse chapter right into the future, to the appearance of Jesus, and there will be a peaceful situation at that time.

Zechariah's vision deserves a closer investigation, particularly of the characters involved and the unfolding drama:

Zechariah: was the one given the vision and having received it, he is responsible for communicating it to those around him and in writing for all who would read his prophecy in the future. In the OT he is mentioned in 2 Chronicles, Ezra, and Nehemiah. In the NT, sadly, Jesus informs us that he was murdered by the Jews, '… between the temple and the altar' (Matthew 23:35). Jesus then had a firm word for the Pharisees, '…you (*are those*) who kill the prophets and stone those sent to you…' (v37). (*Insertion mine*).[260]

Joshua: was standing in front of the angel as a ministering priest, and Satan, or the Devil, was standing at his right-hand side to accuse him (Zechariah 3:1). Satan similarly confronted Job (Job 1:13-19), and Jesus (Matthew 4:3-10). Joshua seems to have been attacked by Satan because he was the High Priest, and heading up spiritual issues and the spiritual life of the nation. He was serving during Zechariah's ministry.

Satan: was allowed by God to resist or accuse Joshua (Zechariah 3:1). He is called in Revelation, '…the accuser of our brothers and sisters, who accuses them before our God day and night, has been hurled down' (Revelation 12:10b). He was present in Zechariah's vision as an adversary. As Pastor David Guzik in the Enduring Word blog put it, 'He (*Satan*), stands against us in spiritual battle (Ephesians 6:10-18). The only thing worse than having Satan as an adversary is to have him as a friend.'[261] (*Insertion mine*).

The angel: was acting for the Lord or may even have been the Lord. He speaks to his helpers to undress Joshua and remove his dirty clothes, and re-clothe him in new clothes.[262] He tells Joshua this action was symbolically removing his sin, and charges him to be obedient to God and so the reward will be the senior position in God's court. Lastly, he assures Joshua that his servant, the 'Branch,'[263] the Messiah or Jesus, will be coming one day. This will herald the total removal of sin from the land and neighbours will get on well and be at peace there with each other (Zechariah 3:4, v6, v9-10).

The Lord: was the angel, or in the angel, making them one and the same person. He rebukes Satan and points out to him that Joshua is a man of faith (v2). Then he promises the 'Branch' to come and details the inscribed stone and how he will remove sin in total on one day. After days of warfare and social unrest, he promises peace (v8-10).

The drama unfolds with the Lord speaking to Satan the **strange** words, '…The Lord rebuke you, Satan!...' (v2). The Explaining the Book blog finds these words unusual and says,

'The Lord … is calling on the Lord to do something. And that's a little unusual. Maybe not what we would expect. I could imagine Joshua calling on the Lord to rebuke Satan. I could even imagine Zechariah doing that. But the Lord himself is calling on the Lord to rebuke Satan.'[264]

The angel may be calling on God to do something, or it may be God the Father is calling on God the Son to act? What is clear is that Satan is being rebuked because of his accusations against Joshua. 'God does allow Satan to attack and harass his people, but He always strictly regulates what Satan is allowed to do.'[265] The words, '…The Lord rebuke you…' (v2) were also taken up by Jude in his short one chapter letter, 'But even the archangel Michael, when he was disputing with the devil about the body of Moses … said, 'The Lord rebuke you!' (Jude 1:9)

Jerusalem is going to be restored. The temple is going to be re-built. Joshua is going to be involved and Satan is not going to stop him! After all, Joshua was snatched out of exile and released into the Promised Land and brought out of the world and into faith. Joshua needed to be cleaned up but so did the religious system of Israel. We can see in this vision and enactment that God is pleased with what he is seeing. The transformation is happening in hearts, lives, temple and worship.

One day God's people will appear before him in white (Revelation 6:11), and 'Fine linen, bright and clean…' (*which*) '…stands for the righteous acts of God's holy people' (Revelation 19:8) (*Insertion mine*). In the creation of the world seven times in six days God said about his creation '…it was very good' (Genesis 1:31), he was saying the same thing in this fresh start for his own people back in their own land.

39 Malachi - *God objects to people robbing him.*

"'Will a mere mortal rob God? Yet you rob me. But you ask, How are we robbing you? In tithes and offerings. You are under a curse – your whole nation – because you are robbing me. **Bring the whole tithe into the storehouse**, *that there may be food in my house. Test me in this," says the Lord Almighty, "and see if I will not throw open the floodgates of heaven and pour out so much blessing that there will not be room enough to store it."'*

(Malachi 3:8-10)

Zerubbabel the governor, or political leader, and Joshua the High Priest, or spiritual leader led the way in re-building the temple, and it was completed in 514 BC. This quickly assumed its former role of being the centre of the nation's light, life and worship. As in the early days, Israel was tasked with reaching out to the nations of the world with a message of hope as Israel revealed God as Lord of all.

Sadly, as the years went by, the people fell into sin and left behind their first love. About 50 years after Zechariah, and 70 years after the temple was finished, their worship had become corrupted, and their dealings with each other were unjust. Malachi, whose name means *my messenger*, was raised up about 434 BC and prophesied to about 414 BC to challenge his people to honour God in their worship and in their relationships with one another. This would allow the world to come to know the Lord as the King. Malachi writes addressing firstly, the priests of Israel (Malachi 1:6, 2:1) and the Levites (3:3), but secondly, he speaks to the ordinary people as well.

In chapter three, Malachi brings a message from God as to what he required and to make it clear that he would be testing the actions of his people against his own moral code by putting them on trial. The people had broken their covenant with him but in his love and mercy he is offering the people another chance, and he is calling for people to turn back to him then he will return to them. Sadly, and in condemnation, God calls his people 'cheats' (Malachi 1:14). The Got Question blog tells us, 'So hardened and cold had the nation grown that they were blind to the fact that they had abandoned their first love for the Lord.'[266] The message seems to include the prophecy foretelling the coming of John the Baptist to prepare the way for the Messiah. This was fulfilled some 400 years later. John was the fore-runner of Christ, the Messiah, and he prepared the way and the people for his coming. The challenge for the Jews to return to God is typified by Malachi highlighting their withholding of tithes which are rightly the Lord's. This coming of the Messiah, as the Bible Study Tools blog reports, will be '…terrible to the wicked, and as trying and purifying to the righteous, expressed by the various similes of a refiner's fire, and fuller's soap; and the end answered by it, their offering a righteous offering to the Lord.'[267]

As a nation, what they were doing was robbing God of what was his (Malachi 3:8). God further says through Malachi that if the people gave him what is his he would bless them with prosperity and protection and make their land 'delightful' (v12). It seems that only part, and not the whole of what was God's, was being given so we meet the unexpected and **strange** words, 'Bring the whole tithe into the storehouse…' (v10a).

Jeremy Myers, author, Bible teacher and blogger in Oregon, observes, 'It appears that the section on tithing in Malachi 3:8-10 is not so much addressed to the people of Israel, who apparently were doing a good job of bringing their tithes and offerings to the storehouse, but to the wicked and wayward priests, … who were removing the tithes and offerings from the storehouse for their own personal gain.'[268] The book of Nehemiah also indicates that the people were bringing their tithes and the priests were stealing them for their own use (Nehemiah 13:12). It is really quite surprising that people should want to steal from God since he sees all that happens and all the earth belongs to him anyway. The Psalms tell us, 'The earth is the Lord's, and everything in it, the world, and all who live in it' (Psalms 24:1). The people, led by the priests, were taking what belonged to God and using it for themselves. The remaining portion is also God's but which he allowed them to keep, and trusted them to manage it well. However, the withholding of both money and food from the storehouse was not limited to just the priests. The people were also not fully committed to Yahweh, their Lord and God, and so they were complicit with the priests, and the priests were dependent on the people for their income and food from the tithe.

Because the whole tithes and offerings were not being brought to God, he told the people, 'You are under a curse – your whole nation – because you are robbing me' (Malachi 3:9). Pastor David Guzik says the situation is clear: 'Because God's people did not give as he commanded, God did not bless them materially or spiritually the way he would have otherwise. Their stingy hearts proved that their hearts were far from God, because God is the greatest giver.' We see this in the way he gave his Son to be the Saviour of the world, (John 3:16; 2 Corinthians 9:15).[269]

All this reminds *us* to bring our financial challenges to God and honour him with our giving; in doing this, our part, he promises to bless us and help us.[270] In fact, God always sees and blesses generous givers. Matthew Henry knows this to be true, 'He who makes trial will find nothing is lost by honouring the Lord with his substance.'[271]

I am convinced that the attitude of heart and mind to giving is absolutely essential and God looks for full commitment. This prompts generous giving and God blesses that abundantly. John O. Reid, (1930-2016) an elder of the Church of the Great God, Missouri, in The Berean Blog tells us,

'God is saying, "Bring your tithes with a right heart and attitude and I will open the sluice, or the floodgates, of blessings and pour them out upon you until you cannot receive it all!" The conditions are a right heart and a right attitude. We do not know if these blessings will be spiritual or physical, but you can bet your bottom dollar that the blessings are going to be there!'[272]

The whole Bible, and especially the words of Jesus, encourages us to be generous in our giving to God just as he is generous to us more than we deserve and more than we can imagine. I suggest Jesus has the last word of the last book of the OT, before the gap of about 400 years before there is another direct word from God:

'Give, and it will be given to you. A good measure, pressed down, shaken together and running over, will be poured into your lap. For with the measure you use, it will be measured to you' (Luke 6:38).

The New Testament

40 Matthew - A Gentile Roman centurion declares the truth about Jesus.

'From noon until three in the afternoon darkness came over all the land. About three in the afternoon Jesus cried out in a loud voice, "Eli, Eli, lema sabachthani?" (which means "My God, my God, why have you forsaken me?")

When some of those standing there heard this, they said, "He's calling Elijah."

Immediately one of them ran and got a sponge. He filled it with wine vinegar, put it on a staff, and offered it to Jesus to drink. The rest said, "Now leave him alone. Let's see if Elijah comes to save him." And when Jesus had cried out again in a loud voice, he gave up his spirit.

*At that moment the curtain of the temple was torn in two from top to bottom. The earth shook, the rocks split and the tombs broke open. The bodies of many holy people who had died were raised to life. They came out of the tombs after Jesus' resurrection and went into the holy city and appeared to many people. When the centurion and those with him who were guarding Jesus saw the earthquake and all that had happened, they were terrified, and exclaimed, "**Surely he was the Son of God!**"'*

(Matthew 27:45-54)[273]

There are times when the 'penny drops;' when things fall into place. I have just had an experience with an *app* on my smart phone which has been exactly that. For an older person, IT has to be deliberately learned since it was not taught at school, so it is not *second nature*. I wasn't at school in the abacus days but was in the era of slide rules and then electronic calculators which were essential. I also carried a pocket English dictionary and an English-French dictionary. I was ready for most eventualities.

I have just learned a little more about the *NHS app* I once downloaded on to my phone but have not really used. I needed to check whether or not it is now possible to make an appointment with my G.P. through this app. Those brought up with computers and apps find information finding and retrieval easy but to some of us who pre-date these skills and experience, it can be a lengthy process. So, what did I discover? I found I could access the NHS site through a login feature, then I needed a password, then a registration code and then I was in to my health records. Then on one particular page the tab was there to click on to make appointments. As one of my relatives used to say, *simple when you know how!* I wouldn't call it *that* easy but I now know the sequence of steps and can hopefully remember and apply the learning in the future. The penny dropped!

As I enter the New Testament and work through it to the completion of our studies of a strange person, incident, teaching or statement in each of the books of the Bible, we begin with a Gentile for whom as he did his job, *the penny dropped.*

Matthew is the first of our gospel writers. He is writing essentially for Jewish readers and shows them that after a long and involved history in which God interacted with his own special people, culminating in a period of silence for 400 years or so to the birth of Christ. God has kept his promises to the Jews, and that the whole of their history and prophesies are fulfilled in the person of the Lord Jesus Christ, the Messiah, who has at last appeared; he is fully God and fully man. In him, heaven has come to Earth and the kingdom of God is being established. Matthew emphasises that Jesus is the son of David, their greatest king, and an ancestor of Abraham, the nation's founder and patriarch. These are the absolute and best credentials.

Matthew points out that Jesus is, therefore, a true Israelite, living an exemplary life, teaching truth as no other person could or would. There is no wonder Matthew says in conclusion to his record of the Sermon on the Mount, 'When Jesus had finished saying these things, the crowds were amazed at his teaching, because he taught as one who had authority, and not as their teachers of the law' (Matthew 7:28-29). Jesus revealed aspects of God which individuals, small groups of people or larger gatherings needed to have revealed to them at certain times. Because he is God, miracles such as healings, were seen and experienced. Things naturally reached a climax in the third and final annual Passover Jesus shared with his disciples on Earth, as recorded by the Gospels. This was followed by his capture, arrest, trial and death sentence. It is at this point we pick up the story and see a professional soldier following orders and coming to a life-changing discovery.

The Governor's soldiers, and probably others also (Mark 15:16), had been mocking Jesus to humiliate him and as sport for themselves (Matthew 27:27-30a), but then he would have been handed over to the Romans to conduct the crucifixion which the Jews were not permitted to perform. An un-named centurion with his detachment of soldiers conducted his grim task (v54). The soldiers were 'guarding Jesus' which was necessary because there were lawless and angry Jewish leaders and some ordinary people who would otherwise have taken the law into their own hands. The soldiers were watching that Roman law and their legal method of execution were upheld. If necessary, they would speed up a crucifixion or confirm death to the Roman governor. The soldiers had already seen or been made aware of how Jesus had been treated at his trial, and were informed of the motives of his accusers.

The Bible Reference blog adds some interesting details:

'An unnatural darkness had come and gone in the middle of the day (v45). Jesus' death was immediately followed by a dramatic earthquake that seemed too connected to be coincidence (v50–51). That combination of eerie events and the odd taunts of the crowd (v40–43) seems to have terrified the attending soldiers. They might fear they are about to experience divine punishment for their involvement.'[274]

As the Revd. Dr. Tim McBride of Georgia tells us, in verse 45 we find that God uses 'astrological and meteorological events (*which are*) indications of the redemptive significance of the moment: Jesus' death is portrayed as a decisive moment of judgement on the nation of Israel, and at the same time a saving death for the whole world.'[275] (*Insertion mine*) The imagery of judgment reflects the warnings over the centuries by the prophets of the Day of the Lord, as the following references indicate preached between 750 and 625 BC (Amos 5:18-20, 8:9; Joel 2:1-2; Zephaniah 1:15).

The centurion saw these signs, and was probably anxious for the eclipse to end so he could see around him and keep control. He also heard Jesus use the words of Psalms 22:1, 'My God, my God, why have you forsaken me? He heard the Jews explanation of this, 'When some of those standing there heard this, they said, 'He's calling Elijah…' (Matthew 27:47). He saw the dignity with which Jesus bore pain and the attempt by others to deaden this with wine vinegar (v48). He witnessed the great excitement of some looking for the great prophet and miracle-worker Elijah to see if he would come and rescue Jesus, and was made aware the Jews were seeing their Scriptures fulfilled in the details of the Messiah's death (Psalms 69:21). The centurion watched Jesus die. It is likely that someone ran to the hill of crucifixion with the news that the great Temple curtain was torn from top to bottom,[276] and he would feel the earthquake and see the rocks split, the tombs open and godly people raised to life.[277] He would also see that they stayed in their graves.[278] A professional soldier who had to report back to his superior would miss none of these details.

So we are told amazing and **strange** words, which other than being from God the Holy Spirit, would be unbelievable. Matthew writes: 'When the centurion and those with him who were guarding Jesus saw the earthquake and all that had happened, they were terrified, and exclaimed, "Surely he was the Son of God!"' The centurion reached his conclusion about this condemned man because of the way he died. He had seen the love of the people watching him, the hatred of those who wanted him to die and his quiet words from the cross exuding love and forgiveness. Last of all the centurion heard Jesus' final words, words of triumph, '…It is finished…' (John 19:30). Seeing the eclipse, earthquake, rocks split and dead people raised, he knew these were extraordinary events linked to an extraordinary person. Even the total eclipse was no ordinary eclipse but was much longer: 12 mid-day to 3 pm.[279] The darkness was an indication of God's judgment and wrath against sin. (Isaiah 51:17; Jeremiah 25:15).

Jesus would have been on the cross for three hours by then (Mark 15:25, 33-34). Pastor David Guzik tells us, 'The first three hours of Jesus' ordeal on the cross were in normal daylight, so that all could see that it was in fact Jesus on the cross, and not a replacement or an impostor.'[280]

All this coincided with what he was undoubtedly told about the massive heavy temple curtain, some 60 feet high, tearing on its own. The centurion was a tough man of war and a leader of 100 warriors, a professional soldier, and he came to understand what he was seeing. He may have known the Jewish Scriptures, but there were certainly those present who were declaring what the Scriptures said and meant and linking them to what *they* were seeing, such as Matthew 27:47 and Psalm 22, and the soldiers would have heard this. Above all, the centurion appears to be convinced of the innocence of Jesus, the lack of justice in this execution, the dignity of this extraordinary person, and in his heart and mind realised that he was seeing the Son of God. Guzik tells us, 'This man had supervised the death of perhaps hundreds of other men by crucifixion, but he knew there was something absolutely unique about Jesus.'[281]

It is worth considering who was there at the cross, and whom the centurion was responsible for as he did his job:

- men and women;
- Jews and Gentiles;
- rich and poor;
- all classes of people;
- soldiers and other professions;
- employed and unemployed;
- leaders and those who were led;
- those with and those without faith;
- religious and non-religious;
- those who loved Jesus and those who hated him;
- those innocent of his death and those guilty;
- those broken-hearted and those mocking him;
- the educated and uneducated;
- those deeply moved and found faith at the cross (such as the thief) and those indifferent at the cross (another thief and other bystanders).

There was tangible evidence of inclusion, and in diversity of those present at the crucifixion: in nationality, race, gender and language. This must be seen as a foretaste of heaven as John the Apostle later wrote in Revelation: 'After this I looked, and there before me was a great multitude that no-one could count, from every nation, tribe, people and language, standing before the throne and before the Lamb' (Revelation 7:9).

A noteworthy explanation belongs to the BBC in one of their televised RE lessons: 'In summary, Jesus died: to save humans from the consequences of sin because no-one else was willing or able to pay the price for the sin of the whole world to restore humans to a right relationship with God.'[282] I believe the centurion came to understand and believe this and came to a personal faith. A decision of this magnitude sets the tone for the rest of the NT books to follow. What a man! What a decision!

41 Mark - *Jesus brings sight to a blind man in a two-stage healing.*

> '*They came to Bethsaida, and some people brought a blind man and begged Jesus to touch him. He took the blind man by the hand and led him outside the village. When he had spat on the man's eyes and put his hands on him, Jesus asked, "Do you see anything?" He looked up and said, "I see people; they look like trees walking around."*
>
> *Once more Jesus put his hands on the man's eyes. Then his eyes were opened, his sight was restored, and **he saw everything clearly**. Jesus sent him home, saying, "Don't even go into the village."'*
>
> *(Mark 8:22-26)*

I know I am the sort of person who likes to do jobs one at a time. I find multi-tasking difficult. If several jobs need to be done, I complete one then move on to the next one. The story I have chosen to investigate in Mark is a miracle performed by Jesus but is not completed at one go. It is in two parts and is therefore different from all the other miracles he performed. It is not a multi-tasking situation but for reasons I hope to make clear, Jesus does not perform and complete a healing quickly then move on to his next task.

Blindness is often seen in the Scriptures as spiritual as well as physical. That is why Jesus often described the Pharisees as being blind - spiritually. Jesus proves here he can heal in both spheres (Revelation 3:18) and restores both faith and sight to a blind man. This is a miracle unique to the Gospel of Mark. Not only that, as Josh Weidmann; Senior Pastor of Grace Chapel, Colorado, tells us, '…it is also the only progressive miracle Jesus performed recorded in the New Testament.'[283] At the time, Jesus was in Bethsaida on the east bank of the Sea of Galilee. This was in the area where Jesus spent much of his time ministering. The people had got to know of Jesus' desire to help individuals, particularly the disadvantaged and so they took to him sick people from their village. One notable person was a blind man. This man was obviously in a condition he couldn't change and from which he couldn't be cured by normal means.[284] As they led him forward in faith they didn't desire much, only for Jesus to touch him, but they expected something to happen. Because the miracle happened progressively, it could be that the man had weak faith, if any at all, and this may account for the miracle happening over a period of time which would have helped the blind man gain faith and trust in Jesus. He was weak, but then God deals kindly with people who are weak, as Paul pointed out in his second letter to the Corinthian Christians (2 Corinthians 12:9).

As would be expected, Jesus led the man by the hand, but perhaps unexpectedly, led him out of the village. Jesus was as Job was, '…eyes to the blind and feet to the lame' (Job 29:15). Matthew Henry tells us that Jesus took over from the friends who had the faith to bring the blind man.[285] This could well be so Jesus could deal with the hesitant man quietly and gently and out of the gaze of the busy and curious villagers. We are not told there were others present and so we must conclude that Jesus wanted to be alone with the man.

We then see Jesus spit right into the man's eyes,[286] and asked him what he saw. Sight was gradually returning and the man couldn't distinguish between people and trees, and the healing was not yet complete, even though the man's faith was increasing (Proverbs 4:18). Sight and faith were both developing. As Matthew Breedon, Teaching Pastor at the Southern Hills Baptist Church, reminds us, 'We are all born spiritually blind and Jesus is the only One who can open blind eyes.'[287] As Paul the Apostle said to the Christians at Ephesus, 'I pray that the eyes of your heart may be enlightened…' (Ephesians 1:18a). As with Jesus, Paul encountered not just physical blindness but spiritual blindness as well.[288]

We are told the man looked up. Before this there was no point ever looking up when he was blind, but here *looking* begins. This must have begun to lift the man's spirits. What a joy he must have felt! This reminds me very much, as at the end of my chapter 15 on Ezra, we read Godfrey Birtill's words in his song, 'Just one touch from the king changes everything!'[289] Jesus didn't make a mistake, he had time, compassion and patience for an individual who needed a loving touch and was not to be rushed. I like the way Josh Weidmann says at this point, 'Jesus was not just a miracle worker, but a Saviour and Lord who was restoring his sight and spiritually touched his heart. Jesus helped him step across the line from unbelief to belief.'[290] The man realised that Jesus knew him intimately and knew what his holistic needs were, as already discovered: sight and faith.

For a second time (Mark 8:23, v25), Jesus put his hands on the man's eyes. Faith was increasing, healing was coming, and sight was restored to perfect vision. We get the impression that the man was once able to see. He knew what people and trees used to look like and the word, 'restored' (v25) shows he was back to how he used to be. He had vision better than before. After years of darkness, the first thing he saw was the face of Jesus, the One who can make faith perfect, 'Fixing our eyes on Jesus, the pioneer and perfecter of faith…' (Hebrews 12:2a). Perfect vision comes from a perfect healing and the **strange** but lovely expression, '…he saw everything clearly' (Mark 8:25c) says all that we need to hear.

Since the man didn't live right in the village, Jesus told him not to go there where people would be awaiting his return to gaze at the man and the result of Jesus' actions, but to go home. Jesus didn't want to be known as a miracle-worker but as the Messiah, the Saviour of the world (Jude 1:25; 1 John 4:14). Jesus expected obedience following faith and healing. It was not the time for the man to be swamped and perhaps overwhelmed nor for Jesus to be praised and worshipped because of a miracle. After the resurrection, things were different. The angel said to the women, '…*Come and see* the place where he lay. Then *go* quickly *and tell…*' (Matthew 28:6-7a) (*Emphasis mine*).

Not only do we see Jesus giving the man special attention and a special experience, we also see Jesus preparing the disciples for their future ministry with teaching and experience but they were slow to understand what he was really saying and doing and processing his warnings about the future. According to Mark, Jesus described himself as a 'bridegroom' who would be taken from them (Mark 2:20); he escaped the Pharisees who were trying to 'kill' him (3:6), and he avoided Judas's betraying intentions until much later in his ministry (3:19). Though the blind man came to faith, as Kelly R. Iverson, Associate Professor

of New Testament at Baylor University in Texas, tells us, '…
the disciples remain confused or at times directly opposed to
the notion of a crucified Messiah.'[291] James and John are prime
examples of misunderstanding by the disciples recorded by
Mark (10:35-40). The healed blind man *saw* what they couldn't
see! One day, after the cross and resurrection, when the two
Mary's and Salome effectively carried the '…come and see…
go quickly and tell…' message from the angel to the disciples
(Matthew 28:6-7), we hear the angel's final words that in
Galilee, '…There you will *see* him…' (Mark 16:7).

42 Luke - *Jesus reveals himself in a study of the Old Testament and by saying grace before a meal.*

'Now that same day two of them were going to a village called Emmaus, about seven miles from Jerusalem. They were talking with each other about everything that had happened. As they talked and discussed these things with each other, Jesus himself came up and walked along with them; but they were kept from recognising him. He asked them, "What are you discussing together as you walk along?" They stood still, their faces downcast. One of them, named Cleopas, asked him, "Are you the only one visiting Jerusalem who does not know the things that have happened there in these days?" "What things?" he asked. "About Jesus of Nazareth," they replied.

And beginning with Moses and all the Prophets, he explained to them what was said in all the Scriptures concerning himself.

As they approached the village to which they were going, Jesus continued on as if he were going further. But they urged him strongly, "Stay with us, for it is nearly evening; the day is almost over." So he went in to stay with them.

When he was at the table with them, he took bread, gave thanks, broke it and began to give it to them. **Then** *their eyes were opened and they recognised him, and he disappeared from their sight. They asked each other, "Were not our hearts burning within us while he talked with us on the road and opened the Scriptures to us?"*

They got up and returned at once to Jerusalem. There they found the Eleven and those with them, assembled together and saying, "It is true! The Lord has risen and has appeared to Simon." Then the two told what had happened on the way, and how Jesus was recognised by them when he broke the bread.'
(Luke 24:13-19a, v27-35)

A few years ago, someone came to our house to see Ruth, my wife, and was surprised to see me because they had heard I had died! This took me by surprise because then, as now, I am very much alive. The incident I have chosen for study in Luke is a little like this. Two people with heavy hearts knew that their friend and teacher, Jesus, had died, so in their case they didn't recognise him as still alive, although it was very dark and they were tired as well as distressed.

The Emmaus narrative describes the growing awareness of two of Jesus' followers who go from despair over his death to faith in his resurrection and serve as a model for the Christian's own journey from doubt and despair to faith based on fact. One disciple is named as Cleopas, the other is unnamed. Darkness and sadness because of recent events prevented them from recognising Jesus until he was revealed at a meal at their home. Mark, in his Gospel seems to write about the same encounter but with less detail, 'Afterwards Jesus appeared in a different form to two of them while they were walking in the country.

These returned and reported it to the rest; but they did not believe them either' (Mark 16:12-13).[292] Matthew and John don't record this incident.

There have been various suggestions by theologians and Church Fathers as to who the unnamed disciple, companion to Cleopas, was as we are not told the name or gender. The two were certainly not part of the original eleven disciples as they returned with their report to the eleven, but they were part of '…all the others' (Luke 24:9).

St Ambrose says Simon or Symeon (Simeon); St Epiphanius says Nathaniel; Arabic Gospel of John says Nicodemus; others say Philip, James and Mary, the wife or daughter of Cleopas. Of course, it could be Luke humbly recording himself but unnamed in the story.

J. Hampton Keathley III (1934-2002), former pastor in Washington, and NT scholar, says that Jesus gave to the disciples his promise of his presence with them and, 'specific revelation regarding his death and resurrection, both of which were essential to these promises. Yet, after his death we find the disciples sad, gloomy, fearful, perplexed, scattered, defeated, and running in retreat with no sense of mission or purpose. They were men in desperate need of the Saviour's touch; they needed his comfort and direction.'[293] These were all signs of grief, but then something amazing happened.

As the two disciples walked towards Emmaus, some seven miles away from Jerusalem, possibly returning from the Passover, deep in despair and *discussion*[294] between themselves, Jesus joined them but they were kept from recognising him. Gregory the Great (540-604), as recorded by Wikipedia,[295] gives a fascinating insight:

'They did not, in fact, have faith in him, yet they were talking about him. The Lord therefore, appeared to them but did not show them a face they could recognize. In this way, the Lord enacted outwardly, before their physical eyes, what was going on in them inwardly, before the eyes of their hearts. For inwardly they simultaneously loved him and doubted him; therefore the Lord was outwardly present to them, and at the same time did not reveal his identity.'[296]

Jesus patiently listened to them as they informed him of the latest news in Jerusalem. Jesus let them open up their hearts to him. They had a hope that Jesus was the Messiah, but that hope in their minds was dashed, and they are surprised he is the only visitor who hasn't heard the news (Luke 24:18) and so he led them in a Bible study centred on what the Writings, the Law and the Prophets, said about the suffering Messiah, '…concerning himself' (v27). He stuck to the Scriptures that they would know so well. He didn't introduce non-Biblical material or human ideas. The Theology of Work blog tells us, 'But the disciples do one thing right in this story – something so apparently insignificant it would be easy to miss. They offer hospitality to Jesus.'[297] They had the presence of Jesus but not the ability to recognise him (Mark 16:12), as with Mary by the garden tomb (John 20:15).

In Christian hospitality to a stranger they pressed Jesus to stay with them because it was so late in the day.[298] It was as they began a meal and he said grace, 'Then their eyes were opened and they recognised him, and he disappeared from their sight' (v31).[299] It is here in his resurrection form that we read those **strange** words, 'Then their eyes were opened…' (v31a). A special action of God prevented them recognising him and equally the special intervention of God the Holy Spirit enabled them *to* recognise him. It was at the table that they were fed spiritually as well as physically. He was remaining with and in them and they were remaining in and with him as John records in the words of Jesus, 'Remain in me, as I also remain in you. No branch can bear fruit by itself; it must remain in the vine. Neither can you bear fruit unless you remain in me' (John 15:4). The grace-saying Jesus and his usual custom of breaking bread in a certain way, and the powerful impact and sight of his nail-pierced hands were the prompts for their hearts and minds to be opened by the Holy Spirit, and when this happened, his work was accomplished in this situation, so he disappeared. He didn't just leave or melt away.

The two disciples had gone from having '…faces downcast.' (Luke 24:17) to having '…hearts burning…' (v32) while Jesus talked and opened up the Scriptures. Jesus having disappeared, the two forgot their tiredness and despondency and returned deep in the night to Jerusalem, much faster than when they left, and found the eleven disciples and others with them still awake and together. They were desperate to share what they had seen, heard and experienced. The best news in all the world certainly couldn't wait until morning. They had the same response as the women at the empty grave who were told by the angel, '…come and see… go… and tell…' (Matthew 28:6-7a). Nothing could stop their missionary zeal, their Christian witness. Arland J. Hultgren, professor of NT, Luther Seminary, St Paul, Minnesota, adds at this point, 'The story ends with the two men going to Jerusalem to report what had happened. But before they can do that, they hear the testimony of the eleven who say that Jesus had been raised and had appeared to Simon Peter (Luke:24:34)'.[300]

Hultgren goes on to explain a profound statement by Luther, 'Why is it that some believe, and others do not? Martin Luther[301] explained it all so well in his explanation to the third article of the Apostles' Creed in his Small Catechism. There, he says, we cannot believe by our own reason or strength; it is by the Holy Spirit that one comes to believe.'[302] It is also a fact that we are seeing the early stages of the formation of the Church. Hultgren calls this *movement* as indicated by ten particular verbs in this story:

- 'two of them were *going*' (v13);
- 'Jesus himself *came up* and *walked along* with them' (v15);
- 'they *approached* the village' (v28);
- 'Jesus *continued* on' (v28);
- 'they *urged him strongly*, "*Stay* with us"' (v29);
- 'he *disappeared* from their sight' (v31);
- 'They *got up* and *returned* at once to Jerusalem' (v33) (*Emphasis mine*).

The two disciples on the road had failed to understand the Scriptures and were not looking deeply enough (Hebrews 5:11-12), so Jesus took them deeper and gave them the most wonderful Bible study anyone has ever had. In comparison, Paul told the Corinthian Christians that it was those who were perishing, and remaining so, who were foolish (1 Corinthians 1:18). However, the two in this story listened to Jesus and responded positively. Pastor David Guzik, Enduring Word blog, concludes about the two travellers: 'They had mutual confirmation of the resurrection of Jesus. Though the risen Jesus was not physically in their midst, his resurrection had been confirmed by more than two witnesses.'[303] In Jewish culture, this proved a point.

43 John - *Jesus walks through walls.*

'On the evening of that first day of the week, when the disciples were together, **with the doors locked for fear of the Jewish leaders, Jesus came and stood among them** *and said, "Peace be with you!" After he said this, he showed them his hands and side. The disciples were overjoyed when they saw the Lord. Again Jesus said, "Peace be with you! As the Father has sent me, I am sending you." And with that he breathed on them and said, 'Receive the Holy Spirit.'*
(John 20:19-22)

There are many things which Jesus did in his life on Earth, including after the resurrection, which are unexpected and remarkable. This incident of Jesus walking into a locked and secure room is one such example and deserves our sincere attention. It follows on after the Emmaus road incident as in Luke's gospel in the last chapter.

John appears to have been written after Matthew which was written about 80-85 AD, and this would fix John's date of writing at 90-95 AD when he would have been quite elderly as he was born about the same time as Jesus. We can therefore see that being about 60 years after the start of the church on the Day of Pentecost, Sunday was now the first day of the week (John 20:19) having replaced the Jewish Sabbath on Saturdays. As the theologian Matthew Henry calls it '…the Christian Sabbath in remembrance of Christ's resurrection.'[304]

This was now the day to meet to share Communion, also called the Lord's Supper, Breaking of Bread, or the Eucharist.

It was early evening and the doors were not just shut, they were locked because the disciples and those with them were living in fear of the authorities, simply referred to as 'the Jewish leaders' (John 20:19).[305] With Thomas absent, the ten had closed their doors and closed their minds. They felt they were under threat since their master and leader had been captured tried and executed. They must have felt they could be next since they were his associates. If he was a rebel leader, they were also members of the rebellion, and so were not safe. The doors were therefore firmly secured. The believers had no joy and no peace.

It is then that we read the **strange** words that despite '… the doors locked for fear of the Jewish leaders, Jesus came and stood among them' (v19b).

The gathered believers had heard from Mary Magdalene and from Peter, their leader, and John, the beloved disciple and special friend of Jesus, but didn't know what to believe. In fact, the believers generally denied the initial reports of Jesus' resurrection. They had all doubted the initial reports of Jesus' resurrection (Luke 24:11).

As the author of his book, John was trying to make sense of it all and convey accurately his faith and the theology, even though he had some doubts at the time, to his readers. He was keen to get the facts right and he was keen to get the theology in his Gospel right. Fr. John McKinnon is a priest of the diocese of Ballarat, Western Victoria. In writing about John, the author, he says, 'The author was using the literary form of narrative to explore the theological implications of the mystery of resurrection. His concern was strictly theological, not historical.'[306]

Into this atmosphere of fear, Jesus appeared and just stood amongst them, not in front to lecture them. The disciples, Luke tells us, there were others '…with them, assembled together' (v33). Jesus greeted them with a single Hebrew word: *Shalom*, 'Peace be with you!' (John 20:19c) because they were '…startled and frightened…' (Luke 24:37). Steven J. Cole, teaching pastor at Flagstaff Christian Fellowship in Arizona, makes an extremely helpful comment:

> '"Peace be with you" was a common Jewish greeting wishing overall well-being on the other person. But in the context here it surely means far more than just a perfunctory greeting. These men were in hiding behind locked doors because of fear of the Jewish leaders who had just crucified their Lord. It was not far-fetched to think that they might be next. They may have been discussing how they could sneak out of Jerusalem without being arrested.'[307]

It is also Luke who tells us that Jesus invited them to actually touch his body to see that it was real (v39-40). When he gave them his words of peace, it was a peace which the world could not give them (John 14:27), but it was a peace they desperately wanted and needed. It would guard their hearts and minds and empower them for the future (Philippians 4:7). The Rev. Dr. Matthew Skinner, Associate Professor of New Testament at Luther Seminary, St Paul, Minnesota, tells us, '…he gives peace that provides solace in the face of persecution, a promise of new possibilities, and confidence in his ability to overcome "the world"' (John 16:33).[308]

He was not a ghost; he was not in their imagination. He was real and in their midst. He was Jesus of Nazareth and was raised from the dead. He was not sitting as a rabbi but standing with power and authority. He stood as King of the Kingdom he had established[309] through his life, death and resurrection. He stood amongst 'friends' (John 15:15). Under pressure, they had deserted him, but he hadn't deserted them. He didn't challenge them for their desertion but simply wished peace upon them. He had forgiven them! MacKinnon says, 'The single word *Shalom* quite simply expressed the essential heart of Christ. His was a totally free, unconditioned, unshakable and limitless love. And in his love, he revealed the essential heart of his Father.'[310]

Jesus had come to them in peace and he had come to them in love. Jesus said when he prayed for the disciples and future believers, 'I have made you known to them, and will continue to make you known in order that the love you have for me may be in them and that I myself may be in them' (John 17:26). Together with coming with peace and love, Jesus also came with unconditional mercy and forgiveness. This is why he showed them his hands and his side. He went through the horrors of execution, shown by his scars: the nail prints and spear-pierced side. In doing so he showed he could forgive and give them new life and citizenship of his kingdom.[311] Jesus carried the marks of his suffering to show his limitless love. They could have been erased in his resurrected body but he chose to keep them for ever. One day, I shall see them for myself! In eternal life and with eternal joy in heaven, Jesus will still have the evidence of his human life and all it achieved on Earth. What the disciples were witnessing was Jesus in his divine body returned to Earth temporarily.

The disciples now knew for certain that it was Jesus their Lord and they were filled with joy '…when they saw the Lord' (John 20:20). This was the fulfilment of what Jesus promised them at the Last Supper, 'I will see you again and you will rejoice, and no-one will take away your joy' (John 16:22b). Joy accompanies genuine faith.

Jesus spoke again *Shalom* (John 20:19, v21). As he had been sent so he was sending them but he knew they couldn't go with power and authority unless they were filled with the Holy Spirit so '…he breathed on them, and some theologians believe this was their point of new birth (Ezekiel 37:9), empowering them for service and mission, and said, "Receive the Holy Spirit"' (John 20:22). Pastor David Guzik informs us, 'Jesus gave His disciples the *Holy Spirit*, bringing new life and the ability to carry out their mission.'[312]

We are strongly encouraged to take the story of the gospel to the nations as H. Ernest Nicol (1862-1928) put so well in his hymn of 1896:

'We've a story to tell to the nations,
that shall turn their hearts to the right,
a story of truth and mercy,
a story of peace and light,
a story of peace and light.'[313]

In carrying out their mission, Jesus promised to be always with the first believers and subsequent Christians who are sent and authorised by the commissioning words: '…surely I am with you always, to the very end of the age' (Matthew 28:20b), with the same peace of God guarding hearts and minds (Philippians 4:7).

44 Acts - *Jesus sitting at God the Father's right hand, stands for Stephen's martyrdom.*

'Now Stephen, a man full of God's grace and power, performed great wonders and signs among the people. Opposition arose, however, from members of the Synagogue of the Freedmen (as it was called) – Jews of Cyrene and Alexandria as well as the provinces of Cilicia and Asia – who began to argue with Stephen. But they could not stand up against the wisdom the Spirit gave him as he spoke.

Then they secretly persuaded some men to say, "We have heard Stephen speak blasphemous words against Moses and against God."

So they stirred up the people and the elders and the teachers of the law. They seized Stephen and brought him before the Sanhedrin. They produced false witnesses, who testified, "This fellow never stops speaking against this holy place and against the law. For we have heard him say that this Jesus of Nazareth will destroy this place and change the customs Moses handed down to us."

All who were sitting in the Sanhedrin looked intently at Stephen, and they saw that his face was like the face of an angel.'

(Acts 6:8-15)

'Then the high priest asked Stephen, "Are these charges true?" To this he replied: "Brothers and fathers, listen to me!"'

(Acts 7:1-2a)

[Stephen gave a potted history of: Abraham, Jacob, Joseph, Moses, Joshua, David and Solomon (Acts 7:2b-53)].

'When the members of the Sanhedrin heard this, they were furious and gnashed their teeth at him. But Stephen, full of the Holy Spirit, looked up to heaven and saw the glory of God, and Jesus standing at the right hand of God. "Look," he said, **"I see heaven open and the Son of Man standing at the right hand of God."***

At this they covered their ears and, yelling at the top of their voices, they all rushed at him, dragged him out of the city and began to stone him. Meanwhile, the witnesses laid their coats at the feet of a young man named Saul.

While they were stoning him, Stephen prayed, "Lord Jesus, receive my spirit." Then he fell on his knees and cried out, "Lord, do not hold this sin against them." When he had said this, he fell asleep.'

(Acts 7:54-60)

One of my favourite paintings is by the Amsterdam-based Dutchman, Rembrandt (1606-1669), 'The Return of the Prodigal Son', painted 1661-1669. However, his very first signed painting completed 1625 at the age of 19 is 'The Stoning of Saint Stephen.' In this his genius is already obvious. The painting is very moving and correctly portrays the Acts of the Apostles sad record of events.

Politically, in the first century, Israel was a very unstable land and when the jobs were being given out by Caesar in Rome for governorships in the parts of his empire, Pilate got the job of managing the Jews. They were considered unruly and required a tough person. He had managed Jesus' trial and crucifixion, but as the Got Questions blog informs us, 'Pilate was more interested in political harmony than justice' (John 19:4, v6, v15-16).[314] After about another three years, Pilate was still in post at the time of Stephen's martyrdom, which was between 33 and 36 AD. Then by 36 AD Pilate had lost control of the Jews in Israel and therefore lost his governorship.

Stephen was quite different from Jesus. He didn't have a history of dispute with the Jewish leaders and was relatively unknown. His stoning would not attract the attention of Rome, unlike the execution of Jesus for which Pilate personally took command, though he acceded to the demands of the Jewish leaders who said they couldn't execute their own people (John 18:31). He probably didn't even hear of this dispute in relation to Stephen amongst the Jews, and wouldn't have been interested if he had done. The mob dispensed their own justice and didn't have the sanction of the Sanhedrin, who when they realised what was happening, were so angry to hear the content of Stephen's sermon, they just let the mob do their worst, and as Got Questions says '...it's possible nobody was thinking logically' (Acts 7:54, v57a).[315] However, the details of this especially important incident must be considered.

The martyrdom of Stephen was an important milestone in the development of the Early Church because here was the first person who died because of his faith in Jesus.[316] Stephen's example fired up the church to evangelise and spread the gospel despite the great persecution that broke out as a result (Acts 8:1). But as Christians fled for their lives, they planted new churches wherever they went. Unfortunately for the Jewish leaders, this was the result of *their* actions and that of the traditional Jews who hated this new faith and attempted constantly to wipe it out.

In Acts six we read of a Foodbank sort of situation which was not being well managed amongst the believers to help those in need, so the 12 disciples gathered people together and decided to appoint seven men to deal with the administration and other similar problems.[317] Stephen was one of those chosen because he was '…a man full of faith and of the Holy Spirit' (Acts 6:5a). With other outstanding attributes Luke tells us as author of Acts,

'Now Stephen, a man full of God's grace and power, performed great wonders and signs among the people. Opposition arose, however, from members of the Synagogue … who began to argue with Stephen. But they could not stand up against the wisdom the Spirit gave him as he spoke' (Acts 6:8-10).

As a result, Stephen was seized and brought before the Sanhedrin who sat in judgement over the false charges brought against him.[318] The Great Sanhedrin met in the Temple in Jerusalem, (Acts 5:20-21). Creating great anger, as they looked intently at him, '…they saw that his face was like the face of an angel' (Acts 6:15b).

The High Priest as chairman of the full Sanhedrin council asked Stephen if the charges were true. This gave Stephen the opportunity to recount the history of Israel from Abraham to Solomon with great boldness and in careful detail occupying nearly all of our long chapter seven of Acts (Acts 7:2-53). Charles Haddon Spurgeon (1834-1892), Pastor of Metropolitan Tabernacle, preacher and author, as a preacher is impressed with the sermon Stephen delivered. He said to his congregation, 'I would have you observe, first, that although Stephen was surrounded by bitter enemies, no doubt railing and cavilling, and muttering their observations to disturb him and distract his mind, yet his defence is wonderfully logical, clear, consecutive, and forcible.'[319]

Stephen began with the face of an angel and when he said the law was received through the ministry of angels the Sanhedrin took great exception[320] and stopped him at that point, both because of the mention of angels and especially as he had pointed out that Jesus had been betrayed and murdered by them as Jewish authorities. The Jesus Film blog expressed their response to criticism:

'This enrages the members of the Sanhedrin. It wasn't the first time Jesus' followers spoke in front of the Sanhedrin and proclaimed him the Messiah - or even the first time Christians criticised Jewish leaders about his death. Peter and John had done so in Acts 4 and got off with a warning. And in Acts 5, the Sanhedrin was ready to execute the apostles until one of their own talked them out of it.'[321]

The Sanhedrin had been there before, faced by bold Christians facing up to them and sharing truths they didn't want to hear. It was more than they could stand. Becky Harling, author and conference speaker, explains, 'Stephen pointed out how the Jewish leaders had been stiff-necked and arrogantly rejected all of God's plans for redemption.'[322] We read, 'When the members of the Sanhedrin heard this, they were furious and gnashed their teeth at him. But Stephen, full of the Holy Spirit, looked up to heaven and saw the glory of God, and Jesus standing at the right hand of God' (Acts 7:54-55). *They* had white-hot anger with a man they hated on Earth; *Stephen* had peace and joy and a vision of his Saviour whom he loved, in glory in heaven. With great poise and dignity, Stephen shared his vision with them, encouraging them to look with him and see Jesus standing at God's right hand. This is the only occasion in Scripture we are told Jesus does this. He is normally, in more than 100 references, seated at God's right hand (for example: Psalm 110:1; Mark 16:19). I believe he was so impressed with Stephen as the first Christian martyr he stood for this martyrdom, willing Stephen on!

And so, Stephen used the **strange** words:

'I see heaven open and the Son of Man standing at the right hand of God' (Acts 7:56).

At this point the council members covered their ears and made a lot of noise to drown out anything further that Stephen might say. He was dragged out of the city and they began to stone him. As all this happened, Stephen had God's grace to enable him to preach and die for his Lord as Paul told the Corinthian Christians, this was all they needed 'My grace is sufficient for you, for my power is made perfect in weakness' (2 Corinthians

12:9a). For Stephen, as with others, the grace doesn't come in advance but at the moment it is needed, (Matthew 10:19).[323]

As he died Stephen asked Jesus to receive his spirit and prayed for his murderers forgiveness. His final words echoed those of Jesus when he was dying on the cross, also recorded by Luke in his gospel, 'Jesus called out with a loud voice, 'Father, into your hands I commit my spirit.' When he had said this, he breathed his last' (Luke 23:46).

The only other reference to Stephen in the NT is when the young man Saul, who later became a rabbi at 30, then became upon conversion the Apostle Paul, mentions Stephen in his own defence after being seized by an angry mob and almost killed. He addressed the crowd, 'And when the blood of your martyr Stephen was shed, I stood there giving my approval and guarding the clothes of those who were killing him' (Acts 22:20).

C.S. Lewis died on November 22, in 1963. One hour later President John F. Kennedy was assassinated in Texas. It was also the same day that Aldous Huxley, the author of the Brave New World, died. Three different people but all individuals before God. It is not how we live but how we die which defines a person. As Spurgeon put it, 'Your story will be defined by how it ends.'[324] Stephen's life and death were victorious because he was filled with the Holy Spirit and was totally committed to God his Father and the Lord Jesus Christ his Saviour.

45 Romans - *We must submit to the authorities, including the ones we don't like.*

'Let everyone be subject to the governing authorities, for there is no authority except that which God has established. The authorities that exist have been established by God. Consequently, whoever rebels against the authority is rebelling against what God has instituted, and those who do so will bring judgment on themselves. For rulers hold no terror for those who do right, but for those who do wrong. Do you want to be free from fear of the one in authority? Then do what is right and you will be commended. For the one in authority is God's servant for your good. But if you do wrong, be afraid, for rulers do not bear the sword for no reason. They are God's servants, agents of wrath to bring punishment on the wrongdoer. Therefore, it is necessary to submit to the authorities, not only because of possible punishment but also as a matter of conscience.'

(Romans 13:1-5)

The thirteenth chapter of Romans provides us with particular challenges: moral, ethical, political and organisational. So we read **strange** and unexpected words, 'Let everyone be subject to the governing authorities, for there is no authority except that which God has established. The authorities that exist have been established by God' (v1). 'Everyone' includes Christians.[325] The Greek word translated 'governing authorities,' is used of a soldier's unquestioning obedience to a commanding officer. The same obedience is expected in Scripture of Christians with the exception of if the command or law of the land is contrary to the word of God. In an interesting conversation between Jesus on trial and Pilate the Governor, and in this case the judge (John 19:10b-11a), we read: '… Pilate said, "Don't you realise I have power either to free you or to crucify you?" Jesus answered, "You would have no power over me if it were not given to you from above."'

In careful study of the Bible, we see that there are four principal authorities on Earth established by God. I am grateful to Bible Studys blog which sets them out as:

'1. The government over all citizens;
2. The church over all believers;
3. The parents over all children;
4. The masters over all employees.'[326]

These seem to me to be very sensible and logical. One of the first challenges of this chapter is how to regard present governments. We know, even from recent history, that there are glaring examples of cruel, selfish, power-hungry, land-grabbing and unjust governments, but what about those at the present time? How should we view Russia invading Ukraine? What about tribal warfare under governments in Somalia, Yemen and a number of Arab, particularly Islamic states? What about some of decisions made by the governments of the UK and USA? What about the constituent levels of governance of the UK, Parliamentary districts, Local Authorities, Parish Councils and even Church Councils? At all levels, those set over us as individuals or as a group can be a blessing or a curse. We must decide where we stand and what we should do if we don't like their decisions or if we feel they go against the Bible's teaching. In the Times[327] there was a picture of a church minister in clerical clothes with a group of protesters. They had hands glued to the road at the entrance to an oil terminal. They did this to stop the passage of lorries and make the point that they felt the oil companies were not acting with the best of high moral and ethical standards making high profits at the expense of customers who felt the financial strain. They certainly got their point across.

The Bible Reference blog tells us, 'Paul is teaching the biblical doctrine of submission to human authorities, something Peter also teaches.'[328] The Apostle Peter wrote, 'Submit yourselves for the Lord's sake to every human authority: whether to the emperor, as the supreme authority, or to governors, who are sent by him to punish those who do wrong and to commend those who do right' (1 Peter 2:13-14). We must therefore be in submission to authorities even if we don't necessarily obey them (Titus 3:1). This is a delicate balance, not to be undertaken lightly. 'Peter and the other apostles...' (Acts 5:29a), were commanded by the authorities not to preach, but they courageously answered the Sanhedrin that they '...must obey God rather than human beings!' (v29b) (see v27-29)

At this, the Sanhedrin were so angry, they wanted to kill the Apostles, but the wisdom of Gamaliel, who was president of the Sanhedrin 30-50 AD,[329] prevailed and he prevented a massacre by pointing out to his colleagues that they may be fighting against God! However, we must also be aware of Peter's reply to the Sanhedrin, when he and John were commanded to be silent: But Peter and John replied 'Which is right in God's eyes: to listen to you, or to him? You be the judges! As for us, we cannot help speaking about what we have seen and heard' (Acts 4:19-20). Later, when the command was repeated, that is when Peter answered, 'We must obey God rather than human beings!' (Acts 5:29b)

It is easy to name dictators, tribal leaders and governments, ideologies and those we would say who have extremist views. Some authorities we consider are good, others we consider evil through the eyes of Western democracies, but Jesus, Paul, Peter and others set out teaching and example to recognise that human government is a legitimate authority, and that God puts leaders there for specific reasons. It is worth remembering that Paul is writing to Christians in Rome who are having a tough time in their faith. Rome was all-powerful over its conquered empire which included the land of Israel.

The book of Romans was written to Christians located in the Empire's capital in the time of the Emperor Nero (54-68 AD). The Bible Reference blog adds, 'Nero is famous for his cruel and unfair treatment of Christians, among other groups. We must not assume that Paul is writing these words lightly. He was aware of the implications of his teaching.'[330] Pastor David Guzik in the Enduring Word blog[331] quotes William Newell,[332] 'Your Saviour suffered under Pontius Pilate, one of the worst Roman governors Judea ever had; and Paul under Nero, the worst Roman Emperor. And neither our Lord nor his Apostle denied or reviled the "authority!"' (Romans 13:1).

Then there are moral dilemmas. Should we withhold taxes if we don't like the way our government is spending our money? Steven J. Cole, retired Pastor of Flagstaff Christian Fellowship, Lake Gregory Community Church, California, 1992-2018, challenges us with the question 'Is it wrong to use force to resist an aggressor?' He answers it in part saying 'So Paul shows that it is proper for the government to protect law-abiding citizens and to punish evildoers.'[333]

Rome was a very cosmopolitan city. Christians there comprised Jews and Gentiles. We have said that Nero hated Christians but the emperor before him, Claudius, also hated Jews and expelled them from Rome at one stage (Acts 18:1-2). Christians and Jews hated Roman rule. The Romans aware of this, viewed them with suspicion and thought they might cause a rebellion against the government which they saw as morally corrupt. Paul was therefore clear in his teaching about being subject to governing authorities. The OT theocracy had gone; dictatorships were rarely kind and just; and democracies varied from bad to good, so Paul does not suggest one type of government was better than another. In theory the Roman Empire was a democracy but the Caesars acted in part as dictators.

The theologian Matthew Henry summarises the types of government, 'Whatever the particular form and method of government are – whether by monarchy, aristocracy, or democracy – wherever the governing power is lodged, it is an ordinance of God, and it is to be received and submitted to accordingly.'[334] Solomon writes in Proverbs, 'By me kings reign and rulers issue decrees that are just; by me princes govern, and nobles – all who rule on earth' (Proverbs 8:15-16).

Pastor Guzik informs us about democracies. He reminds us that in a democracy we there is a sense in which we *are* the government, and should not hesitate to help *govern* our democracy through our participation in the democratic process. We must therefore, as with the Early Christians, trust God in his sovereignty to place over us the government of *his* choosing as given in the verses of the chosen passage above. As he does so, this means that those who rebel against authority are rebelling against God (Romans 13:2). He encourages prayer, '…for kings and all those in authority, that we may live peaceful and quiet lives in all godliness and holiness' (1 Timothy 2:2).

The purpose of government, Paul says, is to protect law-abiding citizens and punish law-breakers (Romans 13:3-4). He completes this thought by saying there are two reasons to be subject to governments: fear of punishment, and a clear conscience before God (v5).

Paul then applies his teaching and gives a practical example of paying taxes to government officials who are servants of God, and as such they are worthy of respect (v6-7).

Jesus also encouraged paying taxes: '…give back to Caesar what is Caesar's, and to God what is God's' (Matthew 22:21).

In Paul's experience on one occasion, faced with an unjust process and likely outcome, he himself appealed as a Roman citizen to Caesar (Acts 22:25; 25:11) as being the correct way forward. Above all, Paul encourages all Christians to rely not on the wisdom of the world but on God's grace and his presence in the conscience to give integrity and sincerity (2 Corinthians 1:12) as mature citizens of an imperfect governance in an imperfect world.

46 1 Corinthians - *Disagreeing Christians are encouraged to agree.*

*'I appeal to you, brothers and sisters, in the name of our Lord Jesus Christ, that all of you **agree with one another** in what you say and that there be no divisions among you, but that you be perfectly united in mind and thought. My brothers and sisters, some from Chloe's household have informed me that there are quarrels among you.'*

(1 Corinthians 1:10-11)

It is not a new thing to have disagreements between Christians. We should not say it's the fault of others or put the blame down to the church we attend or the denomination we are part of. It is really an aspect of being human and because we are sinful people in a fallen world with personalities which may accept Christ as Saviour but we don't always acknowledge him as Lord in all we think, do and say. We can accept Christ as our Saviour in a moment of time but to allow Jesus to be Lord of our lives takes a lifetime.

It is generally accepted that it is the people and not the building which constitutes the church, though buildings are useful as places to meet. When people meet together there can be challenges because of differences and because we are all learning to get on together. The Christians at Corinth were like that. They had their personalities, preferences and presumptions. Paul, the Apostle, did his best to share the gospel with them so they might come to know Christ personally. He taught them and answered their questions as well as he could from a distance.

As part of his travels on his third missionary journey, he stayed at Corinth for a year and a half, and after he had left them, that is when they wrote to him sharing problems and concerns and looking to him as a father-figure for support and guidance. The first book written to the Corinthians, written about 54-57 AD, is a fairly long letter written to this lively Christian church, largely to answer their questions put to him in their letter and to take them further on in their faith into more holy living.

The Bible sets the standard for Christian living. As the Jews went up the hill to Jerusalem annually to celebrate the Passover, they sang what we call psalms 120-134, a sort of travellers' hymn book, and so they are termed Psalms of Ascent. One of these psalms begins, 'How good and pleasant it is when God's people live together in unity!' (Psalms 133:1) David knew the importance of this unity and so did the first Christians and, though it is hard to apply, that is what Paul is addressing in our chosen verses.

In this first chapter, from a loving heart, Paul appeals to them, he pleads with them to be unified and not to allow the present divisions to continue. John Gill in his Exposition of the Bible tells us, '…agreement is absolutely necessary to the peace, comfort, and well-being of a church; for how should "two", and much less more, "walk together", unless they are "agreed?"' (Amos 3:3) Divisions come from strife and strife comes from pride as Solomon confirms, 'Where there is strife there is pride…' (Proverbs 13:10). In the mid-sixteenth century, the theologian John Calvin (1509-1564) writes, 'Now, after preparing their minds for rebuke, acting like a good, experienced surgeon, who touches the wound gently when a painful remedy must be used, Paul begins to handle them more severely.'[335]

Paul is keen to tell the Corinthians to stop tearing each other apart within the body of Christ, (lit. *schism*) based on the Greek word for 'divisions.' To avoid this, Paul uses **strange** words challenging them he tells them to '…agree with one another…' in important things in their thinking (1 Corinthians 1:10). To be '…perfectly united…' is a wonderful aim for unity and peace (v10c). He appeals to them in the name of Christ believing that they would respect his authority and allow him to bring about harmony and love. Paul was saying this disharmony was not the mark of mature Christians and conversely that harmony and agreement is not only right amongst God's people it is a secure thing for the future of the church. As Calvin says, '… for it is the main article of our religion that we be in harmony among ourselves; and farther, on such agreement the safety of the Church rests and is dependent.'[336]

The Greek word for 'perfectly united' (v10c), means fitted and adjusted, in the same way that the parts of the human body fit together and are connected perfectly. It seems that Paul had in mind the Christian love and harmony that he had witnessed in Jerusalem, the centre of the Christian church. In Acts we read, 'Every day they continued to meet together in the temple courts. They broke bread in their homes and ate together with glad and sincere hearts' (Acts 2:46). This is the 'one heart and one soul' he suggests in the words, '…perfectly united in mind and thought' (1 Corinthians 1:10c). Paul cannot stress this too much, and it seems to be a continuing need with the Corinthian church because in his second letter he is still encouraging unity, 'We are glad whenever we are weak but you are strong; and our prayer is that you may be fully restored' (2 Corinthians 13:9).

He is aiming for that full restoration so they return to where they used to be in relationships.

The theologian Matthew Henry identifies what the cause of the divisions is: 'They quarrelled about their ministers. Paul and Apollos were both faithful ministers of Jesus Christ, and helpers of their faith and joy: but those who were disposed to be contentious broke into parties, and set their ministers at the head of their several factions.'[337]

Before we leave this verse ten, it is worth considering one further point raised by Charles Ward Smith in his Bible commentary on this verse, remembering that the believers at Corinth have been called into perfect unity. Smith says, '... that Greek (*word*) koinonia is a difficult word to translate because it has such a depth of meaning. It means oneness, it means communion, it means fellowship, it means common, it means sharing, all of these things. We do not have an English equivalent, and so we use different words at different times as it appears in the text, because all of them are words that define or help define koinonia.'[338] (*Insertion mine*)

Pastor David Guzik has a really helpful summary of verse eleven of this chapter in relation to the message from Chloe's household:

'Chloe was a woman (probably a Christian) whose business interests caused her representatives (those of her household) to travel between Ephesus and Corinth. Paul writes this letter from Ephesus, where these people from Chloe's household visited and told him about the condition of the Corinthian church.'[339]

John Gill in his Exposition of the Bible tells us on 1 Corinthians 1:11:

'...but the whole affair was laid open, and made manifest to him: the thing was a clear point to him; he had no reason at all to doubt of the truth of it; nor could they deny it, the proof was so strong, the evidence so full, being given.'[340]

Chloe was a woman who appears to have lived in Corinth and was a member of the church there. The reference to her suggests she was head of her well-to-do family. She is upset by what is happening in the church with the increasing animosities and discord so she wrote an accurate account to the Apostle Paul. She wanted him to intervene and put a stop to the problems which were not to the good of the church and not to the glory of God. Initially she spoke of ministers by name but she then expanded her comments to include opinions in understanding of doctrines, leading on to practice amongst the church such as with baptism. These were put to Paul by Chloe and in verse 11 he is addressing them.

So Paul graciously and firmly addresses problems raised and, no doubt after thought and prayer, this first letter to the Corinthians is his reply. This first chapter is therefore largely answering Chloe but with a challenge to the whole church.

47 2 Corinthians - *Paul had to cope with near-death experiences.*

*'I have worked much harder, been in prison more frequently, been flogged more severely, and been **exposed to death again and again**. Five times I received from the Jews the forty lashes minus one. Three times I was beaten with rods, once I was pelted with stones, three times I was shipwrecked, I spent a night and a day in the open sea, I have been constantly on the move. I have been in danger from rivers, in danger from bandits, in danger from my fellow Jews, in danger from Gentiles; in danger in the city, in danger in the country, in danger at sea; and in danger from false believers. I have laboured and toiled and have often gone without sleep; I have known hunger and thirst and have often gone without food; I have been cold and naked. Besides everything else, I face daily the pressure of my concern for all the churches. Who is weak, and I do not feel weak? Who is led into sin, and I do not inwardly burn? If I must boast, I will boast of the things that show my weakness.'*

(2 Corinthians 11:23-30)

Paul had already spoken about how tough life was for him in chapter six, and in doing so, he commends himself and his co-workers (2 Corinthians 6:4-10). He says, in outlining his c.v. or *résumé*, he has faithfully represented Christ in every situation and through every kind of suffering. Most suffering was caused by others and some is self-inflicted such as 'hard

277

work' and 'sleepless nights' but these developed in him patience and endurance. It's as if he had suffered for the Corinthians as an example to them and an encouragement to them to continue in their faith. In all his suffering he has been sorrowful but yet always rejoicing and he wants them to do the same.

After the Early Church is established Luke, the author of Acts, brings Paul in at chapter nine as a convert from Judaism, having literally 'seen the light.' Paul's zeal as an extremely strict Jewish Pharisee led him to direct the same zeal in his new Christian life and faith. He was feared as a Pharisee by the Christians he was hunting down (Acts 9:1, v13), then feared as a Christian by other Christians who were not convinced he was a fully converted and a changed person (v26).

Stephen was martyred 33-36 AD, as we found in our study on Acts in my chapter 44, and Paul was converted 34-36 AD. This allows for Paul's three years of preparation for his ministry in Damascus before his introduction to the Apostles in Jerusalem (Galatians 1:18). It was from Damascus he was lowered down the city wall in a basket to escape persecution (2 Corinthians 11:32-33). This was in the reign of Aretas the king between 37 and 39 AD.[341] In summary:

- To the *Jews* Paul spoke about his new faith; the result was they tried to kill him (Acts 9:29);
- To the *Romans* Paul said he had inner sorrow and anguish in his heart (Romans 9:2) because of Israel's history;
- To the *Corinthians*, Paul says he is short of basic necessities (1 Corinthians 4:11) but he wants to have a positive spiritual relationship with them (2 Corinthians 2:1-3).

He uses **strange** words telling them that he has been, '...exposed to death again and again' (2 Corinthians 11:23c).[342]

And so we move on to 'Paul's apostolic credentials,' as Pastor David Guzik calls them[343] in our passage: 2 Corinthians 11:23-30. He was certainly a true Jew, having grown up in Tarsus in Cilicia (Acts 9:11), but suffered greatly since he became a Christian. In humility he says he was the least of the apostles but in fact was pre-eminent amongst them (1 Corinthians 15:9-10) by God's grace. He was in a privileged position. Paul says he was '...exposed to death...' (2 Corinthians 11:23c) a number of times, and one of them was when he was stoned in Lystra (Acts 14:19) to the brink of death because he had been used by God in the healing of a lame man. Jews from Antioch and Iconium strongly resented this happening and led the stoning and dragged him out of the city leaving him for dead, but the believers ministered to him and he recovered sufficiently so that the next day he left for Derbe with Barnabas.

In the book of Acts, where most of Paul's experiences are recorded, we read he made 18 journeys by sea, but the total number could be much higher if unrecorded journeys are added. Travel by sea in fairly flimsy vessels was quite dangerous and he survived a number of shipwrecks. His preaching and healing in towns and cities also stirred up the people who attacked him and persecuted him, such as: Acts 13:50; 14:5; and 16:19. He suffered a great deal from Alexander the metalworker who was not a true brother Christian to Paul and opposed the Gospel message (2 Timothy 4:14-15).

I know what pressure comes from being responsible for a group of people. Paul said he daily felt responsibility for the *churches;* each one had a whole group of people. He identified with weakness and he identified with sinners. He felt his only justifiable boast was his weakness, as he humbly faced up to that as a fault. With these and other hardships, Paul had a very stress-filled life. It all adds up to a c.v. not to be wished on anyone! He could only live like this because he was fully committed to Jesus as his Saviour and his Lord. His view was therefore that troubles in time are brief, compared to eternity, and he was keeping his eyes firmly on Jesus and eternal considerations (2 Corinthians 4:17-18) which made it all worthwhile and the right way to live.

Finally, we must note the theologian Matthew Henry's comment, 'It astonishes us to reflect on (*Paul's*) account of his dangers, hardships, and sufferings, and to observe his patience, perseverance, diligence, cheerfulness, and usefulness, in the midst of all these trials.'[344] (*Insertion mine*).

48 Galatians - *Acts of the flesh must give way to the fruit of the Spirit.*

'The acts of the flesh are obvious: sexual immorality, impurity and debauchery; idolatry and witchcraft; hatred, discord, jealousy, fits of rage, selfish ambition, dissensions, factions and envy; drunkenness, orgies, and the like. I warn you, as I did before, that those who live like this will not inherit the kingdom of God.

*But the fruit of the Spirit is love, joy, peace, forbearance, kindness, goodness, faithfulness, gentleness and self-control. Against such things there is no law. Those who belong to Christ Jesus have crucified the flesh with its passions and desires. Since we live by the Spirit, let us **keep in step with the Spirit**.'*

(Galatians 5:19-25)

In the same way that we rank people, crimes and professions in relative importance (we shouldn't but we do), as Christians, and yet as human beings, we rank sin also in levels or degrees of importance and say that some are much worse than others.

In ranking people, we might say our King Charles III is the number one citizen, and somewhere towards the bottom of the pile is a rough sleeper; we might say murder is the most serious sin, and breaking the speed laws by driving over the limit by a couple of miles an hour is at the other end of law-breaking and doesn't count as being wrong; we might say a nuclear scientist is somewhere near the top profession, and a street sweeper is a long way behind. So, we have Paul writing to churches for which he carries a responsibility, and he lists major sins. But we might say ours, staying in bed too long, being jealous of a lottery winner or grumbling about the weather don't really count as sins. Paul takes a different view. All sin is sin. All are '…acts of the flesh…' (v19a), and Paul has a challenging list to set before the Christians in Galatia. James is also quite clear: 'For whoever keeps the whole law and yet stumbles at just one point is guilty of breaking all of it' (James 2:10). To God, sins do not rank in size and importance. All people are sinners (Romans 3:23). All who live enjoying their sin, '…will not inherit the kingdom of God' (Galatians 5:21b).

In contrast, Paul is saying the Holy Spirit within them will lead to fruitfulness and these fruits (or more correctly 'fruit'), are greater than the moral law. In fact, he strongly advises in **strange** words to '…keep in step with the Spirit' (Galatians 5:25b). We must consider what Paul meant us to understand by life in the Spirit, but first take a look at the context in which the church received his teaching.

Galatia was a province established by the Romans as they conquered Asia Minor. Paul travelled there on each of his missionary journeys and he was always warmly received. However, as time passed he came under some criticism from critics who undermined his leadership and teaching. In his letter to the Christians in Galatia, Paul answered the threat to his position and re-affirmed gospel preaching and Bible-based living.[345] He reminds Gentile church members that they don't need to be circumcised, since this teaching from the Torah applies principally to the Jews and was a mark of the first Covenant, but he does emphasise the pre-eminence of the Spirit-filled life for all who follow Jesus as Messiah; their Saviour.

The theologian, John Gill reminds us that nine of the fruit are mentioned here in Galatia '…and from the whole concludes, that such as are true believers in Christ …are led by his Spirit, and have the fruits of it, (*and*) have the flesh with its affections and lusts crucified…' (Galatians 5:24-25).(*Insertion mine*) [346]

In verses 19-21 we read some serious things with serious consequences in the words Paul uses. Charles Ward Smith in his Bible Commentary therefore uses serious language:

'This is indeed strong language for you who want to live after the flesh. As we go down these things here, these are the things that God will exclude from his kingdom. These things are not allowed in the kingdom of God. If you want to be a subject in God's kingdom, then you cannot do these things. You cannot be ruled and dominated by your flesh.'[347]

John in Revelation says some remarkably similar things.[348] He writes the words he hears from Jesus, 'But the cowardly, the unbelieving, the vile, the murderers, the sexually immoral, those who practise magic arts, the idolaters and all liars – they will be consigned to the fiery lake of burning sulphur. This is the second death' (Revelation 21:8).

It is worthy of mentioning that 'The acts of the flesh…' (Galatians 5:19) is plural 'But the fruit of the Spirit…' (v22) is singular. That fruit is love. From this the other fruit come, more fully expressed by Paul to the Christians at Corinth (1 Corinthians 13:4-8a). Here in Galatians, as with Corinthians,

Paul purposely puts love first. He wants the Galatians to walk in love: to walk in the Spirit. Other qualities and other fruit follow when this quality leads. This is why Paul says there is no law against love. I also know of no law in the UK or any other country which legislates against excessive love in line with God's teaching as in the Bible, unlike the many laws which stand against excesses of actions and words in 'The acts of the flesh…' (Galatians 5:19a). God in his sovereignty and omniscience also includes thoughts, as well as actions and deeds: all are condemned by him if they spring from the flesh. This is why Matthew Henry speaks about 'mortifying' the acts of the flesh but 'cherishing' the fruit of the Spirit.[349] Paul was reminding his readers that they had changed from being dominated by one to the other: from the 'flesh' to the 'Spirit' (1 Corinthians 6:9-11). In particular we see that after Paul lists some of the fleshly acts he applies things to the Galatians with the change they had gone through, 'And that is what some of you were. But you were washed, you were sanctified, you were justified in the name of the Lord Jesus Christ and by the Spirit of our God' (v11). This is why Paul says to keep in step with the Spirit and live in peace with people around them (Galatians 5:25-26).

Though the battle for godly living is fought internally, the results are seen externally. The fruit of the Spirit, especially centred on love, is what lawmakers across the world aim to bring into being. It is sad that most don't realise God has elevated love already and by his grace individuals can accept Christ, be filled with the Spirit and have the power to live a life of fruitfulness based on love. Finally, we would do well to see a summary of the battle as Pastor David Guzik concludes, 'The fruit of the Spirit can always conquer the works of the flesh.'[350]

What does it mean, then, to keep in step with the Spirit? The first thing to note is the use of the word 'step.' This is not the action of standing still but a moving forward in life in the way military service personnel keep in step as they march. In the case of this verse 25, moving forward in the Christian life is with the Holy Spirit who moves and doesn't remain still. I am not thinking necessarily of physical movement, though that might be required, but moving to live and develop into maturity which is the lifetime process already encountered to make Christ Lord of our life as in Paul's letter to the Romans, 'Neither height nor depth, nor anything else in all creation, will be able to separate us from the love of God that is in Christ Jesus our Lord' (Romans 8:39). 'For those who are led by the Spirit of God are the children of God' (v14). From the beginning to the end of the Bible, the Holy Spirit is moving and is never inactive; the moving of the Spirit and moving water are symbols of the Holy Spirit at work as we read in a number of Scriptures:

- At Creation, '…the Spirit of God was hovering over the waters' (Genesis 1:2b).
- On one occasion, the Jews were commanded not to fight until the Holy Spirit moves, 'As soon as you hear the sound of marching in the tops of the poplar trees, move out to battle, because that will mean God has gone out in front of you to strike the Philistine army' (1 Chronicles 14:15).
- Ezekiel saw the water of life '…coming out from under the threshold of the temple…' and was told, '… where the river flows everything will live' (Ezekiel 47:1c, v9c).

- 'As soon as Jesus was baptised, he went up out of the water. At that moment heaven was opened, and he saw the Spirit of God descending like a dove and alighting on him' (Matthew 3:16).
- Jesus offered the water of life, '...whoever drinks the water I give them will never thirst... God is spirit, and his worshippers must worship in the Spirit and in truth' (John 4:14a, v24).
- To move into a life in the Spirit, we must leave behind the '...acts of the flesh...' (Galatians 5:19), which are incompatible with a spiritual way of thinking, speaking and living, which produce the fruit of the Spirit (v22-23).
- Hebrews speaks about _taking off_ the former lifestyle, values and tangled sin (Hebrews 12:1).
- Paul tells the Ephesians about _putting on_ '... the full armour of God, so that when the day of evil comes, you may be able to stand your ground...' Ephesians 6:13b).
- In heaven, John reports, 'Then the angel showed me the river of the water of life, as clear as crystal, flowing from the throne of God' (Revelation 22:1).

Paul, therefore, tells the Galatians to '...keep in step with the Spirit' (Galatians 5:25b).

49 Ephesians - *A message to slaves.*

'Slaves, obey your earthly masters with respect and fear, and with sincerity of heart, just as you would obey Christ. Obey them not only to win their favour when their eye is on you, but as slaves of Christ, doing the will of God from your heart. Serve wholeheartedly, as if you were serving the Lord, not people, because you know that the Lord will reward each one for whatever good they do, whether they are slave or free.'

(Ephesians 6:5-8)

On 25th May 2020, the death of George Floyd (1973-2020) was seen worldwide and many people considered this was an outright racist incident by a white person against a black person in Minnesota.[351] This led to the Black Lives Matter movement and in the UK an attack on a statue of Edward Colston (1636-1721) in Bristol and its subsequent removal by members of the public. **Pamela Parkes** of BBC News tells us that Colston was an English merchant, slave trader, philanthropist, and Conservative Member of Parliament. He followed his father in the family business becoming a sea merchant, initially trading in wine, fruits and textiles, mainly in Spain, Portugal and other European ports, before turning to slave trading from which he became very wealthy. At his death he bequeathed a great deal of money to the city of Bristol where he lived and from where he sailed.[352] Now, 300 years after his death, equality and diversity are high-profile, and current values are vastly different from those tolerated in society in the lifetime of Colston. Anti-slavery activists felt he should not be remembered by a statue.

If we travel back 2000 years we arrive in the first century AD and in 60 AD Paul was writing to the Christians in Ephesus with teaching which may be **strange** to us about slavery. He wrote things such as our chosen words above, 'Slaves obey your earthly masters…' (Ephesians 6:5a). Slavery was commonplace in the first century and has been ever since including right into the present age of the twenty-first century, still taking place in more guarded and sophisticated surroundings, but it is still just as wrong.

The theologian, Matthew Henry, has a good understanding of the situation as he writes, 'The duty of servants is summed up in one word, obedience. The servants of old were generally slaves. The apostles were to teach servants and masters their duties, in doing which evils would be lessened, till slavery should be rooted out by the influence of Christianity.'[353] Another word as an alternative to obedience is the word 'integrity' as used by David in his prayer for the temple about to be built, 'I know, my God, that you test the heart and are pleased with integrity' (1 Chronicles 29:17a).

Lionel Windsor, a lecturer in New Testament at Moore College, Sydney, addresses the issue of slavery: 'Today, slavery is still universally illegal. Yet tragically this illegal slavery continues to be a huge problem in our world. The wickedness of the modern criminal slave trade, especially the sex-slave trade, is widespread even in modern Western countries.'[354]

However, the slavery Paul is speaking of is more widespread and complex than the trans-Atlantic slave trade Colston was engaged with or the present day sex-slave trade and the treatment of illegal immigrants into the UK. The Roman Empire thrived and its slaves were everywhere. They lived in a variety of conditions and were treated in a variety of ways. Some lived in particularly good conditions and as slavery was not always permanent it was not unusual for slaves to be freed or to buy their freedom. However, state-sanctioned slavery meant a slave was tied to their owner and their household. These men and women were not free to make choices about their circumstances or future, so Paul is encouraging them to have the highest possible values and regard for their master or mistress and obey them as if they were serving Christ. In fact, though the immediate instructions come from their master, supremely, all Christian workers work for Christ which elevates their work in importance (Colossians 3:23). Jeremy Myers, writer, teacher and podcast publisher, in his sermon on Ephesians gives his hearers *his* highest priority: 'But our number one goal in work should be to become a better and more fruitful minister and servant in Christ's kingdom.'[355]

Hard as it was to apply, Paul had already said, 'Submit to one another out of reverence for Christ' (Ephesians 5:21) and had given special and detailed instructions to husbands and wives, children and parents, as to how they should treat each other. They must submit to each other as they submit to Christ (Ephesians 6:5-7). The Apostle Peter calls it submitting to masters in reverent fear, '…to those who are good and considerate, but also to those who are harsh' (1 Peter 2:18b).

This is why in various NT letters, Paul encourages slaves to gain their freedom if they can, 'Were you a slave when you were called? Don't let it trouble you - although if you can gain your freedom, do so' (1 Corinthians 7:21). Paul also writes, from his prison cell in Rome to Philemon in relation to his slave Onesimus, 'Perhaps the reason he was separated from you for a little while was that you might have him back for ever - no longer as a slave, but better than a slave, as a dear brother' (Philemon v15-16a). Whether slave or free, all Christians have equal status as citizens of God's kingdom (Ephesians 2:19). In Christ, no one is second class. I believe Paul is saying that wherever people in hard circumstances find themselves, attitudes can still be changed by Christ and power can be given to thrive in all situations with eyes fixed on Jesus as Saviour.

Paul says the highest aim is to serve a master with real reverence, as instructed in Ephesians 6:5, ('…respect and fear…') as if serving Christ personally, and not just serving a human master. After all, Jesus said, 'Take my yoke upon you and learn from me, for I am gentle and humble in heart, and you will find rest for your souls' (Matthew 11:29). Service should come from a sincere heart with no attempt to deceive those set over us. Similarly, employers were commanded to treat slaves well (Ephesians 6:9). In this verse, as Bible Reference blog informs us, Paul specifically addresses, '…those who command servants, or who own slaves…(*he reminds them*) that they are no better than those they oversee, and God will not show favouritism.' (*Insertion mine*)[356]

John Gill's Exposition of the Bible takes the reader on beyond this verse to show them what must come next. The sub-heading in my Bible is 'The Armour of God' (NIVUK):

'From hence the apostle passes to a general exhortation to the saints to behave with firmness and constancy of mind, though they had many enemies, and these mighty and powerful, and more than a match for them; relying on the power and strength of Christ, and making use of the whole armour of God, which he advises them to take, that they might stand and withstand in the worst of times.' (v10-13)[357]

The final verse of our selected passage in Ephesians reminds us that whether slave or free Jesus will judge our work and reward us according to our faithfulness. Matthew tells us in his gospel that Jesus said to his disciples, 'For the Son of Man is going to come in his Father's glory with his angels, and then he will reward each person according to what they have done' (Matthew 16:27). We must remember that the reward for faithfulness on Earth is to continue with responsibility in heaven. Jesus said, recorded in Luke's record of the parable of the Ten Minas, 'Well done, my good servant! ... Because you have been trustworthy in a very small matter, take charge of ten cities' (Luke 19:17). This is a very sobering thought and should encourage all Christians in the C21st to keep on track as much as the teaching kept the Ephesians on track in the C1st.

50 Philippians - *The BBC was founded on words of Paul to Christians in Philippi.*

*'Finally, brethren, ('brothers and sisters' NIVUK) whatsoever things are true, whatsoever things are **honest**, whatsoever things are just, whatsoever things are pure, whatsoever things are **lovely**, whatsoever things are of **good report**; if there be any virtue, and if there be any praise, think on these things. Those things, which ye have both learned, and received, and heard, and seen in me, do: and the God of peace shall be with you.*

(Philippians 4:8-9 KJV)

The BBC was founded on Christian principles. Its broadcasting house in central London was opened in 1932. Above the central archway in the entrance lobby was placed a large inscription in Latin stating the broadcaster's values with the following translation based on KJV wording:

'This Temple of the Arts and Muses is dedicated to Almighty God by the first Governors of Broadcasting in the year 1931, Sir John Reith being Director-General. It is their prayer that good seed sown may bring forth a good harvest, that all things hostile to peace or purity may be banished from this house, and that the people, inclining their ear to whatsoever things are beautiful and honest and of good report, may tread the path of wisdom and uprightness.'

This inscription uses words from Philippians 4:8 and other Scriptures, and despite a refurbishment of 2010, is in the same place today. It shows the founders of the corporation wanted it to be a force for honesty, beauty and good reporting, and so we find **strange** words including *honest, lovely* and *good report.* They form a unique inscription using the Bible version which was high profile at the time. John Reith (1889-1971), who was the BBC's Director General 1927-1938, approved of the inscription but is reported to have said he wasn't sure if the BBC could live up to it.[358]

Whatever version one uses of our chosen verses in Philippians, it is worth comparing with other versions of the Bible. On these two verses, *The Message* is especially clear and very thought-provoking. We read,

> 'Summing it all up, friends, I'd say you'll do best by filling your minds and meditating on things true, noble, reputable, authentic, compelling, gracious – the best, not the worst; the beautiful, not the ugly; things to praise, not things to curse. Put into practice what you learned from me, what you heard and saw and realised. Do that, and God, who makes everything work together, will work you into his most excellent harmonies.' (Philippians 4:8-9 MSG).[359]

Here, Paul challenges the Philippians to cling to everything that is virtuous and commendable. He says if their thinking is right then their lives will be right. He refers them to his teaching and example and the continued presence of God to give them peace. He realises that God's peace is important as is abiding in the presence of Christ which should affect every aspect of life. The point is not to list everything helpful to a Christian but to list what is positive, godly, encouraging and in line with the Bible's teaching. It excludes things which are not.

In verse eight we see the mind should concentrate on what is beautiful. This makes it clear it is possible to control the thought life and think about what is good and uplifting. Natalie Regoli, a speaker, writer and lawyer, and compiler of the Connect Us blog, begins by concentrating on the mind by saying, 'The mind is the starting point for behaviour. When the evil one wants to entice a person to sin, he starts in the mind. He speaks lies and condemnation until he gets the emotional response that he is looking for. Then he whispers suggestions of ways to calm or alleviate the emotion that would cause the person to disobey God in some way.'[360]

I have just been watching the national news on TV and have decided it is really a collection of stories which shock and cover degrading behaviour and treatment of people by people. Having been *immersed* in sinful incidents and seen fallen people in their selfishness I now need to be *immersed* in Christ and his word as I go on into this evening! This will set me on an even course again allowing me to rise into God's beautiful world: from the secular to the spiritual and receive his peace. I notice that Paul J. Bucknell, founder of Biblical Foundations for Freedom, in his blog says something similar and advises '… think about such things' (v8c). He says, 'Contrast this focus to watching a show (*on TV*), where one battles in his conscience that it is not *too* bad.'[361] (*Insertion mine*). The Got Questions blog equally challenges us, 'It seems likely that, if Christians took this verse seriously, our media consumption habits would have to change.'[362]

This thinking is not restrictive but gives mental and spiritual freedom if it is allowed to do that. These are the enduring thoughts Paul would like to leave with the Philippians and so he begins with the word 'finally'. These thoughts are his highest and best for them, and after quite a bit of teaching, these are his closing words of teaching in this letter.

In v9, Paul commends careful vision and putting into practice what has been learned, received, heard or seen. When God's priorities become the Philippians priorities, that leads to peace. Paul had clear principles which he wanted them to emulate. He could say this because the grace of God enabled him to walk close to God. The Apostle John said something similar having the same grace and close walk with God, 'We proclaim to you what we have seen and heard, so that you also may have fellowship with us…' (1 John 1:3a). Paul, John, Peter and other disciples lived what they preached. The goal was to attain Christlike qualities. As Paul said at the end of his second letter to Christians at Corinth, 'Finally, brothers and sisters, rejoice! Strive for full restoration, encourage one another, be of one mind, live in peace. And the God of love and peace will be with you' (2 Corinthians 13:11).

Paul says to the Christians at Rome, '…be transformed by the renewing of your mind. Then you will be able to test and approve what God's will is – his good, pleasing and perfect will' (Romans 12:2b). Regoli says this is abiding in Christ as Jesus taught, 'As the Father has loved me, so have I loved you. Now remain in my love' (John 15:9).[363]

The message is clear: if Christians are thinking about Jesus and Godly qualities it is impossible to concentrate on the diversionary qualities and tactics which come from Satan.

The Bible Reference blog expresses these things succinctly, 'Believers are commanded to live according to God's ways. He does the work, yet gives us work to do. Believers are called to trust the Lord, yet also to serve the Lord. Paul set an example of how to do both. He was faithful in prayer, yet gave every bit of his life to serve the Lord.'[364]

51 Colossians - *Christian households are told how to live.*

*'Wives, submit yourselves to your husbands, as is fitting in the Lord. Husbands, love your wives and do not be harsh with them. Children, obey your parents in everything, for this pleases the Lord. Fathers, do not embitter your children, or they will become discouraged. Slaves, obey your earthly masters in everything; and do it, not only when their eye is on you and to curry their favour, but with sincerity of heart and reverence for the Lord. **Whatever you do, work at it with all your heart**, as working for the Lord, not for human masters, since you know that you will receive an inheritance from the Lord as a reward. It is the Lord Christ you are serving. Anyone who does wrong will be repaid for their wrongs, and there is no favouritism.'*

(Colossians 3:18-25)

It is a challenge for members of Christian families to live together in peace and harmony. I am able to speak with some experience of being a part of a Christian family, although I thought at first Christian families were perfect and in one there would never be a cross word or selfish action.

Whilst a student, I had been invited into the home of a family where the father was the respected pastor of the Baptist Church in the village where he lived with his wife and four daughters. One of them I fell in love with and later married and we then started our own Christian family. I found within both families, there was a need for peace and harmony which had to be worked at and didn't come automatically. This came as a surprise to me. So I can understand Paul's words to the Christian church family at Colossae when he used rather **strange** words telling his readers to work at forming relationships and put their hearts into whatever they were doing. In my wife's family and later in our own, situations developed which required lots of effort to solve and a measure of understanding, unselfishness and love. Over the years a lot of learning had to take place and, as my grand-mother used to say, 'give and take'; we didn't always get things right!

Paul is keen for his readers to have the aim to seek heavenly things and not earthly things: to set their affections on the first not the second. This chapter three of Colossians concludes with practical instructions to achieve this aim.

John Piper (b1946) is an American NT scholar, theologian, pastor, author and college chancellor in Minnesota and, in commenting on the verses in Colossians, referred his readers to similar teaching by Paul to Christians in Ephesus (Ephesians 5:21-22). He says it is vital that the church should submit to Christ and give him due honour. In turn Jesus gives protection and sustenance to his people. This is the example for husbands and wives, especially applying the words, 'Submit to one another out of reverence for Christ' (v21).[365]

Warren Wiersbe (1929-2019) American Bible teacher, conference speaker and writer, describes the position of the husband as,

'...loving leadership. In fact, both the husband and the wife must be submitted to the Lord and to each other (v21). It is a mutual respect under the lordship of Jesus

Christ… This mutual love and submission creates an atmosphere of growth in the home that enables both the husband and the wife to become all that God wants them to be.'[366]

After all, as Paul taught Timothy, '…God's household… is the church of the living God…' (1 Timothy 3:15). This causes me to believe God is vitally interested in what happens in the Christian home.

Matthew N. Taylor, Christian motivational speaker and podcaster, encourages each member of human families to grow more mature in their private lives and relationships and so become, '…fully mature in Christ' (Colossians 1:28b). As the Colossian family home normally consisted of father, mother, children and servants, Paul gives instructions to each group.[367]

Wives are to submit to wise leadership of their husbands who are to love their wives, and children are to obey parents.[368] This is all in an atmosphere of mutual submission and respect. The charge to submit to one another is ever a challenge and the example is always that of Jesus, not only when he was a child but also when he served the disciples and therefore submitted to them in washing their feet (John 13:4-5). It was in this attitude of humility and submission just after the Last Supper experience, that Jesus went via the Mount of Olives to Gethsemane. There in deep and earnest prayer he himself submitted to his father as he prayed, '…My Father, if it is possible, may this cup be taken from me. Yet not as I will, but as you will.' (Matthew 26:39b).

Matt Korniotes, Lead Pastor, Calvary Cherry Creek Church, Colorado, tells us emphatically that, 'If Jesus had not chosen to submit to the Father, all mankind would be lost.'[369] He points out that the root of submission is love. It is never demanded; never requested. It is a choice and Jesus made that choice.

Matthew N. Taylor, in his Seeking Our God blog, points out the importance of motive for obedience which is, '…to please the Lord. Disobedience to parents is designated in the Old Testament as a rebellion against God and was severely punished' (Leviticus 20:9).[370] This obedience by children should not be exploited by 'parents' (Colossians 3:21) or this will lead to discouragement. Slaves, or servants, should equally obey their masters, as employees should obey their employers. As Charles Ward Smith in his Bible Commentary suggests, this is the opposite to a present-day saying, 'The boss is coming, look busy!'[371]

This is Paul's teaching particularly for Christian slaves to obey in Rome, and Colossae. He begins with the words: 'Slaves, obey your earthly masters in everything…' (Colossians 3:22-25; see also Romans 2:9-11). These words are quite remarkable for their day and were certainly not the widespread practice at the time. Andrew Hébert, lead pastor at Paramount Baptist Church, Texas, identifies three important instructions for slaves, and it is to slaves that our chosen special words from our passage are directed:

'Verses 22-25 (*Of Colossians 3*), addresses slaves with three imperative commands:

1) Obey your human masters in everything (v22);
2) Whatever you do, do it from the heart (v23-24a);
3) Serve the Lord Christ (v24b).'[372]
(*Insertion mine*)

Masters and employers are instructed to treat slaves and workers with fairness and respect because they themselves are answerable to their '...Master in heaven' (Colossians 4:1b). As God is omniscient he doesn't miss anything! Human masters watch and would see most things, but God sees everything and acts without favouritism. In everything we are told to fear or respect God who deals with everyone fairly, as a respected prophet said, '"...Consider then and realise how evil and bitter it is for you when you forsake the Lord your God and have no awe of me," declares the Lord, the Lord Almighty' (Jeremiah 2:19b).

Paul, therefore, concludes instructions for a Christian household to learn to live together in harmony by instructing the members of the household to put their heart and efforts into it, he simply says, '...work at it...' (Colossians 3:23).

52 1 Thessalonians - *Christian ministry is commended as being a lay position.*

'Just as a nursing mother cares for her children, so we cared for you. Because we loved you so much, we were delighted to share with you not only the gospel of God but our lives as well. Surely you remember, brothers and sisters, our toil and hardship; **we worked night and day** *in order not to be a burden to anyone while we preached the gospel of God to you. You are witnesses, and so is God, of how holy, righteous and blameless we were among you who believed. For you know that we dealt with each of you as a father deals with his own children, encouraging, comforting and urging you to live lives worthy of God, who calls you into his kingdom and glory.'*

(1 Thessalonians 2:7b-12)

Being a parent is a difficult job. Perhaps one of the hardest there is in society. Having been involved in preparing young people for the outside world – life after school – I can say from experience as a teacher that it is difficult to get the message across to the young people sitting in front of me who are soon to become young adults, how to behave as a parent. How to manage sex, relationships and money, for instance. It all seems irrelevant to the majority until they themselves suddenly become parents and then they wish they had listened better and had the skills to meet the challenge! However, teachers try their best to teach the skills and some young people listen and acquire them.

It seems that Paul tried his best in being involved with teaching young Christians in newly planted churches such as the one at Thessalonica. In his first letter to them, and chapter two, he utilises parenting metaphors. One aspect of his approach is that he doesn't want to rely on them for support, and this is what he means by employing his **strange** words, '…we worked night and day…' (1 Thessalonians 2:9). We must consider what Paul meant by this. Not only did Paul work night and day but he speaks of what else he did constantly as he tells them, 'Night and day we pray most earnestly that we may see you again and supply what is lacking in your faith' (3:10). As young people are lacking in experience and knowledge when encountering adult life and responsibilities for the first time, so these Christians were also lacking in some areas of their faith, having acquired only the basics.

Paul reminds them of his earlier successful visit (2:1) and, despite mistreatment at Philippi and opposition as he moved on to Thessalonica, he pressed on with boldness, faithfulness and integrity (v2). He went forward with God's backing (v3-4) and support (v5) and without seeking any personal glory but rather with the innocence typical of young children (v6-7a). And so we arrive at our chosen verses.

Paul says he is using the gentleness of a nursing mother who would do anything for her baby (v7b-8). The Grace Bible Church, New York, blog explains that the Apostles, '… were *gentle*, in their midst. The word is translated as kind (2 Timothy 2:24) and contrasted with being 'quarrelsome.'[373] A nursing mother with her own baby is a picture of gentleness, kindness and love. As the Fellowship Site blog in their ministry to students informs,

'The mother is not just any mother, but a nursing mother: a mother placed in a situation where the baby is most vulnerable, and most need tender, gentle, sensitive and loving care. Constant attention, regular breastfeeding at odd hours of the night, and patience with the baby's many needs. That heightened state of gentleness describes some of how Paul cared and ministered.'[374]

This was love and was the same love that Jesus had for his disciples when he said, 'A new command I give you: love one another. As I have loved you, so you must love one another. By this everyone will know that you are my disciples, if you love one another' (John 13:34-35).

Paul cares for baby Christians because he has so much love for them. He provides them supremely with the gospel without charge and gives his life and very soul in his tent-making and outreach. A parent has to work hard to provide the support a child needs, and so Paul points out he worked hard amongst them night and day so he didn't have to rely on them for his support. The Bible Reference blog puts it this way 'He would not be a burden to them, but provided for his own needs. Most likely Paul did this by working part-time as a tent maker (Acts 18:3) much as many modern evangelists need to work in some kind of secular field in order to support their ministry work.'[375] In fact, Paul as a tent-maker in Corinth worked with Aquila and Priscilla.[376] His physical and mental toil leading to weariness was worth it to give them encouragement and so they would receive blessing. This is despite the fact that, as he explained to the Corinthians, he could receive from them proper support for the work he was doing amongst them (1 Corinthians 9:3-6). This was Jesus' teaching on one occasion recorded by Matthew: 'Do not get any gold or silver or copper to take with you in your belts – no bag for the journey or extra shirt or sandals or a staff, for the worker is worth his keep' (Matthew 10:9-10).

Paul is confident that God is endorsing what he is saying since his life showed holiness, righteousness and blamelessness (1 Thessalonians 2:9-10). In terms of moral living, Paul lived a holy life (Titus 2:12) because he could reflect on his calling by Jesus who said he was appointing Paul as '…a servant and as a witness…' (Acts 26:16) so his life had to be right.

He then changes the metaphor from a mother to a father involved in child-rearing but to the end of producing lives which are a credit to God, since he knows he is steering young Christians into the Kingdom of God for God's glory (1 Thessalonians 2:11-12). As the mother is involved in the loving and caring, so the father is involved in the planning and preparation with the mother for the child's future and together training the child in godliness and to be a blessing in society, '…to live lives worthy of God…' (v12).

Sadly, some of the parenting in our present society, especially by the father, is not all it should be. What the Fellowship Site told their students is worthy of consideration, since we must ensure Christians receive good support in their faith. They said:

'…fatherhood is (*often*) very broken?
Some fathers are absent.
They do not love like they should.
They hurt instead of protecting.
They take more than they give.' (*Insertion mine*).[377]

Paul concludes his teaching using his parenting illustration to the young believers at Thessalonica. He commends them for their faith and says 'For now we really live, since you are standing firm in the Lord' (1 Thessalonians 3:8), and so he holds them close to his heart and prays for them, 'Night and day…' (v10a). In concluding remarks, he tells these Christians to: 'Rejoice always' (v16); 'Pray continually' (v17). And he states the grace of the Lord Jesus Christ will be with them (v28).

53 2 Thessalonians - *Lawlessness is already at work amongst Christians.*

'Concerning the coming of our Lord Jesus Christ and our being gathered to him, we ask you, brothers and sisters, not to become easily unsettled or alarmed by the teaching allegedly from us – whether by a prophecy or by word of mouth or by letter – asserting that the day of the Lord has already come. Don't let anyone deceive you in any way, for that day will not come until the rebellion occurs and the man of lawlessness is revealed, the man doomed to destruction.

*For the secret power of **lawlessness is already at work**; but the one who now holds it back will continue to do so till he is taken out of the way. And then the lawless one will be revealed, whom the Lord Jesus will overthrow with the breath of his mouth and destroy by the splendour of his coming.'*

(2 Thessalonians 2:1-3, v7-8)

At the time of writing I have witnessed on TV the funeral of Queen Elizabeth II who died at Balmoral Castle in Scotland. Plans of a few decades previously, adjusted from time to time as the years passed and the Queen's health and reign held strong, were finally implemented. The day with all its pomp and precision was very impressive. Westminster Abbey in Central London and St George's Chapel at Windsor were ready. The military and police were ready. The streets lined with a million people were ready. All was ready for the body of the Queen to complete its journey with great ceremony and dignity to its final resting place in a royal tomb in Windsor Castle. There was palpable excitement in the air. 26 million people tuned in to watch on TV in the UK and many more tens of millions across the world. All knew that something enormous was taking place. And so it unfolded as the day progressed.

Jesus existed before time, as John Piper (b.1946), American Pastor and founder of Desiring God organisation, Minnesota, expresses in his sermon:

'Before Time Began, Jesus Was: "In the beginning was the Word" (John 1:1). Those words "In the beginning" in Greek are identical to the first two words of the Bible: "In the beginning, God created the heavens and the earth" (Genesis 1:1). I don't think that's an accident.'[378]

The coming of the Lord Jesus Christ to the Earth has been planned by God since before Creation and the world began. Many prophesies in the OT point to his first coming (an example is Micah 5:2), and second coming, (such as Zechariah 14:4) and many in the NT also point to his return to the Earth (such as Revelation 1:7).

As the signs were all in place for the imminent coming of the body of the Queen along the funeral route, so the signs were in place for the first visit of Jesus to the world and they are in place for his return. However, we must face the facts and say he hasn't yet returned, but agree he will come back at the right time, and note that Paul and other NT writers advise us to live as if it may be soon.

Paul's second letter to the Thessalonians in chapter two tells us that Jesus hasn't come yet, despite some claiming he has come, but rather Paul says in **strange** words that '…lawlessness is already at work…' (2 Thessalonians 2:7), and once it has been identified, '…then the lawless one will be revealed…' (v8). We are further told that this evil person will work '…how Satan works…' (v9). As these are all rather strange facts, we shall explore them further. As we do so, the Fellowship Site blog, we met in 1 Thessalonians informs us, 'Paul is taking these things in his time and tells the people to not be deceived. There is a mystery of lawlessness that is at work and repeatedly in history, we see how lawlessness continues to persist, and continues to repeat itself'.[379] Paul is using words and information from Daniel to support his teaching and there the lawless one is called 'contemptable' (Daniel 11:21-33).

The fulfilment of Daniel's prophecy in history is used by Paul as pointing to this 'lawless one,' called by John the Antichrist (1 John 2:18, v22). Empowered by Satan known as the 'dragon', he appears to be the 'beast' identified in Revelation (Revelation 13:1-8). Certainly, as the Fellowship Site adds, 'Paul wants us to understand the nature of lawlessness and the nature of the Liar of this age. We will live in a time when we will see a counterfeit version of the gospel and of God…'[380]

Lawlessness and the lawless one are features of the end times of the world and of the people in it and, as we look into Revelation, we see that in the Last Days, people will either follow and belong to the Beast, carrying his identifying mark, or they will belong to the Lamb. Though this latter group initially suffer, eventually they will flourish and gain victory with the Lord Jesus, the Lamb (Revelation 19:7). Then the Beast will meet his end (v20). If there is any doubt about this quite complex teaching, I suggest employing the advice from the Study and Obey small group discussion blog, 'You have to learn like the believers in Acts 17:11 to study it on your own and often ask yourselves the question "does the Bible say that?"'[381]

Thankfully, and because of God's grace, the 'the lawless one' described as contemptable and the Antichrist, allied to the Beast and empowered by Satan, also known as the dragon, is being held back' (2 Thessalonians 2:6, v7).[382] But what holds the lawless one and the power of evil back in this world? There are three possibilities in Scripture:

> 1 *Christians* living close to God 'so that you may become blameless and pure, children of God without fault in a warped and crooked generation' (Philippians 2:15).
>
> 2 *Government* 'For the one in authority is God's servant for your good. But if you do wrong, be afraid, for rulers do not bear the sword for no reason. They are God's servants, agents of wrath to bring punishment on the wrongdoer' (Romans 13:4).
>
> 3 *Punishment* of wrong-doers '...angels...' (*and*) 'ungodly people' (Jude v8) '...suffer the punishment of eternal fire...' (Jude v6 – v8) (*Insertion mine*).[383]

However, we read that Jesus will overthrow the lawless one by his breath[384] and destroy him just by the glory and splendour accompanying his coming (2 Thessalonians 2:8). What a sight that will be!

The Apostle Peter provides a brilliant summary to lawlessness: 'Therefore, dear friends, since you have been forewarned, be on your guard so that you may not be carried away by the error of the lawless and fall from your secure position' (2 Peter 3:17).

54 1 Timothy - *The Gospel is a mystery but demands a response.*

*Although I hope to come to you soon, I am writing to you with these instructions so that, if I am delayed, you will know how people ought to conduct themselves in God's household, which is the church of the living God, the pillar and foundation of the truth. 'Beyond all question, **the mystery from which true godliness springs is great**:*

He appeared in the flesh,
was vindicated by the Spirit,
was seen by angels,
was preached among the nations,
was believed on in the world,
was taken up in glory.'

(1 Timothy 3:14-16)

There are always reasons for writing letters. In the pre-internet and social media days when I was getting to know my future wife, I wrote and posted a letter to her every day for a couple of years. I was very much in love with her. I could always find something to say. She equally wrote to me and we still have those letters after more than half a century.

Paul spent some time in prison in Rome and wrote some fine letters to young churches from there. After all, he had the time with little to do, and a heart to bring the gospel to people. When he was released he found that the Christians in Ephesus had lost their grasp of the truth he had been teaching them;

they had distorted the gospel message and acquired teaching from philosophies of the day. They taught that spiritual progress was best gained by rejecting certain foods and even by rejecting marriage. They had not grasped holy living and overlooked immoral behaviour. Paul therefore sent to them his young but spiritually mature colleague Timothy with a letter to share with the church to put things in order until he could get to the young Christians himself and teach truth and correct them in love.

Paul, in these verses, is stressing the importance of the church and he is linking it with God's household, in other words the Kingdom of God.[385] The church, God's family, established after Jesus' ascension and later the descent of the Holy Spirit on the Day of Pentecost, is the visible part of the Kingdom of God. David C.K. Watson (1933-1984) English Anglican priest, evangelist and author writing about the church said, '…it certainly cannot be ignored. When God reigns among his people, they become a city set on a hill and cannot be hid.'[386] Paul wants them to know they are, '…the church of the living God…' (v15; Romans 9:26). They are, in the Greek, *the ekklēsia,* 'the assembly,' 'the called out ones,' which is a high honour and they must live up to this privilege. Pastor Greg Allen (b.1957), of Bethany Bible Church, Portland, Oregon, calls this '…a sacred congregation.'[387]

Gregory Brown, Pastor, author, teacher and university professor in Texas[388] shares his understanding of the purpose of the church,

'For some the church is a social network – a place to meet like-minded people. For others, it's a place to help raise their children. For others, it is a place for social justice – helping the poor, the trafficked, and the unborn. How we view something affects how we treat it. What is God's view of the church and, therefore, God's mission for it?

In 1 Timothy, Paul writes a letter about God's expectations for church conduct. In fact, in 1 Timothy 3:15, he gives three metaphors of the church – three ways God views it. The church is: *a family*; *the assembly of God*; and *the 'support' of the truth.'* (ESV[389]) (*Emphasis mine*)

Martin Luther said, 'At home in my own house there is no warmth or vigour in me, but in the church when the multitude is gathered together, a fire is kindled in my heart and it breaks its way through.'[390]

Timothy is given instructions for the Ephesians so they know as God's people how to live in God's household which is '…the pillar and foundation of the truth' (1 Timothy 3:14-15). The truth is completely within Jesus (John 14:6) and Jesus is the centre of the church as he said to Peter, 'I tell you that you are Peter, and on this rock I will build my church, and the gates of Hades will not overcome it' (Matthew 16:18).[391] Paul builds on the words of Jesus and is sure of the gospel but also considers some things to be a mystery and so uses the **strange** words: '…the mystery from which true godliness springs is great' (1 Timothy 3:16a). Then, he gets into his subject material which contains a great deal of mystery: the gospel and its challenge. He quotes the hymn, as found in 1 Timothy (above), linked to the Early Church.[392]

Steven J. Cole, retired Pastor of Flagstaff Christian Fellowship, Lake Gregory Community Church, California, explains:

'A mystery referred to something that could be known only by revelation, not by speculation. No one can come to know God by human reason alone, but only through the revelation God has given of himself in the person of Jesus Christ. He revealed what perfect godliness is: God dwelling in us and living through us.'[393]

The hymn has six lines (1 Timothy 3:16b) but as Pastor Greg Allen adds:

'No one is absolutely sure whether it was a church hymn that Paul used in his writing, or whether it became a church hymn after Paul wrote these words. But they are wonderful words; because they expresses the message of truth for which we are to serve as pillar and ground in this world.'[394]

Each line, as follows, is clear theology, concise and informative (*Emphasis mine*).

1 *'He appeared in the flesh,'*
Jesus is God revealed in the flesh as reported by John at the start of his gospel, 'The Word became flesh and made his dwelling among us...' (John 1:14a). This appearance of the supreme being as common to all religions, is the true and only God, who came to Earth in human form. This is unique to the Christian faith.

He existed invisibly before Creation and visibly at his birth.

2 'was vindicated by the Spirit,'
'Vindicated' is 'justified' (KJV), 'proved right' (MSG). Jesus was proclaimed to be righteous by the Holy Spirit, as the descending dove at his baptism indicated, and was declared to be the Son of God by the Holy Spirit at his resurrection (Romans 1:4).

3 'was seen by angels,'
Angels (Lit. *messengers* – Revelation 1:20 NIVUK margin) were involved with Jesus at his conception, birth, and following the temptations in the wilderness, in his praying in the Garden of Gethsemane, at his trial where they were on stand-by, at his resurrection from the tomb and at his ascension. There may also have been other unrecorded times when they strengthened Jesus.

4 'was preached among the nations,'
This shows the gospel was not just for the Jews but for all people as Jesus said in his final words to his disciples '...go and make disciples of all nations...' (Matthew 28:19a). The gospel message was and always will be relevant for all people for all time to hear and respond to (1 Corinthians 15:3b-4a).

5 'was believed on in the world,'
The heart of the gospel is as John's summary: 'For God so loved the world that he gave his one and only Son,

that whoever believes in him shall not perish but have eternal life' (John 3:16). The words, 'believes in' suggest received and acted on to possess the eternal life being offered. In other words, it is being offered by grace: God's part, and must be received through faith: our part (Ephesians 2:8-9).

6 *'was taken up in glory.'*
Jesus ascended back to his father in heaven from where he came. In his body he ascended visibly in power and glory and was received by heaven having established his kingdom on Earth. One day he will return to Earth visibly in his heavenly body with the same power and glory.[395]

Having shared basic doctrines with Timothy who in turn will read this letter to the Ephesians, the hearers are expected to hold to the truth taught, and as James wrote, 'Do not merely listen to the word, and so deceive yourselves. Do what it says' (James 1:22). With this challenge addressed to everyone everywhere in every age, we end this chapter agreeing that the mystery is indeed great!

55 2 Timothy - *All Scripture exists because God breathed it into being.*

'But as for you, continue in what you have learned and have become convinced of, because you know those from whom you learned it, and how from infancy you have known the Holy Scriptures, which are able to make you wise for salvation through faith in Christ Jesus. ***All Scripture is God-breathed*** *and is useful for teaching, rebuking, correcting and training in righteousness, so that the servant of God may be thoroughly equipped for every good work.*

(2 Timothy 3:14-17)

Packing children off to school in the morning is a common experience, as my wife can testify having done it for quite a number of years. Parents and guardians check that the child is clean and tidy and they ask a number of what they consider to be necessary questions, such as, to a child in year 7 (age 11): 'Have you got your homework?', 'Have you got your packed lunch?', 'PE kit?', 'Money for the tuck shop?', 'A pound for emergencies?' Then there are instructions. 'Come straight home', 'Try and get on with ….., remember he doesn't come from a loving home like you', 'And be good!' In many ways, Paul is the parent packing off Timothy, his son in the faith, to face the outside world: the world which is normal but therefore hostile to a committed Christian. From a young child, Timothy has been taught the OT and is here in this letter being reminded it can lead to salvation. The Scriptures are from God himself and as Timothy puts them into practice they will ensure he is equipped for life and the future. I can see here quite a parallel between the first and the twenty-first centuries!

Not only do young Christians value good parenting from more mature Christians but the presence of the Holy Spirit is also a tremendous asset as he is such a wonderful and caring teacher. Pastor Tim Potter, the minister of Grace Church of Mentor in Ohio, tells us,

> 'Having a Bible-saturated home is a process. Most importantly, you must know the God of the Bible in Jesus Christ, who is the eternal Word of God. Once you are in Christ, the Holy Spirit becomes your personal divine tutor.'[396]

Having been responsible for improving a number of special schools in the English education system, I had impressed upon me, and I had to pass on to others, the required emphasis on raising the quality of teaching and learning. This was the highest priority. For Christians this is just as important and provides the right focus for growth and preparation for life now and for eternity. Much of our learning in our faith comes from God's word. Timothy knew about good teaching, and in most Jewish homes this was mostly entrusted to the mother. Timothy had been a good learner. We read, '…continue in what you have learned and have become convinced of…' (2 Timothy 3:14). This verse embodies teaching and learning.

The 'Holy Scriptures', as Paul calls the OT (and parts of the NT already circulated),[397] in their scope and accuracy, are absolutely essential for salvation and guidance in living as well as preparation for and the guide book for the future, so it is necessary to examine them further to ensure they are utterly trustworthy.

Paul is sure that Timothy had a good start in his Christian home, with his mother Eunice and grand-mother Lois, and the Scriptures were central there and passed on from generation to generation. As Darryl Dash, Pastor of Liberty Grace Church in Toronto, Canada, says, 'And when Timothy received the message, he too believed. What changed three generations in this family? Paul tells us: "the sacred writings, which are able to make you wise for salvation through faith in Christ Jesus."'[398]

Paul simply tells Timothy to continue in what he has learned and be aware some believers are falling away from sound teaching (2 Timothy 2:16-18). Paul guards against '…quarrelling about words…' (v14) and Timothy is told to 'Avoid godless chatter…' (v16) but to remember that, and here he uses **strange** words, 'All Scripture is God-breathed…'(NIVUK) or 'inspired' (KJV) (2 Timothy 3:16a). An amazing statement!

The Apostles listened to Jesus teaching about the Scriptures, that is the whole Bible, and they trusted its inerrancy and therefore total reliability because it was the work, as Jesus said, of the Holy Spirit (John 14:26; 16:12-13), who would guide them to the truth. Paul, for instance, is sure he is writing what the Lord commissions him to say '…what I am writing to you is the Lord's command' (1 Corinthians 14:37b).

Greg Brown, Pastor, author, teacher and university professor in Texas, explains in his teaching series,

'What does "inerrancy" mean? "Inerrancy" has many definitions:

Wayne A. Grudem (b1948) New Testament theologian, professor, and author said, "The inerrancy of Scripture means that Scripture in the original manuscripts does not affirm anything that is contrary to fact."

Warren Wiersbe (1929-2019) American minister and Bible teacher, adds:

"Whatever the Bible says about itself, man, God, life, death, history, science, and every other subject is true. This does not mean that every statement in the Bible is true, because the Bible records the lies of men and of Satan. *But the record is true.*"[399] (*Emphasis mine*)

As the Bible is pointing people to God for salvation, and it is inspired by God and authorised by God, it is important to understand that it needs to be correct and must be correct since God does not lie and promised salvation before time began (Numbers 23:19; Titus 1:2). The psalmist trusted the Scriptures (Psalms 12:6; 19:7); Jesus certainly trusted the Scriptures (Matthew 4:4).

If we therefore believe God-breathed his word and trusted its recording and transmission to people overseen by the Holy Spirit, we can trust the inerrancy and total reliability of the Scriptures. We can rely upon the teaching from Paul to Timothy in the penultimate verse of chapter three considered in four main points (2 Timothy 3:16) (*Emphasis mine*):

1 The '*teaching*' or doctrine is reliable. God teaches us about himself and what he requires of us. He uses the whole of his word and especially the records of the birth, life, death, resurrection, ascension and return of

Jesus, and the life and teaching of the Early Church and its people.

2 The 'rebuking' happens when someone does wrong. The Scriptures point out errors and correct heresy. Teaching shows what is right and rebuking what is wrong so that behaviour might change. I remember going into a home with a verse framed on the wall, 'Thou God seest me.' (Genesis 16:13 KJV). This verse struck the conscience stating that God doesn't miss anything.

3 The 'correcting' addresses something which is wrong by improvement. Tim Potter explains, 'This term means that God's word is able "to cause something to be or become correct again." The Bible has both convicting and healing ability on its own. It does not have to be made relevant.'[400]

4 The 'training' is in relation to living a godly life. This is what Paul means by righteousness, or right living: the right way to live. As we get to know God's word we get to know God. The wisdom in it greatly helps with decision-making and in the quality of our lives and relationships.

We must ask the question what is the purpose of knowing that Scripture is a result of God's breath of authority, as in 2 Timothy 3:16? This is answered in the next verse. It makes '…the servant of God…thoroughly equipped for every good work' (v17). This carries the meaning of being mature and proficient in Christian service. Jesus sent his twelve disciples out to preach with authority and to drive out demons (Mark 3:14-15). For the disciples it was part of their training: to know God, to make him known, and to stand against Satan and evil.

John Piper (b.1946), American Pastor and founder of Desiring God organisation, Minnesota, expresses in a sermon '...continue in the Scriptures – these holy, God-breathed, inerrant, infinitely valuable words of the living God.'[401] He then points us to truly relevant verses in the Psalms.

'The decrees of the Lord are firm,
and all of them are righteous.
They are more precious than gold,
than much pure gold;
they are sweeter than honey,
than honey from the honeycomb.
By them your servant is warned;
in keeping them there is great reward' (Psalms 19:9b-11).

56 Titus - *Avoid arguments.*

*'But **avoid foolish controversies and genealogies and arguments and quarrels** about the law, because these are unprofitable and useless. Warn a divisive person once, and then warn them a second time. After that, have nothing to do with them. You may be sure that such people are warped and sinful; they are self-condemned.'*

(Titus 3:9-11)

When Paul, the Apostle was released from prison in Rome he knew he must do something about the believers in the church at Ephesus who had gone astray in their Christian beliefs and practice. He therefore left his colleague Timothy with them in the city to help, support and correct them and he had a letter of authority from Paul to do so. Similarly, another church he founded in Crete had problems so he commissioned another colleague, Titus, to work with them as his representative. This letter addressed to Titus and sent in 62 AD is also for the church and is the one we are now looking at.

As I have got older I have decided I am going to try and argue less than I did when I was much younger. I know those close to me sometimes find this unusual or even hard to live with but that is my decision. I just don't feel I get far by arguing so I let more things *go*! The Lord brought clearly to my attention, '...the servant of the Lord must not strive; but be gentle unto all men...' (KJV); '...the Lord's servant must not be quarrelsome but must be kind to everyone...' (NIVUK) (2 Timothy 2:24). Paul stresses how important it is to, 'Avoid godless chatter...'

(2 Timothy 2:16a). This teaching he shares with a number of churches.

The false teachers on the island of Crete are paralleled with Ephesus and they are restricting good practice and introducing controversial activities and argumentative behaviour. This is why Paul uses the **strange** words, '…avoid foolish controversies and genealogies and arguments and quarrels…' (Titus 3:9). Paul points to God's grace to guide their Christian development and new way of life. He wants Titus to restore good practice then move on with Paul to continue to spread the gospel to needy areas in the Western part of the Roman Empire and leave healthy churches behind.

Paul uses particular verbs in our passage: 'avoid' (v9), and 'warn' (v10) are two of them, informing Titus and the church to stand apart from those who are self-appointed teachers in the church. Paul gives his reason for this: that the false teachers are '… warped and sinful; they are self-condemned' (v11b). Controversies, genealogies, arguments and quarrels waste a lot of time. Paul therefore directs two warnings to be given to difficult people and the next action if there is no response is to avoid and resist the divisive person who insists on going their own way. Attitudes which make them self-willed also make them self-condemned.

Paul J. Bucknell, a minister from North Carolina, is keen we should understand for what reasons divisive people should be avoided, 'Why? They simply are unprofitable and worthless. They don't help us so we should avoid them. If we are not careful, those who cannot discern might believe there is some truth to these foolish words.'[402] These are important things and major ways of distorting truth and behaviour. This is sin from sinful people.

Paul the Apostle had already touched on these things at the start of his letter to Titus, and they are so important he returns to the same teaching in his third chapter (v10). In the first chapter, he pointed out that the '…rebellious people…must be silenced, because they are disrupting whole households by teaching things they ought not to teach…' (Titus 1:10-11). Paul commands a severe rebuke (v13).

Verse 9 of Titus 3 according to John Calvin (1509-1564), a French theologian says that questions or controversies are in disagreement with sound teaching: 'There is no necessity for debating long about the exposition of this passage.' He contrasts "questions" with sound and certain doctrine. 'Although it is necessary to seek, in order to find, yet there is a limit to seeking, that you may understand what is useful to be known, and, next, that you may adhere firmly to the truth, when it has been known.'[403] Pastor Ricky Kurth, Pastor of Faith Bible Church, Germantown, Wisconsin, says, 'Everyone knows we should maintain good works (v8), but some in Crete were saying to get believers to do good works that you have to put them under the law. So they constantly affirmed the Law!'[404]

Verse 10 reminds us that divisive people waste so much time of sincere believers. Calvin says it is nothing less than the 'cunning of Satan', although he counsels moderation in taking action over someone who doesn't agree with our opinion (Philippians 3:15). We must take care to recognise and speak against heresy but have wisdom when to keep quiet about differences of opinion. A divisive person teaches division which is doctrine contrary to that taught them by the servants of God and is contrary to that already accepted by God's people as sound and correct teaching.

Verse 11 tells us that if there is no hope of repentance because of divisive people having a 'warped' mind, we must leave them to God and his judgment because they are condemning themselves, as mentioned earlier, even if they can't see it or admit it. Anthony Roe, Pastor of Dapto Church, NSW, Australia, reminds us of the teaching of Jesus and his return to Earth:

'The righteousness of the righteous man will be credited to him, and the wickedness of the wicked will be charged against him.'

The Bible makes clear, 'For the Son of Man is going to come in his Father's glory with his angels, and then he will reward each person according to what they have done' (Matthew 16:27).

Anthony Roe of Faithlife goes on to say,

'God makes it clear that it is not hard to spot such people in the Church. Their thinking is warped; it does not make sense in connection with Scripture. They are sinful in that their aims are not to obey and glorify God in Christ but themselves.'[405]

Paul doesn't mince his words. He simply strongly encourages Titus and the Christians in the church in Crete to avoid arguments. In doing so, he affirms that the Bible can speak for itself since it is '...God-breathed...' (2 Timothy 3:16), and it conveys the '...truth...', '...trustworthy message...' and '...sound doctrine...' (Titus 1:1, v9; 2:1).

57 Philemon - *A runaway slave is converted and returned to his master.*

*'I appeal to you for my son Onesimus, who became my son while I was in chains. Formerly he was useless to you, but now he has become useful both to you and to me. I am sending him – who is my very heart – back to you. I would have liked to keep him with me so that he could take your place in helping me while I am in chains for the gospel. But I did not want to do anything without your consent, so that any favour you do would not seem forced but would be voluntary. Perhaps the reason he was separated from you for a little while was that you might have him back for ever – no longer as a slave, but **better than a slave, as a dear brother**. He is very dear to me but even dearer to you, both as a fellow man and as a brother in the Lord.'*

(Philemon v10-16)

I think if I had been in the police force in Britain, I would have been a detective. I like looking for evidence and piecing things together jigsaw-like to form a picture. I am definitely an evidence-based person in life especially with my Christian faith. This is based on experience and understanding with logic and common sense applied to situations. I work hard to build up a picture which is accurate and therefore believable. I think John Gill, the theologian, is like that as he develops a picture based on details he unearths for his Bible commentary: *Exposition of the Bible*.[406] He does this with the little letter of Paul to Philemon which is brief but has an important and powerful message.

This letter, or epistle, was written by Paul when he was a prisoner in Rome in 60 AD. *Professor N. T. Wright* tells us, 'The Apostle Paul is known particularly for some of his longer letters such as his letter to the Romans. In **...Philemon**, we encounter his shortest letter. But don't let that fool you into thinking there isn't much there! This way of life (*following Jesus*) was in contrast to the normal Roman way of living in the first century AD.' (*Insertion mine*).[407]

John Gill tells us it was '...sent by the same hand as the epistle to the Colossians; seeing the same persons were with the apostle at the writing of both, and send their Christian salutations in the one, as in the other; ... and Archippus, the minister in Colossae, is made mention of in both.'[408] (Philemon v2 and Colossians 4:17)

Philemon may also have been from Colossae since his servant, Onesimus is from there (Colossians 4:9). Philemon certainly owed his Christian life to Paul through his witness and preaching. Now, whilst in chains in house-arrest guarded by soldiers, Paul had a number of visitors and it is thought Onesimus may have been one of them (Acts 28:30). Under Paul's ministry he became a Christian (Philemon v10), and Paul is sending him back to Philemon to properly face the consequences for his behaviour in which he was of little value, and his actions which include stealing from his master and running away. Paul is therefore making a plea to his dear friend Philemon on behalf of his new friend and convert to the faith Onesimus whom he sends back to his master (v12), to put things right as a transformed slave and as a Christian. Paul appeals to Philemon to show love and forgiveness. It is in Paul's **strange** words we read '…better than a slave, as a dear brother…' (v16a). Onesimus had gone from being 'useless' to being 'useful' (v11).[409] Philemon was a Christian employer with a house-church in his home and would know the Bible's teaching in relation to a slave-employee relationship as Solomon wrote, '…rescue them, and you will have to do it again' (Proverbs 19:19b). Matthew Henry in his complete Bible commentary writes, 'There is a spiritual brotherhood between all true believers, however distinguished in civil and outward respects; they are all children of the same heavenly Father.'[410] That is why Paul is so confident Philemon will do even more than Paul asks (Philemon v21).

It is in confinement that God is still able to use Paul for furthering the Kingdom of God, both in his own soul-winning and in encouraging other Christians to do the same and stand firm in their faith. He told the Christians in Philippi '…because of my chains, most of the brothers and sisters have become confident in the Lord and dare all the more to proclaim the gospel without fear' (Philippians 1:14).

Jeff Fairchild, Executive Pastor of the New Life Church at Denton in Texas, concludes his teaching to his congregation under the following *headings* (with my explanation of the headings) indicating how Jesus can change lives for Onesimus and for us:[411]

1 *Our identity*: As Onesimus gained a new father on Earth, where Paul called him '…my son…' (Philemon v10), so he also gained a new Father in heaven.
2 *Our effectiveness*: Onesimus went from being 'useless' to 'useful' (v11).

3 *Our direction*: Onesimus went from running away from his master to running towards God (v15) and returning to his master.

4 *Our value*: Onesimus went from being a slave to being a brother Christian (v16).

5 *Our relationships*: Onesimus went from being on the run in a broken relationship to being settled in a renewed and secure relationship.

6 *Our destiny*: Onesimus went from a temporary relationship with Philemon to a permanent relationship with him and with God, his heavenly Father and Paul his Earthly father (v10, v16).[412]

*'Therefore, since we are surrounded by such a great cloud of witnesses, let us throw off everything that hinders and the sin that so easily entangles. **And let us run with perseverance the race marked out for us**, fixing our eyes on Jesus, the pioneer and perfecter of faith. For the joy that was set before him he endured the cross, scorning its shame, and sat down at the right hand of the throne of God. Consider him who endured such opposition from sinners, so that you will not grow weary and lose heart.'*

(Hebrews 12:1-3)

The verses chosen for study in Hebrews are some of my favourite ones in the Bible. This is partly because I have been in a situation where the room was filled by a cloud of witnesses who were watching events unfold. They were invisible but I could sense their presence very strongly. I was with an elderly Christian who was dying and not only did she see at the foot of her bed a special person who was probably her guardian angel, but I realised that there were many of heaven's citizens in the room with my wife and I as we prayed with and for the person soon to meet her Saviour. It was challenging and comforting at the same time, but we were able to release this saint of God to go to her home with all our love and thankfulness for a life well spent. It was a privilege to be there. That night God took her home.

Dr. Richard J. Krejcir of Pasadena, California, the founder and director of *Into Thy Word Ministries, sets out the following,* 'We are not alone in this journey of faith; we have a great multitude of witnesses in those who have gone before us, upon whose shoulders we stand.'[413] There are some words and phrases in these three verses which are full of surprises and encouragement and which require our special attention.

The illustration used by the writer, quite possibly Paul the Apostle but we don't know that for certain,[414] at the start of this chapter in Hebrews is that of an athlete who trains, competes and runs with energy and determination in order to win the race.[415] The races in Paul's day would have been in front of a large number of spectators cheering them on. The athletes had their eyes on the finish and on the prize. In spiritual terms, the writer had just covered heroes of faith (Hebrews 11) who completed their course, and now the focus is on Jesus (Hebrews 12:2), following his example and not giving up despite exhaustion and special challenges (v3). When Hebrews was written, athletes would discard flowing robes and run naked or wearing little so as not to be hindered or get entangled (v1). These verses encourage continuing in faith, not allowing ourselves to get entangled with the world, and not giving up.

In his Bible Outlines teaching ministry blog, Paul Apple, Church elder in Columbia, Maryland, explains:

'The Christian life is one of ministry. You have received a call to run a very specific race – a course laid out just for you that takes advantage of your unique spiritual giftedness. This life of discipleship to Jesus Christ – the one who said: "Follow Me and I will make you fishers of men" – is filled with dangers and difficulties and the potential for discouragement. At some point – in fact numerous points – there will be the temptation to lay down and quit the race.'[416]

The mention of a cloud, as in the first verse and as generally used in Scripture, is usually a reminder of God's presence and glory.[417] Here we see *cloud* as a crowd of people watching the progress of Christians (v1).

Cloud is also linked with *witnesses* (v1), a word which can also be translated as martyrs, according to Pastor David Guzik.[418] These are people, such as the 18 of the previous chapter of Hebrews and many more, who have persevered in their faith and the writer is saying that they have arrived at their goal and can now testify to God's faithfulness and they have gained their prize.[419] The witnesses are surrounding those in the earthly race to encourage them to keep going to the finish.

We are told in these verses how to run: it is by having staying power or *perseverance* (v1). James the Apostle tells us how to do this, 'Be patient…' (James 5:7); '…stand firm…' (v8); '…don't grumble…' (v9). It is sticking at the task and not giving up. It is knowing that the Lord Jesus was the greatest example of perseverance as '…he endured the cross…' (Hebrews 12:2), so in turn, he won't leave us but be with us every step of the way.[420]

This is why the writer of Hebrews says stay clear of sin and run the race (v1b, v1c); we must not get distracted but keep on course. And so we find in this first verse of our chapter the **strange** words the writer uses, '…And let us run with perseverance the race marked out for us…' (v1c) which brings a challenge. We must persevere in the race by faith following the example of the older Christians. Well might Paul conclude in his second letter to Timothy, 'I have fought the good fight, I have finished the race, I have kept the faith' (2 Timothy 4:7).

I live in a rural area and I know when a tractor is ploughing a field, the farmer doesn't look down at the ground around him but up to the field boundary in front of him, and so he goes in a straight line. Equally in our faith we are commanded to concentrate on Jesus up ahead and keep moving forward, not keep looking down and certainly not allowing ourselves to wander aimlessly through life. He is the one who brought us to faith and can keep us in our faith, this is why Paul tells the Christians at Philippi, '…I press on to take hold of that for which Christ Jesus took hold of me' (Philippians 3:12b). Jesus is the greatest example of faith, living it to perfection (Hebrews 2:10; 12:2). He proves this by seeing the cross as his joy and heaven as his goal, sitting with his Father in heaven as the prize.

It is therefore important to concentrate on Jesus who was opposed by sinful people but who '…gives strength to the weary and increases the power of the weak' (Isaiah 40:29).

The writer to the Hebrews quotes Proverbs 'My son, do not despise the Lord's discipline,

and do not resent his rebuke, because the Lord disciplines those he loves…' (Proverbs 3:11-12; Hebrews 12:5b-6a).

As the third verse in this study simply reminds us, keep our focus on the example of Jesus so we don't grow weary and get discouraged. If we do grow weary in the Christian life, '… the race marked out for us' (Hebrews 12:1c), don't lose heart, keep going.

59 James - *The tongue is small but powerful.*

'The tongue is a small part of the body, but it makes great boasts. Consider what a great forest is set on fire by a small spark. The tongue also is a fire, a world of evil among the parts of the body. It corrupts the whole body, sets the whole course of one's life on fire, and is itself set on fire by hell.

All kinds of animals, birds, reptiles and sea creatures are being tamed and have been tamed by mankind, but no human being can tame the tongue. It is a restless evil, full of deadly poison.

With the tongue we praise our Lord and Father, and with it we curse human beings, who have been made in God's likeness. Out of the same mouth come praise and cursing. My brothers and sisters, this should not be.'

(James 3:5-10)

After the death, resurrection and ascension of Jesus, James, one of his step-brothers became the leader of the church in Jerusalem, the home of the Early Church and the centre of Christianity. He had spiritual maturity, common sense and a deep knowledge of the Scriptures and so he arrived at wise decisions (Acts 15:13-21). He grew up with Jesus and listened to him on many occasions, and may well have been a witness to a number of miracles. Seeing the sinless life of Jesus must have had a profound impact on James and once he was a committed Christian and follower of Jesus (who originally was only his step-brother, but who became his Saviour), he knew he must write down his memories and the teaching of Jesus and share them with Christians scattered throughout the Roman Empire. On some subjects he writes with short powerful sayings, other subjects are developed in more length and depth. The result is a short book or extended letter with topics such as those in wisdom literature such as Proverbs and Ecclesiastes. The teaching in James is both challenging and up-to-date.

The theologian, John Gill, sees the power of the tongue in these verses as being potentially both a danger and a blessing. He says, 'Though the tongue is a little member, and not comparable to a horse, or ship…much mischief is done by it. And what is the most monstrous and shocking, blessing and cursing come out of the same mouth…which is used in blessing God, and cursing men.'[421] This must be seen alongside what James has already said at the beginning of his letter, 'Such a person is double-minded and unstable in all they do' (James 1:8). Blessing and cursing from the same person is an indicator of this double-mindedness and instability. The tongue needs to be surrendered to God and under the lordship of Christ. This is easier said than done! It is easier to speak our minds and we justify ourselves when we do so. This is why Paul gave specific guidance to the Christians at Ephesus, 'Do not let any unwholesome talk come out of your mouths, but only what is helpful for building others up according to their needs, that it may benefit those who listen' (Ephesians 4:29).

Brent Kercheville (b1975), of the Church of Christ, West Palm Beach in Florida says,

'The tongue is this small member but it gets us in a lot of trouble. A modern comparison would be that the tongue is like a steering wheel. It is small, but it controls where we go. The first important point that James wants us to take away from these illustrations is that if we can master our words, we can also master our lives. Winning the battle of the tongue goes a long way to winning all of our other battles.'[422]

The theologian Matthew Henry adds, 'As the helm is a very small part of the ship, so is the tongue a very small part of the body: but the right governing of the helm or rudder will steer and turn the ship as the governor pleases; and a right management of the tongue is, in a great measure, the government of the whole man.'[423] This is why Solomon wrote, 'Do not let your mouth lead you into sin' (Ecclesiastes 5:6a), and so James uses the **strange** words, 'Likewise, the tongue is a small part of the body, but it makes great boasts…' (James 3:5a).

James reflects on the subject of fire and observes the destructive power of one spark (v5b). In the next verse, fire is mentioned three times and evil and hell once each (v6). He is likening the effects of the tongue with the result of fire – a picture of destructive power! In fact it is so destructive, hell itself is capable of setting it on fire. In other words, Satan is capable of manipulating the tongue of the individual to achieve his own ends. These verses in James require careful scrutiny to establish why the tongue gets so much attention.

We must also bear in mind that Jesus knew about the fires of hell and one thing he said about someone being sent there was that it could happen to a person who makes an unjust accusation sincerely from the heart '…And anyone who says, "You fool!" will be in danger of the fire of hell' (Matthew 5:22c).

At the other extreme is the use of fire by God who chose to convey his message of cleansing, love and power to the gathered disciples and other believers of the Early Church on the day of Pentecost where, 'They saw what seemed to be tongues of fire that separated and came to rest on each of them' (Acts 2:3). Fire can be used for negative and for positive purposes.

The tongue though small is powerful and its effect is out of all proportion to its size. It takes the owner into an entire world of evil and can be responsible for very damaging sins. As Pastor David Guzik, of Santa Barbara, California, tells us, 'There aren't many sins that don't involve talking in some way.'[424] The psalmist said of the arrogant, 'Their mouths lay claim to heaven, and their tongues take possession of the earth' (Psalms 73:9). Sometimes we describe people as having a sharp tongue, this is nothing new because the Psalmist said, 'You who practise deceit, your tongue plots destruction; it is like a sharpened razor' (52:2). In great contrast we read Solomon's assessment, 'Gracious words are a honeycomb, sweet to the soul and healing to the bones' (Proverbs 16:24). These potential extremes from the same small body part are certainly very thought-provoking!

James goes on to say how wild animals and sea creatures can be tamed and controlled but the tongue is untameable and has restless energy and can deliver deadly poisonous words (James 3:7-8). David Guzik shares an interesting anecdote, 'A woman once came to John Wesley and said she knew what her talent was and she said, "I think my talent from God is to speak my mind." Wesley replied, "I don't think God would mind if you buried that talent." Speaking forth everything that comes to mind is unwise, poisonous speech.'[425]

What is possible, of course, is for God to influence the mind which operates the tongue with his superior power and he can give the fully committed Christian who depends on their Lord self-control through the indwelling Holy Spirit. To the Christians at the church in Galatia Paul writes, '...the fruit of the Spirit is love, joy, peace, forbearance, kindness, goodness, faithfulness, gentleness and self-control' (Galatians 5:22-23a).

The verses which conclude this study (James 3:9-10) show us the spectrum and extremes of the power of the tongue. It can be used for the highest calling, to praise and bless God, or the lowest evil to curse human beings: all out of the same mouth! The Apostle Peter is an example of reaching these extremes. He proclaimed Jesus as Messiah and the anointed one, and so we read, 'Simon Peter answered, "You are the Messiah, the Son of the living God"' (Matthew 16:16). Later he denied knowing Jesus, 'Then he began to call down curses, and he swore to them, "I don't know the man!"' (26:74).

James clearly knew what he was talking about as he indicates that in ministry he had known exalted praise and worship but had also suffered the depths of bitterness in harsh and critical speech used against him: experiences with which many people can identify! Jesus knew that before we change our words we must change our heart (12:34-35), but the use of our words has profound consequences as seen in a particularly challenging statement from Jesus. He tells us, 'But I tell you that everyone will have to give account on the day of judgment for every empty word they have spoken' (v36).

It is possible to understand why Jesus refused to speak when he was on trial and false accusations were directed at him. He had complete control of his tongue and spoke when he needed to but not to defend himself and protest innocence. Instead, he spoke when he needed to proclaim truth. I think James learned this of Jesus during his growing up years with Jesus at home and so he says, 'My dear brothers and sisters, take note of this: everyone should be quick to listen, slow to speak and slow to become angry' (James 1:19). I trust that God will help me and all of us to be slower to react and remember Solomon's teaching: 'A word fitly spoken is like apples of gold in pictures of silver' (Proverbs 25:11 KJV).

In 1925 Kate B. Wilkinson was prompted by God to write that what we do or say is the result of having the right mindset and so in her hymn, 'May the mind of Christ my Saviour', she included the words 'By his love and power controlling all I do and say.'[426] The Holy Spirit in love and power can bring this control to the person in submission to their Lord.

60 1 Peter - *Peter, the fisherman, knew about building techniques.*

'As you come to him, the living Stone – rejected by humans but chosen by God and precious to him – you also, like living stones, are being built into a spiritual house to be a holy priesthood, offering spiritual sacrifices acceptable to God through Jesus Christ. For in Scripture it says:

> *"See, I lay a stone in Zion, a chosen and precious cornerstone, and the one who trusts in him will never be put to shame."*

> *Now to you who believe, this stone is precious. But to those who do not believe,*

> *"The stone the builders rejected has become **the cornerstone**,"*

> *and,*

> *"A stone that causes people to stumble and a rock that makes them fall."'*
>
> *(1 Peter 2:4-8)*

Peter was one of the first disciples of Jesus and was initially called Simon. When it was revealed to Peter by God the Father who Jesus really was, Jesus renamed him Peter, as the Greek word for Peter means 'rock' (Matthew 16:17-18). Jesus was saying he was to become a rock or foundation of the Church soon to be established. Peter spent his final years in Rome as the leader of the church there in the early 60's AD. He wrote what we call 1 and 2 Peter about 61-63 AD, 30 years or so after Jesus ascension. He had the help of Silas who also worked closely with the Apostle Paul (Acts 15:22-17:15), and who delivered the letters to the persecuted Christians in what is now Turkey, and probably also to those Christian groups and individuals around him in Rome. In the difficult days of the first century, they needed something or someone to rely upon and give them faith and hope.

Though Peter was an experienced fisherman, and he knew his Scriptures, he uses in a metaphor the rather **strange** language for a fisherman, but a term a builder would use as he describes Jesus as a cornerstone which was rejected. He takes his words from those of Isaiah, 'So this is what the Sovereign Lord says: 'See, I lay a stone in Zion, a tested stone, a precious cornerstone for a sure foundation…' (Isaiah 28:16a; 1 Peter 2:6a). The stone, or it can be understood as a rock, might cause stumbling and offence but God sees it as precious and causes it to be identified as such in both these verses. The first prophetically pointing to the coming Messiah and the second to its fulfilment in Jesus.

I live in a cottage dating back to the early C18th and at the base of the walls at a corner facing the main highway the cornerstone sits and protrudes a little to be seen, and upon this two walls at 90 degrees to each other are built. Attached to those is the rest of the house. I am impressed every time I notice it as it has been a secure foundation for the structure for nearly 300 years. When I think of this verse I see Jesus as being a foundation stone and totally dependable as one on which I can build my life and be secure.[427] Jesus stressed his permanence and said, '…surely I am with you always, to the very end of the age' (Matthew 28:20b). He is certainly this and has upheld countless Christians and churches in the last 2000 years. However, I can't be certain this house cornerstone will still be doing its job after 2000 years' service!

Peter chose to use a building term: the cornerstone, rather than terms from his fishing background. This warrants investigation.

Jesus is not an inanimate lifeless rock or stone but is described as '…the living Stone…' by Peter (1 Peter 2:4a). He is precious to his Father (v4b). Between five and six hundred years earlier when King Nebuchadnezzar was on the throne of the Babylonian Empire, he had a dream of a large statue made of various materials but then came a rock which God cut out of a mountain. This rock smashed the statue. The materials represented kingdoms each replacing the one before it. Finally, Daniel showed the king that God's kingdom would ultimately prevail symbolised by the rock destroying the statue. This dream or vison of the king was a Messianic prophecy pointing forward to Jesus as God's Messiah (Daniel 2:44-45). The king recognised this interpretation as being correct and greatly honoured Daniel as a result of his wisdom and counsel.

Jesus as this rock or stone was chosen to establish his kingdom before the world began and this truth was revealed to the first disciples of Jesus (1 Peter 1:20-21). As Messiah or Saviour, Jesus was rejected by people but was chosen by God and was valuable to him (1 Peter 2:4). In a sermon, Rev. Shine Thomas, founder and Pastor of City Harvest AG Church, Bangalore, India, explains, 'Peter is telling us that Jesus is the rejected stone, rejected by men. Both by the Roman and Jewish authorities.'[428]

Wayne S. Walker for Expository Files, based in California observed: 'A house needs a good foundation, so the foundation of God's spiritual house, the church, is Jesus Christ.'[429]

Paul writing about the importance of a good foundation for the Christian life said,

> 'By the grace God has given me, I laid a foundation as a wise builder, and someone else is building on it. But each one should build with care. For no-one can lay any foundation other than the one already laid, which is Jesus Christ.'
>
> (1 Corinthians 3:10-11)

Peter described Jesus as being the living stone and then describes the Christian recipients of his letter as being living stones as well (1 Peter 2:5a). They are rejected by people but not by God and are actually '…God's elect exiles…' (1 Peter 1:1a). They are a copy of their Master, their example. They are being built by God into a spiritual house, and as this happens they build up each other. They are holy and priests who offer to God not animal sacrifices but spiritual sacrifices through the mediation of Jesus Christ (1 Peter 2:5b). These sacrifices are the sacrifices of showing love which are always acceptable to God.

Brent Kercheville (b1975), of the Church of Christ, West Palm Beach in Florida asks some searching questions of what Christians should be:

'This image is a call to our holiness. We are holy priests offering sacrifices to God. So what are we offering to God? Are our offerings acceptable? I cannot help but be reminded of Romans 12:1-2 that describes our lives as living sacrifices being offered to God. We are holy priests and our lives are to reflect that spiritual worship to God.'[430]

Peter quoting Isaiah, as mentioned earlier, asserts that the cornerstone must be right and doing its supportive job well so that everything built on it will endure and not collapse at a later date. This is true of buildings and true of people.

Amongst my craft tools I have a lengthy high quality spirit-level. The little bubbles of air are an accurate indicator of whether or not my work, whatever I am constructing is vertical or horizontal. I try hard to work accurately. Things for me must be right. With God the building he is building in people in their lives, must be right. The measure and standard for that work is our Lord Jesus Christ.[431] He is the example. If we build on him, we may be rejected by people but we need never be ashamed. As my house, as mentioned earlier, built on its cornerstone has stood the test of time, so a life built on Jesus will do also. Peter tells us clearly '…the one who trusts in him will never be put to shame' (1 Peter 2:6b). Paul says the same thing in his letter to the Roman Christians (Romans 10:11).

Peter points out from two Bible references (1 Peter 2:7 and v8) what will happen if people choose not to believe in Jesus and reject him: 'The stone the builders rejected has become the cornerstone' (Psalms 118:22). These people were building their lives but without a proper foundation. They did not recognise Jesus as the cornerstone placed by God on which to build. Jesus quoted this verse from Psalms when teaching using parables (Matthew 21:42). It reminds me of a song with a misguided and rather self-centred message called *My Way*. The end of each verse concludes with the words 'I did it my way.'[432] The Scriptures hold firmly to the position that to do things your own way is not God's way 'There is a way that appears to be right, but in the end it leads to death' (Proverbs 14:12; 16:25). Peter quotes this verse when he and John are hauled from their preaching in the Jerusalem temple and taken before the Sanhedrin. These judges were amazed at their use of the Scriptures and concluded that as they were uneducated men they must have been with Jesus (Acts 4:11-13). After deliberation and threats the Sanhedrin released them.

The second reference Peter uses (1 Peter 2:8) is from Isaiah where Jesus is seen as '…a stone that causes people to stumble and a rock that makes them fall' (Isaiah 8:14b). Brent Kercheville goes on to say,

> '…if you reject Jesus as the basis for your life, you are going to be tripped up. You are going to stumble. When your life is not built upon Jesus, you are going to find all sorts of problems and disasters. We get ourselves into so many messes because we are choosing to do things our own way. We are not aligning our lives to Jesus, the cornerstone.'[433]

The cross of Jesus presents a similar challenge. It is foolishness to those who are perishing but salvation to those who are being saved (1 Corinthians 1:18). Shine Thomas concludes 'So come to Christ and *be built up* every day of your life.'[434] (*Emphasis mine*). When I leave my house today, I will look afresh in wonder at the cornerstone. We must also take a fresh look at God's cornerstone and remember we can rely on him for stability and support.

61 2 Peter - *Faith can be extended.*

*'For this very reason, make every effort to **add to your
faith** goodness; and to goodness, knowledge; and to
knowledge, self-control; and to self-control, perseverance;
and to perseverance, godliness; and to godliness, mutual
affection; and to mutual affection, love.'*

(2 Peter 1:5-7)

The soil in my garden looks to me to be quite fertile but my wife
knows that it sometimes lacks essential ingredients for particular
plants. So to the soil she will sometimes add compost, often
home-made, or other nutrients. The plants do much better if
they are fed, watered and generally nurtured in compost-added
soil. The right sort of supplement works wonders; the plants
may otherwise be less than their best.

In his sermon on these verses in the second letter of Peter
chapter one, Dr. Martin Lloyd-Jones (1899-1981), a Welsh
Minister principally at Westminster Chapel, London, explains
that Christians can become discouraged in their faith and
attempts to deal with this are met with fatigue and depression.
He says, 'Causes for this spiritual depression come from
having the wrong view of faith and sheer lack of diligence.
Christians must safeguard their time with the Lord, be diligent
to grow deeper in faith and in the knowledge of the Lord, and
supplement faith with virtue.'[435] There is a need for adding to
faith virtue or goodness and a number of other qualities along
the path to spiritual maturity; this is explained by Peter in the
above three verses of his second letter.

Peter was a highly respected minister and leader of the Early Church. He had spent a great deal of time with Jesus and had been personally taught by him so he knew he could speak with authority against false teachers (2 Peter 2:1,v10) and also give sound advice on moving forward in faith. He therefore writes to those who have faith but are struggling with words which would be **strange** if faith was acquired automatically. Progress comes with effort and determination. As Pastor David Guzik in the Enduring Word blog says, 'We are supposed to give all diligence to our walk with the Lord.'[436]

Peter writes '…make every effort to add to your faith…' (2 Peter 1:5). David Guzik affirms that this literally means '…in the ancient Greek, *Lead up hand in hand*; alluding, as most think, to the *chorus* in the Grecian dance, who danced with joined hands.'[437] This is confirming what John Gill the theologian wrote in his Exposition of the Bible commentary.[438]

Basic faith can be added to which means in spiritual terms that there can be growth with concentrated effort. It is in these verses that we see what must be added to faith in order for the individual to grow into maturity. This means to leave behind the world with its values of pride and corruption and go forward into God's own nature to which we are called and which Peter refers to as '…precious promises…' (v4).

So, to faith, Peter says, add goodness or 'virtue' (KJV). David Treybig, Pastor of The Church of God in Austin, Texas, likes the addition of virtue and says, 'The perfect example of moral virtue for Christians is Jesus Christ himself. As a human, he always had the perfect balance of kindness toward humans who needed encouragement and strength to stand for what was right.'[439] To show goodness requires energy and effort.

This is what Luke meant in Acts when he said that the Jewish Sanhedrin leaders, '…saw the courage of Peter and John and realised that they were unschooled, ordinary men, they were astonished and they took note that these men had been with Jesus' (Acts 4:13), as used in the last chapter on 1 Peter. The goodness of Jesus was seen at close range and absorbed by Peter and showed itself in courage when under pressure.

Knowledge is the next quality to add. It is knowledge of Jesus which leads to living a Godly life (2 Peter 1:5) and this pleases Jesus. It is this which leads to wisdom and therefore we have the ability to identify and to reject false teaching as Solomon said, 'The fear of the Lord is the beginning of wisdom, and knowledge of the Holy One is understanding' (Proverbs 9:10). Salvation is itself linked with knowledge of the truth and as Paul told Timothy this comes from knowledge of God's word (1 Timothy 2:4). It is encouraging to note that when Christ returns to establish his reign on Earth, '…the earth will be filled with the knowledge of the Lord as the waters cover the sea' (Isaiah 11:9b).

To knowledge is added self-control or moderation and the ability to please and obey God. Paul linked this self-control to righteousness and judgement when he addressed Felix, the governor or procurator of Judea. Felix, together with his Jewish wife, Drusilla, came for a private audience to hear Paul.[440] But this challenging preaching put the governor *on the spot* and made this Roman official afraid when he heard the truth about Jesus, so he asked Paul to leave his presence (Acts 24:24-25). There was only so much truth he could take!

Self-control is needed for every area of life, none more so than watching television, for example. If I am not careful I can be drawn into watching something which is quite unhelpful to my spiritual life and I have to make a determined effort to use the remote control and stop. This is why Paul speaks of making the body our slave as opposed to being our master (1 Corinthians 9:27) in order to be worthy of the prize: that is, the crown of eternal life (v25).

The next quality to be added is perseverance or 'patience' (KJV). It was especially important for Peter's persecuted Christian audience to hear this. Being a Christian can be difficult but, 'a spiritually mature Christian doesn't give up' as David Treybig writes.[441] James in leading the Jerusalem church was so experienced with trials he writes: 'Consider it pure joy, my brothers and sisters, whenever you face trials of many kinds, because you know that the testing of your faith produces perseverance. Let perseverance finish its work so that you may be mature and complete, not lacking anything' (James 1:2-4). To persevere through trials, although they are uncomfortable and undesirable, is absolutely essential and leads to spiritual growth.

For the person who perseveres, there is the result of Godliness, which means being like God. Peter had already linked Godliness to knowledge and goodness (2 Peter 1:5), and it includes living up to the standards of God based on the commands of God. Paul was firm with Timothy in instructing him to '…train yourself to be godly' (1 Timothy 4:7b), and in linking a number of these qualities together writes: '…pursue righteousness, godliness, faith, love, endurance and gentleness' (6:11b). This shows the consistency of the teaching amongst the leaders of the Early Church: people like Peter, Paul, James and John.

Peter then moves on adding '...mutual affection...' (2 Peter 1:7), called in some Bible versions 'brotherly love.' This is the love Christians should have for each other. The writer to Hebrews simply says 'Keep on loving one another as brothers and sisters' (Hebrews 13:1). In doing so, this fulfils the command of Jesus 'Whoever does God's will is my brother and sister and mother' (Mark 3:35).

The last and highest quality to add to faith is that of '...love' (2 Peter 1:7d). Pastor David Guzik describes this as 'love being the capstone of all God's work in us.'[442] Love is, and should be, the key characteristic of Christians and was certainly expected by Jesus when he said 'A new command I give you: love one another. As I have loved you, so you must love one another. By this everyone will know that you are my disciples, if you love one another' (John 13:34-35). Scholars tell us that the Greek word for love in this context specifically between people is *philadelphia* and that the word used as Jesus did in showing love to everyone as in 'God so loved the world that he gave his one and only Son, that whoever believes in him shall not perish but have eternal life' (John 3:16) is *agape*. I am aware of this love extending not only to Christians but also to all people.[443] As the Godhead, particularly Father and Son love everyone in the whole world, so we must love fellow Christians '...the family of believers' (Galatians 6:10b) with the same love, and also love all people with God's life and love in us. (1 John 4:12)

What we are seeing is that through the adding of the qualities listed, faith is being extended and therefore we move on to maturity. The absence of these qualities stops us being effective and causes us to be unproductive, especially in knowing the

Lord Jesus Christ (1 Peter 2:8). This makes us limited in what we can see, do and be as a Christian.

At one time I worked for the Royal National Institute for Blind people and on my first day my induction included being bind-folded and being a wheel chair user with someone to move me around. I was vulnerable, humbled and very dependent on my 'carer.' It was incredibly challenging to experience sight loss and immobility at the same time for me. It reminds me I want the filling of the Holy Spirit and the freedom and sight he brings and I really want the life to the full that Jesus offers (John 10:10). But I and others must trust him and see all he has to give us and know that he is the one who can open the heart to respond to him (Acts 16:14) and enable us to extend or add to our faith.

62 1 John - *John encourages his friends to love one another.*

*'Dear friends, **let us love one another**, for love comes from God. Everyone who loves has been born of God and knows God. Whoever does not love does not know God, because God is love. This is how God showed his love among us: he sent his one and only Son into the world that we might live through him. This is love: not that we loved God, but that he loved us and sent his Son as an atoning sacrifice for our sins. Dear friends, since God so loved us, we also ought to love one another. No-one has ever seen God; but if we love one another, God lives in us and his love is made complete in us.'*

(1 John 4:7-12)

From a youthful age I used to visit my grandparents. I have some interesting memories of them which helped serve as roots for my Christian life.

Near Barnsley in Yorkshire, my grandmother, Mary-Ella lived on her own and had somehow survived without state benefits since my grandfather Isaac died as a miner when the pit props gave way along the underground passageway to the coal face deep underground. From being able to walk and talk I was guided to kneel at her lap and pray with my Grandma before going to bed. She was of the Victorian era and was certainly God-fearing, kind and stern. It was good discipline. We always did it. I travelled there by bus. The terraced house had no electricity and no garden. It was rented from the Coal Board.

There were two gas lights downstairs and candles upstairs. I used to collect for her firewood at each visit.

Near Sheffield in Yorkshire my other grandparents lived. They were also God-fearing. As I could walk there from home, I went quite often. My Grandma, Annie, also of the Victorian era, was small, cheerful and very loving and caring. My Grandad, John, after whom I am named, lived out his faith. He shone with the Lord. He sang his faith, he played it in hymns on the piano and he was a man of great stature morally, physically and spiritually but he didn't press his faith on me. Those grandparents had a house rented from the council with a garden and rented what Grandad called an *accumulator*. This was a sort of big battery which we took to a hardware shop each Saturday in a wheel barrow and exchanged for another one which was charged up. That provided electricity for the house: one plug socket and one light bulb! Another thing I remember was their outside toilet across the yard. When my Grandad used it he always wrote a message on paper and left it there. It said, *God is love*. It was always there to be found by the next user.

What a blessing it is to have grandparents who care, pray and love, and build a foundation into the lives of children and grandchildren. Upon these beginnings my faith was formed and I accepted Christ as my Saviour in teenage years. Every individual is capable of a close and unique relationship with God, and by his grace, mine is in place.

The Apostle John, the writer of three letters named after him as well as the Gospel and Revelation, often takes the theme of love. We have a dog who likes attention and if she isn't getting enough of it, she simply leans against you focussing on your eyes. She is happy, secure and much loved. John the

Apostle was like that. At the Last Supper Passover meal he leaned into Jesus (John 21:20b) and on several occasions John writes about himself to give his eye-witness authority to his writings and humbly describes himself as '…the disciple whom Jesus loved…' (John 21:20a). Others, such as Mary, Martha and Lazarus knew how much Jesus loved them and used the same expression, 'So the sisters sent word to Jesus, "Lord, the one you love is ill"… Now Jesus loved Martha and her sister and Lazarus' (John 11:3, v5).

We must note how Jesus got things right, including love. In a powerful Sunday sermon just before one Christmas, a church in America centred on this very message as many churches do. In no uncertain terms, the minister of The First Baptist Church of Scott City, Missouri, declared: 'True love begins with God. 1 John 4:19 says, "We love because he first loved us."'[444]

This was the kind of deep love John had seen from his close contact with Jesus for three years and it made a lasting impression on him. In fact, it seems he was always thinking about love and therefore writing about it.

Jason C. of Power to Change, in his ministry to students blog, brings attention to a particular verse in John's first letter, 'This is love: not that we loved God, but that he loved us and sent his Son as an atoning sacrifice for our sins' (1 John 4:10). He writes to his students: (*This shows*) 'the initiative of God. Who loved first? God loved first. This isn't meant to be a dive into predestination or whatever, but to really take a look at the initiative that God takes in his love.' (*Insertion mine*)[445] The greatest expression of God's love is through the death of his son, the Lord Jesus Christ to satisfy the desire of God to forgive people for their sin. He then looks for a response in each individual of repentance and a turning to God in faith accepting the sacrifice of Jesus and allowing him to be Saviour and Lord of our lives. However, we must always think things through and not just accept anything. Paul expected the Christians in Berea to carefully consider his preaching and to compare it with the Scriptures, '...they received the message with great eagerness and examined the Scriptures every day to see if what Paul said was true' (Acts 17:11b).

Pastor Nate Holdridge of Calvary Monterey Church in Monterey, California, reminds us, John had already made two appeals to his readers to show love. 'The first appeal was attached to God's light, and if we want to walk in the light, we should love one another (1 John 2:9-11). His second appeal was attached to our nature, that if we are born again, we will love others (1 John 3:10-24).'[446] Godly love is a sign of being born again. It is theory put into practice by God's grace and with his help.

In our chosen passage John is even more blunt and strongly encourages love for one another with the love which comes from God (1 John 4:7). It is in this verse that John writes words **strange** to read, '...let us love one another...' John says this three times in these verses (v7, v11, v12). These words are strange because they are not an option nor a command. They are certainly not an aim or even given as a potential action. They are a statement of fact and are part of our '...reasonable service' (Romans 12:1b KJV). It's as if all obstacles are removed so we must *just do it*, as a famous advert says.[447] As Nate Holdridge adds 'John hits it harder than he has up to this point'[448] and John develops his theme: 'Whoever does not love does not know God, because God is love' (1 John 4:8). This is real and sincere love and is in contrast to that which the media portrays which is often debased and sexual, superficial and selfish. Raymond Charles Stedman (1917-1992), Pastor, and author and leader of the Peninsula Bible Church in California wrote, 'Who will deny that love is the dominant theme of the age in which we live? Everyone talks about love, though not everyone practices it.'[449]

Matthew Henry the theologian in his commentary on these verses is almost overwhelmed by the immensity of God's love and the difficulty of putting it all into words,

> 'None of our words or thoughts can do justice to the free, astonishing love of a holy God towards sinners, who could not profit or harm him, whom he might justly crush in a moment, and whose deserving of his vengeance was shown in the method by which they were saved, though he could by his almighty Word have created other worlds, with more perfect beings, if he had seen fit.'[450]

Perfect love is seen in the horrific death on the cross of God's only son. Jesus was sent '...into the world...' by his Father and was the '...atoning sacrifice for our sins' (v9-10). John Stott (1921-2011), Anglican minister, international speaker, theologian and author wrote:

> 'I could never myself believe in God, if it were not for the cross...He laid aside his immunity to pain. He entered our world of flesh and blood, tears and death. He suffered for us. Our sufferings become more manageable in the light of his.'[451]

We read that God took the initiative and accepted Jesus as the 'atoning sacrifice.' This can be understood as the '*at-one-ing*' as my wife's father, a Pastor, would explain. Atonement means *at-one-ment*. This is the way, and the only way, that individual people can be *at one* with God and right with him: accepted by him and forgiven by him (v10). It is in the manner that Jesus died that 'God's love and holiness intermixed, and the cross was the result. At the cross, his love and justice were satisfied. Our sins were dealt with.'[452]

If we have come to know that God loves us, that is the only encouragement we need to reach out and love others (v11). This verse is the answer to excuses we might make if we can't love a particular person, 'Dear friends, since God so loved us, we also ought to love one another' (v11). Though no one has seen God, as he lives in us so we experience his love and naturally in our new nature, which is *his* nature, we love others. This love for others is not affected by ethnicity, gender, orientation, age, political affinity, status, profession, faith or financial position. We must love each person as a unique creation of God, unconditionally. This is why John rounds off these immediate thoughts, 'No-one has ever seen God; but if we love one another, God lives in us and his love is made complete in us' (v12).

I like the way Isaac Walsh of Dulinsgrove Church, Charlotte, North Carolina puts it in a Sunday sermon, 'Since God loves, so should we love. This is only possible by receiving a new heart from Christ. And then through faith, study, surrender, submission and sanctification, we will learn to love like he did because we are in the presence of love.'[453]

63 2 John - *John looks forward to Christian fellowship.*

*'I have much to write to you, but I do not want to use paper and ink. Instead, I hope to visit you and talk with you **face to face**, so that our joy may be complete.'*

(2 John v12)

The Apostle John appears to have written his Gospel, three letters and Revelation around the same time, and possibly in that order, during the last decade of the first century. Matthew Henry definitely fixes a date of 90 AD for 2 John, and considering its content, this seems perfectly reasonable.[454]

John was writing in this letter to warn churches that false teachers may arrive and try to spread their ideas and practices. He writes to this church as an elder and addresses it as a lady and its members as her children (v1). John describes his own community as her sister (v13). This was one literary style of the Early Church, as used also by Peter (1 Peter 5:13). He is keen to warn the church not to support the false teachers in any way (2 John v7-11), and he further develops the theme of love as in his first letter.[455] Though these five documents are the ones which survive in our NT canon, there may have been more as John was a prolific writer although he preferred to see people (3 John v13-14). Bible Reference blog picks up this point 'Despite his writing talent, John prefers personal contact. He uses a Greek phrase almost always translated as "face to face"...*stoma pro stoma*, which literally means "mouth to mouth." The idea is two people directly communicating without any barriers or distance. It means to speak in person, directly.'[456]

This is why I have identified those **strange** words, '…face to face…' (2 John v12; 3 John v14). Paul writes to the Christians at Corinth about the great advantage of personal contact 'For now we see only a reflection as in a mirror; then we shall see face to face…'(1 Corinthians 13:12a). He also says how he longs to see the Christians in Rome for mutual encouragement (Romans 1:11-12).

In his commentary of 1895, Charles John *Ellicott* (1819–1905), says of John, 'His heart is full of things to write, but he hopes soon to have unlimited conversation.'[457]

John mentions paper (Egyptian papyrus, and not the more costly parchment) and ink (a mixture of soot, water and gum), according to Ellicott. Papyrus was gradually replacing scrolls at the end of the first century AD and was developed in Egypt as Ellicott points out quoting William Smith (1813-1893), an English Lexicographer, who was his source.[458]

In these days of advancing technology I have numerous ways to communicate just using my mobile phone without leaving my seat. I can open it with facial or fingerprint recognition, and use text, social media, conferencing, video and voice calls. I can take and send photographs; I can get my phone to speed dial and use speech to text activation. I can employ the skills of predictive text; I have safety features like ant-virus and many useful apps loaded to aid communication. I can even send Emoji's without explanation and use the seemingly unlimited internet which I can access for information and which I can also share. No doubt there are other things my phone will do which I am not aware of and as the future unfolds there will be increasingly sophisticated developments. However, I still like to meet up with people and have 'face to face' communication as John longed for two thousand years ago. For that contact I must get out of my seat! As with John's readership there are people who appreciate hand written letters. Now, this is *almost* a dying art! There is no wonder our communication workers unions in the UK are resisting technology where they can because jobs are being lost and the workforce depleted.

John Gill the theologian in his Bible commentary writes on this verse twelve, 'In seeing one another's faces, and through hearing the things that may be talked of; and since the conversation would doubtless turn on divine and evangelic things, so fulness, or a large measure of spiritual joy, may be here intended.'[459]

At the end of a sermon on 2 John v12, Dr. Grant E. Richison, Baptist minister, speaker, writer and theologian in Florida, informs his congregation:

'PRINCIPLE: There is joy in Christian fellowship.
APPLICATION: Far too many of us endure religion rather than enjoy the richness of Christian fellowship.'[460]

We must note in John's closing words of this letter that personal contact bring him a lot of joy. It does for me too!

64 3 John - *One selfish church leader can do a lot of harm.*

*'I wrote to the church, but Diotrephes, who loves to be first, will not welcome us. So when I come, **I will call attention to what he is doing**, spreading malicious nonsense about us. Not satisfied with that, he even refuses to welcome other believers. He also stops those who want to do so and puts them out of the church.'*
(3 John v9-10)

This short letter, probably written from Ephesus towards the end of John's life, and at the end of the first century AD, speaks particularly about two men in key positions in the church. It conveys thanks and encouragement to one named Gaius who appears to be a leader, possibly an elder. It is also a letter to the whole church of which Gaius is a part. John was pleased to be visited by other members of the church who commended Gaius and brought attention to his faithful Christian life and example.

There is also a second man whom John is concerned about: Diotrephes, who is a church leader. He may even have been the leading elder of the church and is spreading mischief and rejecting visiting Christians and barring some from the church. He is opposing John's authority which causes John sadness.

It is in relation to Diotrephes that John uses **strange** words '...I will call attention to what he is doing...' (v10). This suggests there are those in the church who are unaware or mystified by his actions and John wants to bring discipline and order on this important and urgent matter to the church members. John uses language about Diotrephes which shows he is particularly selfish (v9), and John says he is acting with great wickedness in actions and words (v10).

Ian Mackervoy (b1935) of Woodlands Evangelical Church, Oakwood, California points out using the EASY Bible that:

'John had already sent a letter to the church. Diotrephes was a local leader ... (*and*) would have sent the letter to Diotrephes for him to read it to the members. But the members never heard the contents of that letter. Perhaps Diotrephes destroyed it. We can guess what was in the letter...Diotrephes refused to do as John had asked. He also would not let the members of the church help these visitors.' (*Insertion mine*)[461]

This is a sad situation where someone for selfish reasons is asserting his own authority and not honouring God. Diotrephes did not seem to share leadership with anyone. He didn't care about anyone else and refused to honour John or any other visiting Christians. As the letter that John sent was missing he needed to alert Gaius and the church members even before his visit that 'Diotrephes' actions directly contradicted Jesus' and the New Testament's teaching on servant leadership in the church' as Ken Cayce, preacher and blogger from St Louis, Missouri, points out (Matthew 20:20-28).[462]

Peter in his first letter, goes as far as to say that leaders as shepherds must not lord it over church members but to be examples to them regarding them as sheep (1 Peter 5:3).

Sadly, the character and actions of Diotrephes (3 John v9-10) are in stark contrast to those of Gaius who displays the highest Christian qualities and integrity (v1-8). These two men were not normally considered to be in the same church but may have been in neighbouring churches. Gaius knew of the church but not what Diotrephes was doing there and so John was telling him. Austin Doucette, Student Ministry leader, Cornerstone Moorpark Church, California, explains:

> 'John had sent (*an*) approved workman to minister effectively in Diotrephes' congregation, rightfully expecting proper Christian hospitality in return. But Diotrephes, likely in his fear of losing primacy, must have seen these servants as threats and thus refused to receive them.'[463] (*Insertion mine*)

Gaius knew the truth which he had learned with and from the Apostles, particularly John and Paul. He was baptized by Paul and travelled with him (1 Corinthians 1:14; Acts 19:29). Later on, he hosted Paul and the whole local church in his home (Romans 16:23). His loving approach to others is now being commended by John (3 John v5-6). This is why at his visit John will hold Diotrephes to account to answer for his bad behaviour. He could not be allowed to continue to excommunicate those who resisted him. John is suggesting a public rebuke as Paul taught Timothy when facing this sort of situation 'But those elders who are sinning you are to reprove before everyone, so that the others may take warning' (1 Timothy 5:20).

With Diotrephes, when truth is rejected, fellowship is broken and he was failing to provide normal Christian hospitality.[464] This is identified by Jeffrey Kranz, from Bellingham, Washington, a blogger helping ministry in churches through technology, who says, 'He'll hold Diotrephes accountable for his words and deeds (3 John v10).'[465]

Some concluding words from Austin Doucette make a clear point:

'John included verses 9 and 10 in his epistle to Gaius specifically to condemn Diotrephes' arrogant attitude, slanderous words, and inhospitable actions. The despotic church leader is described to Gaius as rejecting proper submission to apostolic authority in his quest for primacy… Although Diotrephes was a brother in Christ …he was also a deeply egocentric man who required face to face rebuke from John himself.'[466]

As stated in 2 John, and here in 3 John v14, the Apostle values 'face to face' contact so that praise, instruction or rebuke can be given as appropriate and in doing so, it reduces misunderstanding and carries more authority. For distinct reasons both Gaius and Diotrephes would benefit from John's presence, and as I indicated in my last chapter (2 John), despite advancing technological means of communication, personal contact is to be preferred when and where possible.

65 Jude - *There will be judgement for sinful angels.*

*'The angels who did not keep their positions of authority but abandoned their proper dwelling – these he has kept in darkness, bound with everlasting chains for **judgment on the great Day**.*

(Jude v6)

Jesus had a number of brothers and sisters. James is well known and became leader of the church in Jerusalem. He wrote a very full letter and clearly had in mind his experience of growing up with Jesus. Less is known about Jude but his short letter is nevertheless challenging. It is not certain whom the recipients were but his references to Israel's history, angels and some cultural details indicate they may well have been Jewish Christians. As with John, he addresses the problem of false teachers who reject the authority of Christian leaders and he encourages believers to stand firm against them.

One of his interesting emphases is his insight into angels: specifically fallen angels using **strange** words about their judgment day which shows they will receive their own judgment. That is the subject of this chapter as we look into what truth had been revealed to Jude about them.

Jude knew that his readers understood angels and knew that a considerable number had fallen from their positions of authority, that of closeness to God in heaven. Jude is now making it clear that they were banished to Earth with Satan, the devil, their leader and master.

John Gill (1697-1771), an English Baptist, biblical scholar, and staunch Calvinist theologian, writes on this verse about the fallen angels: '…they were among the thrones, dominions, principalities, and powers; were a superior rank of creatures to men, and who beheld the face, and enjoyed the presence of God.'[467] These angels were unwilling to be subject to God, their Creator, and so were banished from heaven and sent to hell, from where they are able to cause havoc and temptation on Earth in a battle through the ages to defeat God.

Peter explains this as he says, 'God did not spare angels when they sinned, but sent them to hell, putting them in chains of darkness to be held for judgment' (2 Peter 2:4). The 'everlasting chains' Jude speaks of is the restraining hand of God who can bind them or loose them at his pleasure together with their master, Satan. They are restricted in a prison-like state until their final day. They are in the prison of darkness away from the close presence of fellowship with God awaiting the judgement of God. John Gill tells us the Jews call this *the day of the great judgment*, adding:

> 'The Judge will appear in great glory; great things will be done, the dead will be raised, and all nations will be gathered together, and the process will be with great solemnity; the thrones will be set, the books opened, the several sentences pronounced, and, all punctually executed.'[468]

The momentous day of judgment will one day come; but the day is not here yet. We are still in:

'...the year of the Lord's favour' and not yet at '...
the day of vengeance of our God' (Isaiah 61:2a, v2b).
It is interesting that when Jesus began his ministry
at Nazareth he read the scroll given to him in the
synagogue and found in it the place he wanted to read
from. He chose to stop at 'the Lord's favour' (Luke
4:16-17, v19).

He didn't read the next part as it was not yet time for 'vengeance'

The OT prophet Joel described the judgment day as a great
and dreadful day (Joel 2:31), and Jesus spoke of hell as being
a place of weeping and gnashing of teeth (Matthew 25:30).[469]

Grant E. Richison, Baptist minister, speaker, writer and
theologian in Florida, informed his congregation:

'One day Christians will judge angels. We will assist the
Saviour at the Great White Throne Judgment. Our case
will not come up at that judgment because it was settled
out of court (Jesus took my hell that I might have his
heaven). After the Millennium is over, God will cast the
devil and his angels into the lake of fire and brimstone
(Revelation 20:10-12).'[470]

James Jordan (b.1949) is an American Protestant theologian
and author. He feels it is worth mentioning that '...not all the
demonized angels are "cast into hell, committed to pits of
darkness, reserved for judgment," as Peter writes. This same
Peter says that Satan is still loose, and prowls around like a
roaring lion (1 Peter 5:8).'[471]

Whether all fallen angels are free or a number are bound and others with Satan are free, is unclear. What we do know is that they are all outside of God's love and kingdom by their choice. Humans and angels will be subject to the judgment of God. We do well to stay by choice close to God depending on his mercy and grace.

66 Revelation - *Jesus rides a white horse.*

*'I saw heaven standing open and there before me was **a** **white horse, whose rider is called Faithful and True**. With justice he judges and wages war. His eyes are like blazing fire, and on his head are many crowns. He has a name written on him that no-one knows but he himself. He is dressed in a robe dipped in blood, and his name is the Word of God. The armies of heaven were following him, riding on white horses and dressed in fine linen, white and clean. Coming out of his mouth is a sharp sword with which to strike down the nations. "He will rule them with an iron sceptre." He treads the winepress of the fury of the wrath of God Almighty. On his robe and on his thigh he has this name written: King of kings and lord of lords.'*

(Revelation 19:11-16)

On May 5, 1941, the Ethiopian Emperor Haile Selassie rode into a liberated Addis Ababa on a white horse. He was known by Ethiopians as the King of Kings. Recently, I read about him in my newspaper. Selassie was a Christian. He rode into the city in restored power and authority to take his rightful place.

When he was on an official visit to Britain in 1954 he took an unannounced detour to open a pottery in Godmanchester, Cambridgeshire, England. There, he found Squadron Leader Geoffrey Curran, whom he knew because of their contact during the Second World War. After the war Curran eventually became a potter and the two of them remained in touch because Curran had collaborated so closely with the Emperor.

Curran was attached to the Gideon Force, a British and Ethiopian special forces brigade. 'He was also a special duties intelligence officer, sent to Ethiopia to help eject the fascist Italian Army from the capital and restore Emperor Haile Selassie to the throne.' Selassie arrived in a Bentley which 'bore the standard of the Lion of Judah.'[472]

In Revelation chapter 19, the verses in our selection describe a **strange** picture of a rider on a white horse in a position of power and authority. To understand why, we need to look at the context.

When I was quite young I went with my father to my football team's home matches in the Northern city where I grew up. As we travelled in heavy traffic and neared the stand, I knew the match had started and a tremendous roar went up from the 50,000 or so spectators. The noise was like thunder or the sound of a very busy motorway. Something had happened. I wondered if a goal had been scored. It certainly made us walk as fast as possible to get into the ground and see for ourselves.

The first thing we read of in Revelation 19 is '…the roar of a great multitude in heaven shouting…' (Revelation 19:1a). There would be many more than the spectators in my football crowd! The shout of Hallelujah is really one of congratulations because of the victory of Christ over his enemies, and to honour his salvation and the righteous justice and judgment of God (v1-3). The 24 elders and four living creatures join in the congratulations as they worship God for this victory (v4). Then the great multitude join in with their congratulations because God is now reigning as king over his kingdom, and the wedding of Jesus the Lamb to his bride, the church, has come (v5-8). The righteous acts of God's holy people are displayed in the purity of the bridal costume.

The angel commands all this to be recorded by John who almost begins to worship the angel before being stopped from doing so. The angel re-directs John to worship God only (v9-10).

We now see an open vista of heaven (v11) and a link with chapter four where John writes 'After this I looked, and there before me was a door standing open in heaven...' (Revelation 4:1a). It is as if everything before this chapter 19 in the book of Revelation is leading up to this point where the full and complete *Revelation* of Jesus is unveiled and he returns to Earth in power and glory. Joe Beard, Pastor of McCleary Community Church, Washington, in his sermon entitled: *The King is Coming* adds: 'Here in verse 11 it is not a door that is open in heaven, but heaven itself is opened, the gates have been thrown wide and standing in the open heavens was a white horse with a rider sitting on him.'[473] Joe Beard goes on to say that this is a very special rider on a white horse, the Lord Jesus Christ named as Faithful, True and the Word of God.[474] He is leading his army who are also on white horses. They are following him into battle. The titles for the rider can only be applied to Jesus.[475]

Jesus is therefore the One on the white horse. White is the symbol of purity, holiness and victory. He is seated like a Roman general would be after a successful conquest, riding in triumph through Rome. He has penetrating eyes; eyes of judgment; eyes which miss nothing. Pastor David Guzik in the Enduring Word blog quotes C.H. Spurgeon, ministering at the Metropolitan Tabernacle, London and preaching a sermon entitled: *Jesus Christ returns to a hostile earth*. It included the words: 'Christ's kingdom needs no deception: the plainest speech and the clearest truth – these are the weapons of our warfare.'[476]

John MacArthur (b.1939), an American pastor at Sun Valley, California, explains why the robe is '…dipped in blood…' (Revelation 19:13). MacArthur writes, 'The blood is the blood of his slaughtered enemies (Isaiah 63:1-6). Why are his garments blood spattered before the battle has begun? This is not his first battle. This is his last battle. His war clothes bear the stains of many previous slaughters.'[477]

Jesus is crowned in splendour with royal crowns and is armed with a sharp sword coming from his mouth (Revelation 19:15). This sword is his only weapon and it represents his words which can be as sharp and piercing as his eyes. In fact, the special name for Jesus added to the others is '…The Word of God' (v13b). In just and righteous judgment, Rita Finger, Professor of NT, tells us, 'the Rider expresses God's words to defeat the nations with his army dealing out the fury of the wrath of God (v11-15).'[478]

Jude is clear that the army is formed from God's people '… his holy myriads ' (Jude v14b). John now notes he sees further names ascribed to Jesus, 'On his robe and on his thigh… King of kings and Lord of lords' (Revelation 19:16b RSV).[479]

John Gill (1697-1771), a theologian, makes it clear that Jesus is the supreme King over the kings and Lord over lords of the world. He writes:

'…he (*Jesus*) the General is described, by the horse he sat upon, a white one; by the characters he bears, faithful and true; by what he did, judging and making war in righteousness; by his eyes, which were as a flame of fire; by his having many crowns on his head; by having a name, or names unknown, and particularly one, which is the Word of God; by his habit, a vesture dipped in blood; by the armies he was at the head of, riding on white horses, and clothed in fine linen; by a sharp sword coming out of his mouth, with which he should utterly destroy the nations; and by having a name on his vesture and thigh, King of kings, and Lord of lords.' (*Insertion mine*)[480]

Jesus is king and he is starting his Millennial Reign,[481] as predicted in Psalm 2:4-9. God says within those verses, 'I have set my king on Zion, my holy hill' (v6). He will reign with firmness and be all-powerful immediately putting down any rebellion.

Pastor Joe Beard has a concluding word:

'Finally, as King of kings and Lord of lords this is Jesus Christ's official title, as the Son of Man, he is the rightful heir of all things. This title reveals that Jesus Christ is the supreme, glorious Sovereign of all the earth, of all things. What does this mean for you and me? Because we are part of the church, the bride of Christ, we will reign with him. We will celebrate his reign and worship him for all eternity, first in his millennial kingdom, then in the wonder and glory of the new heavens and the new earth.'[482]

Jesus is therefore riding a white horse in splendour and the most majestic way of travelling in authority known at the time.

He is given a name or names superior to those of anyone else describing him as King of kings and Lord of lords. This is why Paul told the Christians in the church at Philippi, 'Therefore God exalted him to the highest place and gave him the name that is above every name' (Philippians 2:9). Names, or rather titles for the Godhead, are especially applied to Jesus with whom we most easily identify in the trinity, since he is the One of the trinity who became human so that we might understand him; we know that he has shared our humanity. It is worth noting that names and titles in the style of Revelation 19:16 '…King of kings and Lord of lords,' have appeared in various Scriptures:

> *Moses* wrote: 'For the Lord your God is God of gods and Lord of lords…' (Deuteronomy 10:17a).
> *Daniel* wrote: 'The king (*Nebuchadnezzar*) said to Daniel, "Surely your God is God of gods and the Lord of kings…' (Daniel 2:47a). (*Insertion mine*)
> *Paul* wrote to Timothy: '…our Lord Jesus Christ…the King of kings and Lord of lords (1 Timothy 6:15b).
> *John* wrote what he saw written on Jesus: '…King of kings and Lord of lords' (Revelation 19:16b).

The name on the robe and thigh of Jesus is his exalted and victorious name. It stands in great contrast to that of the Beast, who received his power and authority from the kings of the Earth. 'They (*The world's rulers*) have one purpose (*to*) give their power and authority to the beast. They will wage war against the Lamb, but the Lamb will triumph over them because he is Lord of lords and King of kings…' (Revelation 17:13-14a). (*Insertions mine*)

On Saturday May 6 2023 at 11 am, Samuel Strachan given the title: 'Child of His Majesties Chapel Royal, following the choir singing Psalm 122, addressed the King. He began the first spoken part of the Coronation of His Majesty Charles III setting the scene of this glorious event by saying:

'Your Majesty, as children of the kingdom of God we welcome you in the name of the King of kings.'

The King replied:

'In his name and after his example I come not to be served but to serve.'[483]

And so the most powerful king on Earth acknowledged Jesus as King of kings.

Finally, I end Revelation and our studies of the books of the Bible with words chosen and set to magnificent music by George F. Handel (1685-1759), at the end of the last verse of the Hallelujah chorus. The choir proclaims of Jesus multiple times in song:

'King of kings,
and Lord of lords.
Hallelujah!'[484]

Conclusion

This brings to an end our study of a **strange** person, event or teaching in each book of the Bible. There are many more remarkable things in the Bible to discover, but only 66 have been chosen to explore and encourage. The question is, how to apply what has been learned?

Before that question can be answered, it is worth making a last visit to some of the issues raised in my *Introduction*.

I believe the OT is an accurate record of God's dealings with his people and of their experience of and response to their God who chose them as a special people or family for himself. Where some people see errors in this Testament, I see the same issues not as an inaccuracy but as a failure to understand the Bible: God's word. It must be said that to fully comprehend God's word, we first need to know the author. I wonder if critics of God and his word actually know him, rather than knowing about him? It is also worth saying the obvious. That is to understand God's word we need to dig deep and cover all our excavations into the Scriptures with prayer and apply God's wisdom which he can impart to us if we know him and ask him for it. We will then get to know how to apply what we learn.

Having covered the 39 books of the OT we moved on to the NT and its 27 books. A number of these books are letters and several of them are very short but contain a powerful message. This reminds me of a Physical Education teacher at a school of 3500 pupils and adults I once taught at. She was head of department and at five feet tall packed a very hard punch with words and organised some tall and strong young men and women with ease by the force of her personality. She was not to be messed with! So, in the NT there is a Man who stands metaphorically speaking *head and shoulders* above all others. We read of his unique birth, life, death, resurrection and ascension and are told of his coming again to Earth to complete the Kingdom he started whilst divine yet in his human body.

On numerous occasions, I have been pleased to write about the Bible's own authority about itself endorsed by God, Father, Son and Holy Spirit. The Bible also stands *head and shoulders* above all other books because it has the authority of God behind it. If it is God-breathed (2 Timothy 3:15-16) then we must accept it and live by it. If the Bible as we have it is not from God then it is the work of a whole collection of imposters. At worst, this theory suggests that one or more people carefully co-ordinated their efforts through the centuries. What we actually have is the work of a group of at least 40 authors who worked to record teaching and facts to produce the best-selling book in the world. For imposters to pull off this organised feat would be impossible. It doesn't make sense. No, the Bible is a library of books which people have died for and continue to die for as its teaching, expectations and challenge are literally *out of this world!* Simply, it is priceless and has the highest moral and spiritual standards of any book to live by. It speaks of a wonderful Saviour who still lives and empowers through the Holy Spirit the faith he began. It is a book of salvation and the only faith among faiths with the perfect answer to sin. It explains for those who have eyes opened by God, wonderful truths about life and eternity explaining what God is like and what human beings are like. Briefly, the Bible has through it the stamp of God's approval and his inspiration.

However, in all our digging, delving and deliberating, I came across some **strange** things. I found many examples which were interesting and reduced them to one from each book of the Bible. The determined reader could find more simply because the Bible is like no other book; it is complex but yet so simple. It has to be simple as it needs to be understood by all people who approach it by faith in all races and at all levels of intelligence through all the ages, and yet is complex enough to satisfy the learned who dwell deep to find answers. The earliest parts of it cover life as far back as 4000 BC and the latest parts cover life to the end of the first century AD then by prophesy on to the end of the world. It is thought Moses wrote the first five books, the Pentateuch, about 1445 BC and John the Divine (the Apostle) the last book, Revelation about 95 AD. Then the revealing from God of his salvation stopped. He had caused to be written all he wanted to say.

As the Highway Code does not deal with cookery and a book of plant classification is not a dictionary so the Bible is not a science book. So we err when we expect it to solve scientific issues. The Bible is a book, in fact *the* book of salvation applicable to every single person who ever lived and will ever live. In respect of salvation it is a unique library of books.

In case you wish to challenge this fact and say what about those who have never read it or those who can't gain access to it or those who don't have it in their own language, there are two things to say by way of an answer. The first is that for those who have the Bible there is no excuse for them denying God and his claims on our obedience to him and acceptance of his

Son as our Saviour and Lord. The second is that I am happy to leave those without the privileges I have both of possessing God's word and his Holy Spirit within me giving the ability to understand it, to God's perfect judgment. So, I must allow God to be God and reach the lost in his way and his time. For those who die without the knowledge of God through his word, God will know how to judge them when they are before him in a personal audience when they die. As Hebrews tells us, '… people are destined to die once, and after that to face judgment' (Hebrews 9:27); death and judgment will happen. When the time comes, I am convinced he will make the right decision about their future about which destiny they will go to.[485]

Salvation is always available throughout the whole Bible by faith through God's grace (Ephesians 2:8-9). Faith is trust in the Lord Jesus Christ. Before his physical birth he existed with his Father in heaven. After his birth, he lived as a perfect human being *and* as God for 33 years on Earth before returning to his Father in heaven. Salvation has therefore always been before the birth of Jesus by looking forward to God's provision of a sacrifice *to come* or as now, looking back to Jesus who *was* the sacrifice for our sin upon the cross on which he died before rising from death and ascending to heaven. From there, he will one day return to Earth and take full and final control as King of his Kingdom.[486] All this is because of love, as one of the greatest verses in the Bible says, 'For God so loved the world that he gave his one and only Son, that whoever believes in him shall not perish but have eternal life' (John 3:16). The *wonderful thing* is that we can all come to know and love him as he loves us. The *sad thing* is that not all turn to him in sorrow for sin, accepting Jesus as Saviour, allowing the Holy Spirit to fill and transform them, and grant then eternal life and save them by their faith through his grace.

> And what of the strange things in the Bible? Are they
> believable? Are they real?
> You might say *Really?* My reply is, yes, **Really!**

My prayer is that God may bless you and bring his work in you to completion to bring glory to him.

Notes

Introduction

1. Bob Hartman; The Storyteller Bible; Lion; 2018.
2. city.org.nz; *Bible Overview; All 66 Books*; City Kit; City Church Christchurch, NZ; 10 01 2022.
3. Don Stewart, b.1939; a Pentecostal Minister and televangelist, Arizona; blueletterbible.org.
4. Old Testament dating relies principally on John C. Whitcomb; Old Testament Kings and Prophets; BMH Books; 1977; and: bookshop.org/books/chart-old-testament-kings-and-prophets-paper; 2021. John C. Whitcomb (1924-2020) was professor of theology and Old Testament at Grace Theological Seminary, Winona Lake, Indiana, for 38 years.
5. 'Therefore, since through God's mercy we have this ministry, we do not lose heart. Rather, we have renounced secret and shameful ways; we do not use deception, nor do we distort the word of God. On the contrary, by setting forth the truth plainly we commend ourselves to everyone's conscience in the sight of God' (2 Corinthians 4:1-2).
6. Oxford Languages Dictionary; OUP; 2022.
7. Oxford Languages Dictionary, Ibid.

Chapter 1

8. I have used the term 'vignettes' in the sense of 'brief evocative descriptions, accounts or episodes'; Oxford Languages and Google Dictionary; OUP; 2023, revised annually.
9. Genesis 3:9 KJV.

10. Matthew Henry; Commentary on the whole Bible (Concise); Genesis 3; First published 1706; Edition used: Marshall, Morgan and Scott; 1980; quoted by: biblestudytools.com.

11. God's control of events on Earth is seen in the gospel, or good news. Jesus, God's only Son, came to Earth to live a sinless life and die on the cross and rise again to take away the sin of the world and please a holy God. This is salvation: the work of a Saviour. It remains an offer for all people but must be received by the faith of the individual. 'For God so loved the world that he gave his one and only Son, that whoever believes in him shall not perish but have eternal life' (John 3:16).

Chapter 2

12. Matthew Henry; Commentary on the whole Bible (Concise); Exodus 14.

13. Charlie Garrett; Exodus; 06 09 2015; superiorword.org.

14. Charlie Garrett; Exodus; Ibid.

Chapter 3

15. Summary of Religions and Beliefs; University of Bolton; Chaplaincy; Worldviews; .bolton.ac.uk.

16. David Instone-Brewer; Solving the problem of holiness; Premier Christianity; June 2022; p68.

17. David Instone-Brewer; Ibid.

18. Matthew Henry; Commentary on the whole Bible (Concise); Leviticus 19.

Chapter 4

19. Lia Martin; biblestudytools.com; 11 02 2021.

20. Lia Martin; biblestudytools.com; Ibid.

Chapter 5

21. Christianity.com is a Christian web portal, part of Salem Web Network, providing articles on current topics; Richmond, Virginia; christianity.com; 2022.
22. The Torah is the compilation of the first five books of the Hebrew Bible, namely the books of Genesis, Exodus, Leviticus, Numbers and Deuteronomy. In that, The Torah is The Pentateuch or the Five Books of Moses.
23. The consensus of dating for Moses gives his birth as 1524 BC; the Exodus took place when he was 80 in 1445 BC; and he died in 1405 BC. This is based on Exodus 7:7 – when he spoke to Pharaoh with his brother Aaron; Deuteronomy 34:7 – his death aged 120; and 1 Kings 6:1 – giving the date of the Exodus and start of the temple re-building. answers.com.

Chapter 6

24. The Book of Jashar is 'also known as the "Book of the Upright One" in the Greek Septuagint and the "Book of the Just Ones" in the Latin Vulgate… probably a collection or compilation of ancient Hebrew songs and poems praising the heroes of Israel and their exploits in battle… mentioned in Joshua 10:12-13 when the Lord stopped the sun in the middle of the day during the battle of Beth Horon. It is also mentioned in 2 Samuel 1:18-27 as containing the Song or Lament of the Bow, that mournful funeral song which David composed at the time of the death of Saul and Jonathan. In recording *the Beth Horon* battle, Joshua included passages from the Book of Jashar not because it was his only source of what occurred, rather, he was stating, in effect, *If you don't believe what I'm saying, then go read it in the Book of Jashar. Even that book has a record of this event.* (gotquestions.org) (*Emphasis mine*)

25. John Gill, (1697-1771) was an English Baptist, a biblical scholar, and a staunch Calvinist. His commentary, '*Exposition of the Bible*,' was printed in nine volumes, (1746-1763).

26. John Gill is reported by the Bible Study Tools group: biblestudytools.com.

27. oakpointe.org; 30 09 2015.

28. We see God working within natural laws and also bypassing laws, such as with the virgin birth, resurrection and ascension of Jesus, for instance.

29. Matthew Henry; Commentary on the whole Bible (Concise); Joshua 10.

30. Mike Bagwell; Joshua 10; drmikebagwell.org; 14 10 2017.

31. Mike Bagwell; Joshua 10; Ibid.

32. Matthew Henry; Commentary on the whole Bible (Concise); Joshua 10.

Chapter 7

33. Unclean foods are those prohibited that may not be consumed in any form include all animals – and the products of animals – that do not chew the cud and do not have cloven hoofs, e.g. pigs and horses; fish without fins and scales; the blood of any animal; shellfish, e.g., clams, oysters, shrimp, crabs and all other living creatures that creep; and those fowl listed in the Bible, e.g., vultures, hawks, owls, herons. All other foods may be eaten. Yehudi A. Cohen; Rules and customs in world religions: Judaism; The Editors of Encyclopaedia Britannica; Judaism; 1768; (Now only published on-line with annual revisions); britannica.com; 2022.

34. Bible Study Tools; California; Judges 16; biblestudytools.com.

35. David Guzik, Pastor, Santa Barbara, California; Commentary on Judges 16; enduringword.com; 2018.

36. See 1 Samuel 5:1-5, where the Ark of God is put alongside Dagon's statue in the temple of Dagon.

37. Lou Nicholes; Word of Life, International Youth Fellowship, NY; family-times.net.

38. David Guzik; enduringword.com. 2018.

39. David Guzik; enduringword.com. Ibid.

40. Matthew Henry; Commentary on the whole Bible (Concise); Judges 16:25-31.

Chapter 8

41. John C. Whitcomb (1924-2020); Old Testament Kings and Prophets; BMH Books; 1977; and: bookshop.org/books/chart-old-testament-kings-and-prophets-paper; 2021.

42. Bethlehem means *House of Bread*.

43. Iain Gordon; Leadership Team member of Living Waters Church, Tauranga, NZ; jesusplusnothing.com.

44. Matthew Henry; Commentary on the whole Bible (Concise); Ruth 1:1-5.

45. The names of the two sons and wives are interesting and fit their characters: Mahlon (sickly) and Kilion (pining); Ruth (friendship) and Orpah (stiff-necked).

46. David Guzik, Pastor, Santa Barbara, California; Commentary on Ruth 1; enduringword.com; 2018.

47. David Guzik. Ibid.

48. The good seed of conversion that Jesus spoke about found root in Ruth but not in Orpah! (Matthew 13:3-9)

49. Matthew Henry; Ruth 1:1-5.

Chapter 9

50. 12 judges are mentioned in the Book of Judges (and one other leader) and two in 1 Samuel.

51. The ancient Jewish historian Josephus said Samuel was 12 years old.

52. Jesus quotes Isaiah to explain his reason for teaching in parables:

'Be ever hearing, but never understanding;
be ever seeing, but never perceiving.
Make the heart of this people calloused;
make their ears dull and close their eyes.
Otherwise they might see with their eyes,
hear with their ears,
understand with their hearts,
and turn and be healed'
(Isaiah 6:9-10).

53. Don Fleming; Bridgeway Bible Commentary; Bridgeway Books; commentary on 1 Samuel 3:1-10; 1988, 1994, 2005.
54. Note, on the third occasion of answering God, Samuel doesn't use the word Lord because God was not yet his Lord.
55. Abraham (Genesis 22:1); Jacob (Genesis 46:2); Moses (Exodus 3:4); Isaiah (Isaiah 6:8); and Ananias (Acts 9:10).
56. dailyverse.knowing-jesus.com/1-samuel-3-10.
57. Don Fleming; Bridgeway Bible Commentary.
58. Roger Nam; Professor of Hebrew; workingpreacher.org; 18 01 2015.
59. Roger Nam, Ibid.
60. Roger Nam, Ibid.
61. Dr. Ralph F. Wilson; pastor@joyfulheart.com; jesuswalk.com; 2022.
62. Alfred Lord Tennyson; Wikipedia.org.

Chapter 10

63. David Guzik, Pastor, Santa Barbara, California; Commentary on 2 Samuel 5; enduringword.com; 2018.
64. 'For the Lord promised David, "By my servant David I will rescue my people Israel from the hand of the Philistines and from the hand of all their enemies" '(2 Samuel 3:18).
65. Bryce Morgan; ewayofgracechurch.com; 21 07 2013.

66. David Guzik, 2018.

67. Matthew Henry; Commentary on the whole Bible (Concise); 2 Samuel 5.

68. Through the ages, Jerusalem has been and will always be a target for the forces of the world and the powers of evil: 'They marched across the breadth of the earth and surrounded the camp of God's people, the city he loves' (Revelation 20:9).

69. As Paul said to the Christians at Philippi, 'Therefore, my dear friends, as you have always obeyed – not only in my presence, but now much more in my absence – continue to work out your salvation with fear and trembling, for it is God who works in you to will and to act in order to fulfil his good purpose' (Philippians 2:12-13).

70. Bryce Morgan; 2013.

Chapter 11

71. Ellicott's Commentary for English Readers; Edited work of 28 scholars. The full work can be downloaded at: biblicalstudies. org.uk.

72. Ellicott; Ibid.

73. Geoff Fox; Senior Elder; Haven Church, Gorran Haven, Cornwall; Sermon on 1 Kings 10; 22 05 2022.

74. Geoff Fox; Ibid.

75. Wealth became one of the snares to Solomon who, himself, warned of its dangers in his teaching (Ecclesiastes 5:10).

76. The Pulpit Commentary; a work a work produced in 23 volumes over 30 years; studylight.org/commentaries/eng/tbi/1-kings-10; Published 1905-1909.

77. Joseph S. Exell, Spence-Jones, Henry Donald Maurice. Commentary on 1 Kings 10. The Pulpit Commentary; 1897. studylight.org/commentaries/eng/tpc/1-kings-10; biblestudytools.com.

78. John Murfitt; The Kingdom; 2022.
79. Geoff Fox; 2022.

Chapter 12

80. Joseph S. Exell, Spence-Jones, Henry Donald Maurice; Commentary on 2 Kings 6. The Pulpit Commentary; 1897; studylight.org/commentaries/eng/tpc/2-kings-6.
81. theologyofwork.org; 02 06 2014.
82. Bible Outlines; bibleoutlines.com.
83. Matthew Henry; Commentary on the whole Bible (Concise); 2 Kings 6.

Chapter 13

84. David Guzik; The Enduring Word Bible Commentary; enduringword.com; Commentary on 1 Chronicles 29; 2021.
85. David Guzik; Ibid.
86. biblestudytools.com.
87. studylight.org/commentaries/eng/tpc/1-Chronicles-29.

Chapter 14

88. Charles Ward Smith; as reported in: studylight.org. 2014.
89. bible.knowing-jesus.com/topics/Fire-From-Heaven.
90. James and John knew their nation's history so well, they asked Jesus to give them permission to call down fire from heaven on the disrespectful Samaritans (and some manuscripts here add, '…just as Elijah did') (Luke 9:54).
91. Worthy Bible Commentary; incorporating commentaries written by well-known and popular theologians, such as Matthew Henry, were designed to aid in the study of the Bible; acquired and published by Hachette Book Group; 2 Chronicles 7; 13 08 2018.

Chapter 15

92. toughquestionsanswered.org; 08 08 2016.
93. David Guzik; The Enduring Word Bible Commentary; enduringword.com; Commentary on Ezra 1; 2021.
94. studylight.org.
95. Godfrey Birtill; *Just One Touch From The King*; King Lyrics Album; 2007.

Chapter 16

96. Nehemiah is essentially the king's bodyguard and protects the king from being poisoned. In this position he would have regular contact with the king which would make him a person of influence in court over the monarchy, as was Esther (Esther 7:1-3).
97. David Guzik; The Enduring Word Bible Commentary; enduringword.com; Commentary on Nehemiah 2; 2018.
98. The life of both the King and Nehemiah depended on safety in terms of the wine and food not being poisoned. If anything was amiss, Nehemiah would be very ill or die and so the king would avoid that drink or food!
99. Matthew Henry; Commentary on the whole Bible (Concise); Nehemiah 2.
100. Joint editor of The Pulpit Commentary; a work produced in 23 volumes over 30 years; studylight.org/commentaries/eng/tbi/Nehemiah-2. Published 1905-1909.
101. biblehub.com.
102. Dr. Thomas L. Constable's Expository Notes on Nehemiah 2; reported in: studylight.org/commentaries/eng/dcc/nehemiah-2; 2012. Constable is a retired professor of Dallas Theological Seminary; Texas.
103. Nehemiah did as the Apostle Paul taught, 'Pray continually.' (I Thessalonians 5:17)

104. Nehemiah may have been in Jerusalem for 12 years from his sending by and from Artaxerxes to returning back to him. Compare: Nehemiah 5:14 with Nehemiah 13:6.

105. John Gill (1697-1771) was an English Baptist, a biblical scholar, and a staunch Calvinist. His commentary, Exposition of the Bible, was printed in nine volumes, (1746-1763). Nehemiah 2; biblestudytools.com.

106. The ESV Bible (English Standard Version; Crossway); 2001, 2007, 2011, 2016. On-line Bible notes, Berkshire, UK; biblenotes.org.uk.

Chapter 17

107. Amy G. Oden, Saint Paul School of Theology, Oklahoma; workingpreacher.org; 30 09 2012.

108. At these occasions in Persian society, eating a main-course was only a small part of the meal, most of the time was occupied by drinking and desserts.

109. David Guzik; The Enduring Word Bible Commentary; enduringword.com; Commentary on Esther 7; 2018.

110. Joseph S. Exell; Spence-Jones, Donald Maurice Henry. "Commentary on Esther 7". The Pulpit Commentary; studylight.org/commentaries/eng/tpc/esther-7; 1897.

111. Iain Gordon, Leadership Team member of Living Waters Church, Tauranga, NZ; jesusplusnothing.com.

Chapter 18

112. Uz was just north of Edom – which was southeast and outside of Israel. The friends who visit Job are Gentiles, according to the Explaining The Book Blog; WordPress.com.explainingthebook. com; 22 10 2017.

113. Paul in his letters to the churches quotes Job twice but in the NT only James mentions him by name (James 5:11). Melchizedek

appears in Genesis 14:18-20 and is quoted in Psalms 110:4 and is named a number of times in Hebrews, such as 5:6, 6:20, 7:1-3, v15-17, v21.

114. David Guzik; Commentary on Job 1; enduringword.com; 2018.
115. Explaining The Book; 2017.
116. Kirsten; Blog for women; sweetteaandsavinggraceblog.com.
117. We do well to take note of Satan's activity as 1 Peter 5:8 warns.
118. Explaining The Book; 2017.
119. David Guzik; enduringword.com; 2019.
120. christianity.com.

Chapter 19

121. The Message Bible (MSG); Eugene Peterson; NavPress; 2002. 'The Message is a reading Bible translated from the original Greek and Hebrew Scriptures by scholar, pastor, author, and poet Eugene Peterson. Peterson spent ten years working on The Message after teaching in seminary and preaching in churches for more than thirty years. Thoroughly reviewed and approved by twenty biblical scholars, The Message combines the authority of God's Word with the cadence and energy of conversational English.' (NavPress.com; 2022).
122. 'Omniscience: the state of knowing everything;' Oxford English Dictionary; OUP; updated: 2022.
123. 'Omnipresence: the state of being widespread or constantly encountered;' Oxford English Dictionary; Ibid.
124. The ESV Bible (English Standard Version); Crossway; 2001, 2007, 2011, 2016.
125. David Guzik; The Enduring Word Bible Commentary; ewm@ enduringword.com; 2020.
126. John Murfitt; Two Destinies; Zaccmedia; 2022.

127. The righteous are Christians who have accepted Christ as Saviour and serve him as their Lord.

128. John Murfitt; Two Destinies; 2022.

129. Jonathan Edwards; Works, Vol. II, p.880; quoted in: Psalm 139; shawnethomas.com; 26 02 2012.

130. On April 12, 1961, aboard the spacecraft Vostok 1, Soviet cosmonaut Yuri Alekseyevich Gagarin becomes the first human being to travel into space. During the flight, the 27-year-old test pilot and industrial technician also became the first man to orbit the planet, a feat accomplished by his space capsule in 89 minutes.

131. Steven J. Cole; bible.org; 1993.

132. Meg Bucher; Psalms 139; crosswalk.com; 06 11 2020.

Chapter 20

133. Got Questions Ministries; Proverbs 17:28; gotquestions.org.

134. letgodbetrue.com; 09 11 2019.

135. Got Questions; Adam; gotquestions.org.

136. John C. Whitcomb; Old Testament Kings and Prophets; BMH Books; Solomon; 1977; and: bookshop.org/books/chart-old-testament-kings-and-prophets-paper; 2021.

137. Matthew Henry; Commentary on the whole Bible (Concise); Proverbs 17.

138. Matthew Henry; Proverbs 17:28; Ibid.

139. John Gill; Gill's Exposition of the Entire Bible; quoted in: biblestudytools.com.

140. Calvarychapeljonesborough.org; 01 05 2012.

141. Pastor Travis D. Smith; heartofashepherd.com; 17 07 2015.

Chapter 21

142. I heard a learned academic who was an agnostic say that he thought a week for all that Christians' claim God achieved in

creation was far too short a time, at which point his academic colleague who was a Christian replied he personally thought it took God a long time to achieve the whole of the heavens and Earth and the whole of the details of creation, since God is omnipotent and he is God, and he could have done it much faster! It depends on your perspective!

143. The Adam Clarke Commentary; Ecclesiastes 3:11; 1832; quoted in: studylight.org/commentaries/acc/ecclesiastes-3.

144. gotquestions.org; 04 01 2022.

145. The song: *Turn, turn, turn* includes the recurring words, '…and a time to every purpose, under heaven.' It was written by Pete Seeger and released by Columbia Records.

146. Written by H, using Ecclesiastes 3:11; hopereflected.com; 26 09 2016.

147. Matthew Henry; Commentary on the whole Bible (Concise); Ecclesiastes 3:11.

148. Adam Clarke; 1832.

149. The Editor in Chief; Ecclesiastes 3:11; connectusfund.org; 05 04 2020.

Chapter 22

150. The words of Song of Songs chapter two, verse four: 'Let him lead me to the banquet hall, and let his banner over me be love,' have been used to write a chorus by Kevin Prosch, American Christian musician; 1991. The chorus begins: 'He brought me to his banqueting house and his banner over me is love.'

151. L. Craig Harris writing on Song of Songs 2; threeminutebiblestudy. blogspot.com; 16 08 2013.

152. L. Craig Harris; Ibid.

153. John Gill (1697-1771), an English Baptist, a biblical scholar, and a staunch Calvinist. His commentary, *Exposition of the Bible*,

was printed in nine volumes (1746-1763).Song of Solomon 2; as quoted by: biblestudytools.com.

154. David Guzik; enduringword.com/biblecommentary/song-of-solomon-2; 2018.

155. 'He will raise a banner for the nations and gather the exiles of Israel; he will assemble the scattered people of Judah from the four quarters of the earth' (Isaiah 11:12).

156. Matthew Henry; Commentary on the whole Bible (Concise); Song of Solomon 2:4.

Chapter 23

157. The Middle Ages are generally felt to be the C5th-C15th.

158. britannica.com.

159. Charles Darwin; 'On the Origin of Species by Means of Natural Selection, or the Preservation of Favoured Races in the Struggle for Life,' John Murray; p.162; 1859.

160. En.wikipedia.org.

161. Got Questions; gotquestions.org.

162. The 'I' in Proverbs 8:27 is wisdom and also a pre-incarnate reference to Jesus.

163. Albert Barnes Bible commentary: The Whole Bible, was published in14 volumes by Estes and Lauriate between1847-1885. The edition referred to is: Kindle; 10 09 2015.

164. stackexchange.com 31 10 2020.

165. Denis Bratcher; The Circle of the Earth; Isaiah 40:22; Christian Resources Institute; crivoice.org/circle. 2018.

166. Dominic Statham; creation.com/isaiah-40-22-circle-sphere; cmnw.org.uk; 11 08 2016.

167. quora.com/How-much-is-earths-curvature-after-1-km. (1Km is a little over half a mile, and 8cm is just over three inches).

168. John Murfitt; The Kingdom; 2022.

Chapter 24

169. Matthew Henry; Commentary on the whole Bible (Concise); Jeremiah 10:13.
170. David Guzik; The Enduring Word Bible Commentary; ewm@ enduringword.com; 2021.
171. Charles Ward Smith; as reported in: studylight.org; 2014; Jeremiah 10:13.
172. Charles Ward Smith; Jeremiah 10:13; Ibid.
173. John Calvin; The Institutes of the Christian Religion; (Commentary on Jeremiah 10); 1536; as quoted by: studylight. org/commentaries/cal/jeremiah-10.
174. The opening scene of William Shakespeare's tragedy Macbeth. Written 1606 and published 1623 sounds very similar. However, this is a long time after Jeremiah's ministry (627-575 BC), using the same words.

    First witch: 'When shall we three meet again? In thunder, lightning, or in rain?' The Editors of Encyclopaedia Britannica; britannica.com; 1768; (Now only published on-line with annual revisions).
175. John Calvin; 1536.
176. See chapter 19: Psalms, first paragraph on these three attributes of God.

Chapter 25

177. Kernow Choc; The Cornish Slang you need to know; kernowchocolate.co.uk; 21 05 2018.
178. crossway.org/articles/waiting-on-the-lord-is-not-a-waste-of-time; 09 05 2020.
179. Mark Vroegop; *Dark Clouds, Deep Mercy;* Crossway; 2019.
180. Mark Vroegop; Ibid.

181. The Pulpit Commentary of 1897; quoted by Study Light in their Comprehensive overview of Bible Commentaries; studylight.org/commentaries/eng/tpc/lamentations3-25.

182. dailyverse.knowing-jesus.com/lamentations-3-25.

183. 'Some faced jeers and flogging, and even chains and imprisonment. They were put to death by stoning; they were sawn in two; they were killed by the sword. They went about in sheepskins and goatskins, destitute, persecuted and ill-treated – the world was not worthy of them' (Hebrews 11:36-38a). It is traditionally held by scholars that Jeremiah was captured, tortured and killed by being stoned to death by Jews in Egypt. britannica.com.

184. John Murfitt; Two Destinies, Zaccmedia; 2022.

185. John Gill's Exposition of the Bible; Lamentations 3; as quoted by: biblestudytools.com.

Chapter 26

186. history.com; 21 07 2010.

187. bhf.org.uk; 2022.

188. Michal Elizabeth Hunt; agapebiblestudy.com/Ezekiel36; 2017.

189. David Guzik; blueletterbible.org/Comm/guzik_david/StudyGuide2017-Eze/Eze-36; 2017.

190. Charles Haddon Spurgeon, (1834-1892), Pastor of Metropolitan Tabernacle, London for 38 years, renowned preacher and author. This sermon was preached when the Tabernacle had its previous name: The New Park Street Pulpit. It is: Volume 4; No. 212; The New Heart; 1858.

191. Michal Elizabeth Hunt; 2017.

192. abideinchrist.com/messages/eze36.

193. C.H. Spurgeon; 1858.

194. edenproject.com.

Chapter 27

195. Dr. J. Mike Minnix, Founder and Editor of PastorLife, North Carolina; fluent in Hebrew, Greek and Aramaic; pastorlife.com.
196. Their Hebrew names had special significance, as each was connected to the God of Israel.
    - Hananiah means, "God is gracious," changed to "Shadrach," meaning, "Illuminated by the sun god."
    - Mishael means, "Who is like God?" changed to Meshach, meaning, "Who is like Venus?"
    - Azariah means, "The Lord is my helper," changed to Abednego, meaning, "The worshipper of Nego," or Nebo, the Babylonian god of wisdom.
    (Adapted from: sermonnotebook.org.)
197. Pastor Alan Carr of North Carolina made an interesting observation regarding the likely outcome for uncompromising Christians as he states:
    'Everyone who wants to live a godly life in Christ Jesus will be persecuted.' (2 Timothy 3:12).
    'If we are going to live *godly*; if we are going to live for Jesus, then we are going to be persecuted. There will be furnaces of criticism, furnaces of intimidation, furnaces of hatred, furnaces of temptation, furnaces of trials like you cannot imagine. These furnaces will become more numerous and far hotter as society continues to flee from God and from the guidelines he laid down in his Word. That is just the way it is!' sermonnotebook. org; 2002.
198. It is interesting that three young men went into the fire and three young men came out but Nebuchadnezzar saw four men in the flames. It is worthy of consideration where the fourth man went?
199. GotQuestions.org and LearnReligions.com; 06 04 2022.

200. sarahcoleman.com.au; 01 09 2020.
201. Sarah Coleman is persuaded:
    - God can rescue me from cancer... Even if he doesn't, I will not bow down.
    - God can restore my marriage... Even if he doesn't, I will not bow down.
    - God will cause me to prosper... Even if he doesn't, I will not bow down.
    (sarahcoleman.com; 2020.)
202. Dr. J. Mike Minnix; pastorlife.com.
203. en.wikipedia.org

Chapter 28

204. On into the future, Jesus was valued at 30 pieces of silver, but to God his father, he was priceless (Matthew 26:14-15).
205. David Guzik; enduringword.com; 2018.
206. Raisin cakes are 'used in the feasts in pagan worship' (Hosea 3:1AMP). Amplified Bible; Zondervan; 1965; 1987; 2015.
207. biblestudytools.com.
208. bible.org; 13 Feb 2008.
209. Matthew Henry; Commentary on the whole Bible (Concise); Hosea 3; quoted in: blueletterbible.org.

Chapter 29

210. John C. Whitcomb; Old Testament Kings and Prophets; BMH Books; 1977; and: bookshop.org/books/chart-old-testament-kings-and-prophets-paper; 2021.
211. Matthew Henry; Commentary on the whole Bible (Concise); Joel.
212. Isaiah was prophesying the same outpouring of the Holy Spirit about 100 years after Joel, 'I will pour out my Spirit on your offspring, and my blessing on your descendants' (Isaiah 44:3).

213. Charles Ward Smith; Smith's Bible Commentary; Joel 2:28; in studylight.org. 2014. (See his comments on Solomon's temple in my chapter on 2 Chronicles).
214. gotquestions.org.
215. See the Christian Student Group: thefellowship.site; 08 07 2020.

Chapter 30

216. John Gill's Exposition of the Bible; Amos 8; as quoted by: biblestudytools.com.
217. Dr. Justin Imel, Sr., Minister, Church of Christ, Deer Park; Texas; 'The coming famine of God's Word;' drjustinimelsr.com.
218. Never Thirsty; Tucson, Arizona; neverthirsty.org.
219. Antiochus Epiphanes was a king of the Seleucid Empire centred in Greece. He reigned over Syria from 175 BC until 164 BC, and brutally persecuted the Jews, which led to the Maccabean revolt. Antiochus made a decree outlawing Jewish rites and worship, ordering the Jews to worship Zeus rather than Yahweh. In total disrespect, Antiochus raided the temple in Jerusalem, stealing its treasures, setting up an altar to Zeus, and sacrificing pigs on the altar. When the Jews expressed their outrage over the profaning of the temple, Antiochus responded by murdering a great number of the Jews and selling others into slavery. (Based on gotquestions.org.)
220. The Hebrew translated 'seeking' (NIVUK), also means 'reeling.' As used of the reeling of drunkards, of the swaying to and fro of trees in the wind, and the searching of people bewildered.

Chapter 31

221. Charles R. Swindoll; insight.org/resources/bible/the-minor-prophets/obadiah.

222. biblestudytools.com.
223. oxfordreference.com.
224. bibleref.com/Obadiah.

Chapter 32

225. biblestudytools.com/Jonah.
226. Nineveh, founded by Nimrod (Genesis 10:11), at nearly 60 miles wide including all the adjoining cities, was the largest city in the world. It was destroyed in 612 BC by the amalgamation of five nations led forward by the Babylonians. Now, the Iraqi city of Mosul occupies half of the original site by the Tigris river. Though Jonah gives the population as 120,000 (Jonah 4:11), these may have been children, the elderly and those with learning disabilities who 'cannot tell their right hand from their left' (v11). Scholars have calculated a total population of more than half a million. This puts into perspective, the scale of the task allotted to Jonah who appears to be a lone evangelist.
227. britannica.com-Jonah; 20 07 1998.
228. Ashurdan III (772–754 BC).

Chapter 33

229. Definition of a peg to hang (something) on: something (such as a fact or issue) that is used as support or a reason for something said or done; merriam-webster.com/dictionary; American dictionary1828; now on-line with annual revisions.
230. gotquestions.org.
231. Knowing Jesus; dailyverse.knowing-jesus.com/micah-4.
232. Knowing Jesus; Ibid.
233. David Guzik; enduringword.com/bible-commentary/micah-4; 2018.
234. The wall, called the Isaiah Wall, is a piece of the Berlin Wall, a gift of Germany, unveiled at the UN garden, United Nations

headquarters building, on the fourth of April, 2002. The UN was established in 1945 and its HQ was built in New York and opened 1952.

235. Matthew Henry; Commentary on the whole Bible (Concise); Micah 4:3.

236. Knowing Jesus; dailyverse.knowing-Jesus.

Chapter 34

237. fullofeyes.com/project/nahum.

238. David Guzik; enduringword.com/bible-commentary/nahum-1; 2018.

239. In relation to weather phenomena, notice some of the things God is easily able to do:
   - stop the clouds and rain; if there's idolatry (Deuteronomy 11:16-17);
   - cause extreme weather; lightning, hail, snow, clouds, stormy winds (Psalms 148:7-8);
   - cause a drought; neither dew nor rain will happen (1 Kings 17:1);
   - appear in the whirlwind, storm, clouds and rainfall (Nahum 1:3);
   - cause the sun to shine and rain to fall (Matthew 5:45);
   - produce calm; as the wind and waves obey Jesus (Mark 4:4);
   - answer prayer for rain or drought; from Elijah's prayers (James 5:17-18).

240. Matthew Henry; Commentary on the whole Bible (Concise); Nahum 1:6.

241. The Message Bible (MSG); Eugene Peterson; NavPress; 2002.

242. The Amplified Bible is an English language translation of the Bible produced jointly by Zondervan and The Lockman

Foundation. The first edition was published in 1965. It is largely a revision of the American Standard Version of 1901.

243. dailyverse.knowing-jesus.com/nahum-1.

Chapter 35

244. David Mathis; citieschurch.com; 22 11 2015.
245. David Platt; radical.net/podcasts/pray-the-word/yet-i-will-rejoice-in-the-lord-habakkuk-317-18; 02 02 2019.
246. christianity.com/bible/niv/habakkuk/3-17-18.
247. David Mathis; 2015.

Chapter 36

248. drjustinimelsr.com/sermon-on-zephaniah-314-20.
249. John Gill (1697-1771); Exposition of the Bible; Zephaniah 3; as quoted by: biblestudytools.com.
250. Kathryn M. Schifferdecker; Commentary on Zephaniah 3:14-20; workingpreacher.org; 13 12 2009.
251. John Murfitt; Two Destinies; *Introduction*; Zaccmedia; 2022.

Chapter 37

252. Zerubbabel was the political governor or overseer and Joshua was appointed as high priest of the restoration community and was a descendent of Aaron. Both were in the right place at the right time and had the right backgrounds.
253. 'Now Haggai the prophet and Zechariah the prophet, a descendant of Iddo, prophesied to the Jews in Judah and Jerusalem in the name of the God of Israel, who was over them. Then Zerubbabel son of Shealtiel and Joshua son of Jozadak set to work to rebuild the house of God in Jerusalem. And the prophets of God were with them, supporting them' (Ezra 5:1-2).
254. The Amplified Bible; Zondervan and The Lockman Foundation; 1965.

255. biblestudytools.com/haggai/passage/?q=haggai+1:2-7.

256. Dr. Constable's Expository Notes; recorded by: studylight.org/commentaries/eng/dcc/haggai-1.

257. André van Belkum; lifehopeandtruth.com/bible/holy-bible/old-testament/the-prophets/minor-prophets/haggai.

258. Stephen Cole; bible.org/seriespage/lesson-1-putting-first-things-first-haggai-1-1-15; 21 08 2013.

Chapter 38

259. biblestudytools.com/zechariah/passage/?q=zechariah+3:1-5.

260. The only other Zechariah in the Bible is the father of John the Baptist.

261. David Guzik; enduringword.com/bible-commentary/zechariah-3; 2018.

262. The special clothes for the High Priest are given in Exodus: 'These are the garments they are to make: a breastpiece, an ephod, a robe, a woven tunic, a turban and a sash. They are to make these sacred garments for your brother Aaron and his sons, so that they may serve me as priests' (Exodus 28:4).

263. The 'Branch,' considered to be Jesus, is alluded to in: Isaiah 11:1; Jeremiah 23:5; and Zechariah 3:8; 6:12.

264. explainingthebook.com/zechariah-3-commentary-verses-1-5; 27 01 2019.

265. David Guzik; 2018.

Chapter 39

266. gotquestions.org/rob-God.

267. biblestudytools.com/malachi/passage/?q=malachi+3:8-10.

268. Jeremy Myers; redeeminggod.com/malachi-3-tithing; 25 01 2012.

269. David Guzik; enduringword.com/bible-commentary/malachi-3; 2001.

270. Tithing principles are set out in Hebrews 7:5-9, 1 Corinthians 16:2 and 2 Corinthians 9:1-7, for giving to God's work and people in need generally from a cheerful heart.

271. Matthew Henry; Commentary on the whole Bible (Concise); Malachi 3:8.

272. theberean.org/index.cfm/main/default/id/6571/ver/niv/malachi-3-8-10.

Chapter 40

273. Mark and Luke also include this story but not John. Mark's wording is very similar to Matthew but Luke says the centurion describes Jesus as a 'righteous' man, which the centurion may also have said.

274. bibleref.com/Matthew/27.

275. timmacbride.com; 02 04 2015.

276. God's end to man's, symbolically opening the access for people to approach God by faith by removing the barrier. The curtain was believed to be 60 feet high and four inches thick. It separated the Holy of Holies from the rest of the temple. Only the High Priest could go beyond the curtain once a year to conduct sacrifices in the immediate presence of God (Exodus 30:10; Hebrews 9:7). The curtain represented the barrier posed by sin (Isaiah 59:2).

277. The raising of the dead bodies is predicted in Ezekiel 37:12-13.

278. Those raised to life stayed in their graves for three more days from the Friday to the resurrection of Jesus on the Sunday (Matthew 27:53).

279. It was obviously supernatural because it was day time and a time of a full moon which was always when Passover was held. It therefore couldn't have been a natural eclipse of the sun.

280. David Guzik; enduringword.com/bible-commentary/matthew-27; 2018.
281. David Guzik; Ibid.
282. bbc.co.uk/bitesize; The death of Jesus, lesson 8; 03 12 2018.

Chapter 41

283. joshweidmann.com/healing-blind-man-bethsaida.
284. This need for healing because normal physical means could not lead to a cure, was also the case with the deaf and mute man brought to Jesus. The request of the friends was similar: for Jesus to touch him. The response of Jesus was similar: to take the man on one side and use spittle as part of the healing of faith and disability. The result was similar: complete and perfect healing (Mark 7:31-35).
285. Matthew Henry, Commentary on the whole Bible (Concise); Mark 8:23.
286. This use of spittle may have been to separate his eyelids which blindness may have caused to be in a fixed position.
287. southernhillslife.org/get-connected/resources/sermons-and-podcasts/sermon/08-11-2020/the-opening-of-blind-eyes-mark-8:22-26.
288. In 1997, Paul Baloche (b1962), wrote a song based on this verse and called it, 'Open the eyes of my heart, Lord'; Integrity Music. It has come to prominence since Christopher Duffley sang it in America's Got Talent at Concord, New Hampshire in 2007. The challenging thing about that is that Christopher who was ten years old and on the Autistic Spectrum is blind.
289. Godfrey Birtill; *Just One Touch From The King*; King Lyrics Album; 2007.
290. Josh Weidmann; Ibid.
291. bibleodyssey.org/en/passages/main-articles/healing-of-a-blind-man-mark-822-26.

Chapter 42

292. It would be interesting to consider what Mark means by saying, '…Jesus appeared in a different form…' (Mark 16:12). Perhaps his resurrection body? This is also a reason why the two travellers didn't recognise Jesus on the road to Emmaus. It is beyond the scope of this present study to investigate further.

293. bible.org/article/christ-our-companion-luke-2413-35; 15 06 2004.

294. The Greek word for *discussion* is also used by Mark in 9:10, where the disciples are similarly confused.

295. en.wikipedia.org/wiki/Road_to_Emmaus_appearance; 06 05 2022.

296. Gregory I, Pope; Homily 23; Reading the Gospels with Gregory the Great: Homilies on the Gospels, 21-26; Translated by Santha Bhattacharji; St Bede's Publications; 2001.

297. theologyofwork.org/new-testament/luke#the-road-to-emmaus-luke-2413-35.

298. It is often in Christian hospitality and especially around a meal table that Christ is seen and experienced amongst his people sharing in a meal and fellowship.

299. The words and actions of Jesus are the same as those at the last Supper, (Luke 22:19 and 24:30).

300. Arland J. Hultgren; workingpreacher.org; 06 04 2008.

301. Martin Luther (1483-1546), German priest and theologian.

302. Arland J. Hultgren; 2008.

303. enduringword.com/bible-commentary/luke-24; 2018.

Chapter 43

304. Matthew Henry, Commentary on the whole Bible (Concise); John 20.

305. In all the schools I have worked in there has been several doors, mostly to store-rooms, which had to have a notice on them saying: *Keep locked shut.* It was that sort of situation where the believers were in hiding. The doors were firmly locked shut!

306. John McKinnon writing on John 20:19-23; johnmckinnon.org; 2016.

307. bible.org/seriespage/lesson-102-mission-possible-john-2019-23; 2015.

308. workingpreacher.org/commentaries/revised-common-lectionary/day-of-pentecost/commentary-on-john-2019-23; June 12, 2011.

309. John Murfitt; The Kingdom; 2022.

310. John McKinnon; 2016.

311. John Murfitt; The Kingdom; 2022.

312. enduringword.com/bible-commentary/john-20; 2018.

313. Nicol, a civil engineer and hymn writer of 130 hymns, also wrote under the name of Colin Sterne (by re-arranging the letters of his name)! This one is used by permission of Hymnary.org.

Chapter 44

314. gotquestions.org/stoning-of-Stephen; Colorado Springs; 04 01 2022.

315. gotquestions; Ibid.

316. In the example of Stephen, we are shown how to live and how to die as Christians.

317. It is generally considered the seven we would now know as deacons with Stephen as the Archdeacon because he is put first and has such outstanding qualities.

318. The Sanhedrin was established by Moses to assist him in decision making and lasted until its dissolution in 358 AD. The Lesser Sanhedrin had 23 elders or members who sat as a tribunal in

every city in Israel. The Great Sanhedrin had 70 members and a chairman and acted as a supreme court taking appeals to the decisions of the Lesser Sanhedrin, and dealt with major national spiritual matters. With the stoning of Stephen, it seems the full Sanhedrin took offence and wanted to execute him.

319. C.H. Spurgeon; The Metropolitan Tabernacle Pulpit Sermons; Volume 13; No. 740; Stephen's Martyrdom; 1867.

320. Pharisees and Sadducees were the two groups in the Sanhedrin. It was the Sadducees in the Sanhedrin who didn't believe in angels.

321. jesusfilm.org/blog/stoning-of-stephen; Florida; 23 05 2022.

322. Becky Harling; crosswalk.com/faith/bible-study/lessons-we-ca-learn-from-the-life-and-stoning-of-stephen. 04 01 2022.

323. Thomas Hawkes was burned at the stake in 1555, for not renouncing his faith in the gospel of Christ. He had adamantly told his followers before his death that God's grace would be sufficient. He promised them that as a sign, if the flames were bearable and if faith was worth it, he would raise his hands towards heaven and clap 3 times. As the flames were consuming his skin and he was suffering in utter agony, his followers waited for a sign. Finally, Thomas lifted his charred hands and clapped three times. God's grace was indeed sufficient. (With thanks to: Becky Harling of Crosswalk; Ibid. for re-telling this story).

324. C.H.Spurgeon, writing on Acts 7:59-60; 1867.

Chapter 45

325. Paul writing during the 'reign' of the wicked Emperor Nero makes no exceptions. It is the institution of governments that God set up not just individual rulers.

326. bible-studys.org/romans-chapter-13.

327. The Times; News U.K. Ltd; London; founded 1785; 24 08 2022.

328. bibleref.com/Romans/13.

329. en.wikipedia.org/wiki/Sanhedrin.

330. bibleref.com.

331. David Guzik; enduringword.com/bible-commentary/romans-13; 2018.

332. William R. Newell; Romans Verse by Verse; Moody Press; 1979.

333. Steven J. Cole4bible.org/seriespage/lesson-88-government-and-you-romans-13; 2012.

334. Matthew Henry, Commentary on the whole Bible (Concise); Romans 13.

Chapter 46

335. John Calvin; Commentary on 1 Corinthians 1:10; Calvin's Commentary on the Bible; Edition used: 1840-1857. Reported by: studylight.org/commentary.

336. John Calvin; Commentary on 1 Corinthians 1:10; Ibid.

337. Matthew Henry; Complete Bible Commentary on 1 Corinthians 1:10; 1706.

338. Charles Ward Smith; Smith's Bible Commentary; Commentary on 1 Corinthians 1:10; 2014.

339. enduringword.com/bible-commentary/1-corinthians-1; 2018.

340. John Gill's Exposition of the Bible; 1 Corinthians 1:10-11; as quoted by: biblestudytools.com

Chapter 47

341. Aretas (2 Corinthians 11:32) was king of the Nabataeans with a capital at Petra, a Jewish seaport (en.wikipedia.org.).

342. The order of the books in the NT giving Paul's suffering in his new Christian life is different from the dates the books were written and circulated: 1 Corinthians 54-55 AD; 2 Corinthians:

55-56; and Romans: 57; Acts 62-64. (JC Whitcomb; See Textual note 3 following the Contents page.)

343. David Guzik; enduringword.com/bible-commentary/2-corinthians-11; 2018.

344. Matthew Henry, Commentary on the whole Bible (Concise); 2 Corinthians 11:23-30.

Chapter 48

345. At this time of about 48 AD, according to JC Whitcomb (see my Introductory notes), the Bible consisted of the OT and fragments of notes in the possession of the Early Church and in the hands of the Apostles and their close colleagues as they travelled round the Roman Empire. Galatians is considered to be the first NT book, or Letter, in writing. Scholars generally agree that Mark, written in 60 AD, was the first Gospel.

346. John Gill's Exposition of the Bible; Galatians 5:19-25; as quoted by: biblestudytools.com.

347. Charles Ward Smith; Smith's Bible Commentary; Commentary on Galatians 5; 2014.

348. John Murfitt; Two Destinies: *Part 2 Hell*; Zaccmedia; 2022.

349. Matthew Henry; Complete Bible Commentary; Galatians 5:19-25; 1706.

350. David Guzik; blueletterbible.org/Comm/archives/guzik_david/StudyGuide2017-Gal; 2013.

Chapter 49

351. En.wikipedia.org.

352. bbc.co.uk/news/uk-england-bristol-424048; 25 08 06 2020.

353. Matthew Henry, Commentary on the whole Bible (Concise); Ephesians 6:5-8.

354. lionelwindsor.net/ephesians-6-5-8; 18 12 2019.

355. Jeremy Myers; redeeminggod.com/sermons/ephesians/ephesians_6_5-8. Myers supports his view with an interesting illustration. 'William Carey, the founder of modern missions, was a cobbler. He was once accused of neglecting his business because his missionary efforts took so much time. He responded by saying, "Neglecting my business? My business is to extend the kingdom of God. I only cobble shoes to pay expenses."'

356. bibleref.com/Ephesians-6-5.

357. John Gill's Exposition of the Bible; Ephesians 6:5-8; as quoted by: biblestudytools.com.

Chapter 50

358. John Reith, according to the National Records of Scotland was a Scottish engineer, former army officer and broadcaster, and was knighted then later became Lord Reith; nrscotland.gov.uk.

359. The Message Bible (MSG); Eugene Peterson; NavPress; 2002.

360. Natalie Regoli; connectusfund.org/philippians-4-8; 22 03 2022.

361. Rev. Paul J. Bucknell; foundationsforfreedom.net.Philippians 4.8-9.

362. gotquestions.org; 04 01 2022.

363. Natalie Regoli; connectusfund.org; 2022.

364. bibleref.com/Philippians-4-8.

Chapter 51

365. John Stephen Piper; Marriage - a Matrix of Christian Hedonism; desiringgod.org/messages/marriage.

366. Rev. Warren Wendall Wiersbe; The Bible Exposition Commentary; David Cooke; 1989; 2001.

367. Matthew N. Taylor; seekingourgod.com/colossians-318-25; 29 05 2020.

368. Jesus set the example by obeying Mary his mother and Joseph his step-father (Luke 2:51).
369. Matt Korniotes; calvarycherrycreek.org/media/r2r2rbp/colossians-3-vs-18-25.
370. Matthew N. Taylor; 2020.
371. Charles Ward Smith; Smith's Bible Commentary; Commentary on Colossians 3; 2014.
372. Dr. Andrew Hébert; preachingsource.com/sermon-structure/colossians-3-18-4-1; 17 10 2017.

Chapter 52

373. gracebibleny.org/a-model-for-ministry-1-thessalonians-27-12; 25 10 2020.
374. thefellowship.site/archives/with-the-end-in-mind/spiritual-mothering-and-fathering; 18 09 2019.
375. bibleref.com/1-Thessalonians/2/1-Thessalonians-chapter-2.
376. 'Tent-making was a good trade for Paul to have because he could find work wherever he might be, and that became his common practice. He was not against receiving support from established churches as he did from the Philippians' (2 Corinthians 11:9). bibleref.com.
377. thefellowship.site; 2019.

Chapter 53

378. desiringgod.org/messages/in-the-beginning-was-the-word/excerpts/before-time-began-jesus-was.
379. thefellowship.site/rachives/with-the-end-in-mind/deception-about-the-day; 27 11 2019.
380. thefellowship.site; Ibid.
381. studyandobey.com/inductive-bible-study/thessalonians-studies/2thessalonians2-1-8.

382. For a full and frank discussion on 'the lawless one' in connection with the Church and Tribulation, preceding the Second Coming of Christ (Revelation 19:20-21), see: Ray Stedman (1917-1992). Steadman is an American pastor and author, founder of Ray Steadman Ministries, California. raystedman.org/new-testament/thessalonians/the-man-who-claims-to-be-god; 14 02 1988.

383. This three-point summary uses some information from the Fellowship Site blog for which I am grateful: thefellowship.site; 2019.

384. God's breath is in evidence in various parts of the Bible, such as:
    1. All night long God used a strong east wind to divide the Red Sea (Exodus 14:21); see chapter 2: Exodus;
    2. God used a wind in the trees to sound like a marching army (2 Samuel 5:22-25); see chapter 10: 2 Samuel;
    3. God the Holy Spirit used the sound of a violent wind from heaven (Acts 2:2); see chapter 10: 2 Samuel;
    4. The breath of Jesus will destroy the lawless one (2 Thessalonians 2:8);
    5. God breathes the whole of Scripture (the Bible) to bring it into being (2 Timothy 3:16); see chapter 55: 2 Timothy.
    There is no wonder Edwin Hatch (1835-1889), a vicar and hymn-writer used John 20: 22 where we read Jesus, '…breathed on them…' as inspiration for his famous hymn written in 1878, 'Breathe on me breath of God.'

Chapter 54

385. John Murfitt; The Kingdom; 2022.
386. David C.K. Watson; I Believe in the Church; Eerdmans; Church; 1979; p61.
387. bethanybible.org/new/bible-study/am/2014-05-21/the-church-and-the-truth---1-timothy-314-16; 21 05 2014.

388. Greg Brown; bible.org/seriespage/9-god-s-mission-church-1-timothy-314-16; 31 05 2018.

389. The English Standard Version (ESV); Crossway; 2001, 2007, 2011, 2016.

390. Martin Luther is quoted by RK Hughes and B Chappell; 1 and 2 Timothy and Titus: to guard the deposit; Crossway; 2000; p91.

391. This is the first reference to the church in the NT.

392. The start of the church is commonly dated 31 AD and the book of 1 Timothy written about 31 years later in 62 AD.

393. bethanybible.org/seriespage/lesson-11-why-church-important-1-timothy-314-16; 12 04 2013.

394. bethanybible.org.Ibid.

395. I have built on Steven J. Cole's framework summary of 1 Timothy 3:16b in six points based on Paul's use of the hymn; bethanybible.org.Ibid. I have used some of his thoughts together with my own.

Chapter 55

396. Tim Potter; gracechurchmentor.org/sermons/series/morning-worship/1302-2-timothy-3-14-17; 12 07 2020.

397. 2 Timothy seems to have been written 64 AD, and by then some books and letters had made their appearance in the following circulation date order: Galatians, 1 and 2 Thessalonians, James, 1 and 2 Corinthians, Romans, Mark, Colossians, Ephesians, Philemon, Luke, 2 Peter, Philippians, Titus, 1 Timothy, Acts, 1 Peter and Hebrews. Peter brings attention to the letters from Paul, '…our dear brother Paul also wrote to you…. He writes the same way in all his letters, speaking in them of these matters. His letters contain some things that are hard to understand, which ignorant and unstable people distort, as they do the other Scriptures, to their own destruction' (2 Peter 3:15b-16).

398. dashhouse.com/bible-matters-life-2-timothy-314-17; 12 11 2017.

399. Greg Brown; bible.org/seriespage/10-why-abide-god-s-word-2-timothy-314-17; 10 12 2018.

400. Tim Potter; 2020.

401. John Piper; desiringgod.org/messages/all-scripture-is-breathed-out-by-god-continue-in-it; 11 08 2012.

Chapter 56

402. Paul J. Bucknell; Biblical Foundations for Freedom; foundationsforfreedom.net/References/NT/Pauline/Titus/Titus3/Titus3_09-11.

403. John Calvin; Commentary on Titus 3:9; Calvin's Commentary on the Bible; 1840-1857, as quoted by: studylight.org-commentaries/cal/titus-3.

404. bereanbiblesociety.org/things-to-avoid-like-the-plague.

405. sermons.faithlife.com/sermons/398238-titus-3:9-11-avoid-the-divisive.

Chapter 57

406. John Gill, (1697-1771) was an English Baptist, a biblical scholar and a staunch Calvinist. His 'Exposition of the Bible' was printed in nine volumes (1746-1763); Philemon.

407. N.T. Wright is the author and contributor to the international media and Professor of New Testament and Early Christianity, St Andrews University, Scotland. ntwrightonline.org/portfolio-items/philemon; 2018.

408. John Gill's Exposition of the Bible; as quoted by Bible Study Tools; biblestudytools.com/kjv/philemon/passage/?q=philemon+1:10-16.

409. Slavery is not here condemned but it is seen in the context of a loving Christian home and framework. High standards of

relationships and treatment of a slave are expected because slave and master are both now '…in the Lord' (Philemon 16b).

410. Matthew Henry; Commentary on the whole Bible (Concise); quoted in: christianity.com/bible/commentary/mh/philemon/1.

411. I have added my thoughts to Jeff Fairchild's headings; newlifedenton.org.

412. newlifedenton.org/2018/11/jesus-changes-everything-philemon-110-16.

Chapter 58

413. Richard J. Krejcir; Hebrews 12:1-3; intothyword.org.

414. It is beyond the scope of this present book to give all my reasoning but I think there are lots of signs that Paul is the author of Hebrews.

415. The Olympics, for instance were well established having started in 776 BC at Olympia in Southern Greece. A place where the Greeks went to worship their gods. These games were to honour Zeus, the king of the gods.

416. bibleoutlines.com/blog/hebrews-121-3-persevere-in-faith-by-focusing-on-jesus; 27 08 2020.

417. The cloud, shows how God is with and over his people (Exodus 13:21-22; 14:20b). It signifies the judgement of God in the Second Coming to Earth of Jesus (Ezekiel 30:3). We are also told that God sits on a cloud in heaven in his kingly reign (Revelation 14:14, v16).

418. David Guzik; Enduringword.co./bible-commentary/Hebrews-12; 2018.

419. Paul's aim was , '…to finish the race and complete the task… the task of testifying to the good news of God's grace' (Acts 20:24b). After all he was '… running a good race…' (Galatians 5:7a) and wanted others to do the same.

420. An example of perseverance is seen in Noah whom the Bible says spent 120 years building the ark and preaching to scoffing unbelievers. At the same time, God was waiting patiently for him to finish. (Genesis 6:3; 1 Peter 3:20)

Chapter 59

421. John Gill, (1697-1771) was an English Baptist, a biblical scholar, and a staunch Calvinist. His commentary, 'Exposition of the Bible,' was printed in nine volumes, (1746-1763); reported by: biblestudytools.com/msg/james/passage/?q=james+3:5-10.
422. Westpalmbeachchurchofchrist.com/new-testament/james/james_3_1-12; 04 07 2010.
423. Matthew Henry, Commentary on the whole Bible (Concise); James 3; as reported in: blueletterbible.org/Comm/mhc/Jam/Jam_003.cfm.
424. David Guzik; enduringword.com/bible-commentary/james-3. 2018.
425. David Guzik; enduringword.com; Ibid.
426. Kate Barclay Wilkinson (1859-1928) a member of the Church of England, was involved in a ministry to girls in London and a participant in the founding of the Keswick Convention Movement in 1875; hymnary.org.

Chapter 60

427. The foundation stone has to be specially cut out of very dense material to take the weight of the house. It has to be well-positioned to support all that is to be built on it. See Ephesians 2:19-22. If it is not of strong enough material or has flaws in it, it would be rejected as it was unable to do its job.
428. Shine Thomas; cityharvestagchurch.in/living-stone; 28 04 2020.

429. Wayne S. Walker; Expository Files 21.2; bible.ca/ef/expository-1-peter-2-4-8; 02 2014.

430. westpalmbeachchurchofchrist.com/new-testament/1peter/1peter_2_4-8; 22 03 2009.

431. This is God's spirit-level: the Holy Spirit 'level'.

432. *My Way* was written by Claude François in 1968 to a French tune, and was popularised by Frank Sinatra who released it in1969 with Reprise Records.

433. Westpalmbeachchurchofchrist; 2009.

434. Shine Thomas; 2020.

Chapter 61

435. D. Martyn Lloyd-Jones was an evangelical minister who preached and taught in the Reformed tradition. mljtrust.org/sermons-online/2-peter-1-5-7/discipline.

436. David Guzik; enduringword.com/bible-commentary/2-peter-1; 2018.

437. David Guzik; Ibid.

438. John Gill, (1697-1771) was an English Baptist, a biblical scholar, and a staunch Calvinist. His commentary, Exposition of the Bible, was printed in nine volumes, (1746-1763); biblehub.com/commentaries/2_peter/1-5-7.

439. lifehopeandtruth.com/life/blog/2-peter-15-7-spiritual-maturity-explained; 21 02 2022.

440. Felix Antonius, was procurator of Judea 52–60 AD. He was appointed to the procuratorship by the emperor Claudius; en.wikipedia.org.

441. lifehopeandtruth.com; 2022.

442. David Guzik; enduringword.com/bible-commentary/2-peter-1; 2018.

443. A Greek–English Lexicon; Liddell and Scott; OUP; 1843.

Chapter 62

444. firstbaptistscottcity.org/2013/12/09/sermon-1-john-4-7-12-this-is-love.

445. p2c.com/students/articles/we-love-because-god-first-loved-us-1-john-4-7-12; 31 08 2020.

446. nateholdridge.com/through-the-bible; 14 09 2021.

447. Nike, 1987.

448. nateholdridge; 2021.

449. Ray Steadman Ministries; raystedman.org/new-testament/1-john/love-made-visible; 11 06 1967.

450. Matthew Henry, Commentary on the whole Bible (Concise); 1 John 4:7-12; as reported in: christianity.com/bible/niv/1-john/4-7-12.

451. John Stott; The Cross of Christ; IVP; 2021 (first published 1987); p. 326.

452. Nateholdridge; 2021.

453. dulinsgrovechurch.org/2020/02/12/1-john-4-7-12-love-love-love; Dulinsgrove is a Seventh Day Adventist Church;12 02 2020.

Chapter 63

454. John C. Whitcomb; Old Testament Kings and Prophets; BMH Books; 1977; bookshop.org/books/chart-old-testament-kings-and-prophets-paper; 2021.

455. His themes of love, life and light are well developed as themes in all his writings.

456. bibleref.com/2-John/1/2-John-1-12.

457. Charles John Ellicott (1819–1905); Ellicott's Commentary for English Readers; Cassell and Company; first published 1895; revised and extended 1905 (8 volumes). Ellicott was a

distinguished English theologian and Church of England priest. www.bibleref.com/2-John/1/2-John-1-12.

458. 'The papyrus-tree grows in the swamps of the Nile to the height of ten feet and more. Paper was prepared from the thin coats that surround the plant…The different pieces were joined together by the turbid Nile water, as it has a kind of glutinous property. One layer of papyrus was laid flat on a board, and a cross layer put over it; these were pressed, and afterwards dried in the sun. The sheets were then fastened or pasted together. There were never more than twenty of these sheets fastened together in a roll; but of course the length could be increased to any extent. The writing was in columns, with a blank slip between them; it was only on one side. When the work was finished, it was rolled on a staff, and sometimes wrapped in a parchment case.' Sir William Smith; Dictionary of Greek and Roman Antiquities; 1842, with revisions to 1890; Little Brown and Company; p. 567.

459. John Gill (1697-1771) was an English Baptist, a biblical scholar, and a staunch Calvinist. His commentary on 2 John v12 is reported in: studylight.org/commentaries/geb/2-john-1; 1999.

460. Grant E. Richison; versebyversecommentary.com; 19 10 2001.

Chapter 64

461. EASY: easyenglish.bible/bible-commentary/3john; April 2005. (EASY is the Easy Version Bible; Mission Assist; Worcestershire; UK; 2018.)

462. bible-studys.org/3-john-chapter-1.

463. molinism.com/3-john-9-10; 27 12 2021.

464. Hospitality was expected in a Roman world where local inns were dirty, dangerous, and depraved. It would have been expected for friendly local people to offer up lodging to any

traveller especially Christians. Not to do so was thoughtlessness or selfishness.

465. overviewbible.com/3-john; 04 08 2013.
466. molinism.com; 2021.

Chapter 65

467. John Gill; Exposition of the Bible; reported in: biblestudytools. com/jude/1-6.
468. John Gill; Exposition of the Bible. Ibid.
469. John Murfitt; Two Destinies; Part 2: Hell; Zaccmedia; 2022.
470. versebyversecommentary.com/2008/03/09/jude-6; 09 03 2008.
471. James B. Jordan is the Director of Biblical Horizons ministries and scholar-in-residence at Theopolis Institute, Birmingham, Alabama; theopolisinstitute.com/who-were-the-angels-of-jude-6; 12 01 1989.

Chapter 66

472. The Times; *King of Kings secret pottery visit*; 18 10 2022. The Times; News U.K. Ltd; London; founded 1785.
473. mcclearycommunitychurch.com; 14 08 2018.
474. In John chapter one, four times Jesus is called 'the Word' (John 1:1-14).
475. This rider and horse are not the same as those in Revelation 6:2, where the 'crown' worn there is a laurel wreath like the one awarded to the winner of a race. This is one example of the differences between the two references. Rob Phillips, author and speaker writes in his blog explaining the symbolic colours of the horses in his *Once Delivered* blog. He begins with the victory symbol (white horse), and continues 'It's more likely that the rider in Revelation 6:2 symbolises the quest of Rome's neighbours, particularly the Parthians, to expand their empires,

leading to war (red horse), famine (black horse), and epidemic disease (pale horse); oncedelivered.net/2015/12/29/the-rider-on-a-white-horse-revelation-1911-16/; 29 12 2015.

476. enduringword.com/bible-commentary/revelation-19; 2018.

477. John MacArthur; Because the Time is Near: John MacArthur explains the book of Revelation; Moody Publishers; 2007.

478. Dr. Reta Halteman Finger writing about *the Word of God*. She is associate professor of NT and is a writer and speaker. Christian Feminism Today blog; Indianapolis. eewc.com/the-rider-on-the-white-horse-revelation-19-11-16.

479. RSV is the Revised Standard Version of the Bible; OUP; 1946, 1952, 1971.

480. John Gill was an English Baptist, a biblical scholar and a staunch Calvinist. His commentary is called: Exposition of the Bible. Gill's comments are reported by Bible Study Tools: biblestudytools.com/nkjv/revelation/passage/?q=revelation+19:11-16.

481. It is not possible here to discuss the *Millennial Reign of Christ* with its variety of scholarly views.

482. McCleary Community Church; 2018.

483. The Times; News U.K. Ltd; London; founded 1785; 06 05 2023.

484. The Messiah oratorio was written in 1741, taking wording from the KJV of the Bible. At the end of his manuscript Handel wrote the letters "SDG" - *Soli Deo Gloria*, "To God alone the glory." There is no wonder that the custom of standing for the *Hallelujah* chorus originates from a popular belief that, at the London premiere, King George II did so in agreement with the words that Jesus is 'King of kings.' All present would therefore have been obliged to stand, when the king stood. *Hallelujah* is repeated in song five times at the end of the last stanza. This

is a fitting end to the 66th remarkable book of our remarkable library of books: the Bible.

485. John Murfitt; Two Destinies; (A traveller's guide to heaven and hell); Zaccmedia; 2022.

486. John Murfitt; The Kingdom; (A traveller's guide to the Kingdom of God); 2023.

Milton Keynes UK
Ingram Content Group UK Ltd.
UKHW020020011223
433475UK00009B/142